William Palmer, William J. Birkbeck, Aleksyei S. Khomyakov

Russia and the English Church During the Last Fifty Years

Containing a Correspondence Between Mr. William Palmer, Fellow of Magdalen

College, Oxford, and M. Khomiakoff, in the years 1844-1854

William Palmer, William J. Birkbeck, Aleksyei S. Khomyakov

Russia and the English Church During the Last Fifty Years

Containing a Correspondence Between Mr. William Palmer, Fellow of Magdalen College, Oxford, and M. Khomiakoff, in the years 1844-1854

ISBN/EAN: 9783337161972

Printed in Europe, USA, Canada, Australia, Japan

Cover: Foto ©Lupo / pixelio.de

More available books at **www.hansebooks.com**

Russia and the English Church

DURING

THE LAST FIFTY YEARS

VOLUME I.

CONTAINING

A CORRESPONDENCE BETWEEN MR. WILLIAM PALMER

FELLOW OF MAGDALEN COLLEGE, OXFORD

AND M. KHOMIAKOFF, IN THE YEARS 1844-1854

EDITED BY

W. J. BIRKBECK, M.A., F.S.A.

MAGDALEN COLLEGE, OXFORD

PUBLISHED FOR
THE EASTERN CHURCH ASSOCIATION

RIVINGTON, PERCIVAL & CO.
KING STREET, COVENT GARDEN
LONDON
1895

S.B.N. - GB: 576.99190.2

Republished in 1969 by Gregg International Publishers Limited
Westmead, Farnborough, Hants., England

Printed in offset by Franz Wolf, Heppenheim/Bergstrasse
Western Germany

PREFACE

ONLY a few words are necessary by way of Preface to the following collection of letters, in order to explain the purpose of the Eastern Church Association in publishing them. They have been selected as the best means of putting before English Churchmen a point of view in matters of theology, of which they are for the most part very ignorant. Many of us are acquainted with the Anglican or Roman or Nonconformist way of looking at things. We ignore even the existence of the Russian Church, in many ways the most vigorous and powerful of all Christian bodies, with a very clear and definite theology of its own. The following letters between a very friendly but very definite Russian layman and William Palmer, once Fellow of Magdalen College, Oxford, will serve to put before English people a theological position different from that to which they are accustomed. It is felt too that the publication of these letters may do something to preserve the memory of one of by no means the least interesting members of the Oxford Movement, one who was an early pioneer in work towards reunion, who at a time when such ideas were, even more than at present, looked on as Quixotic and visionary, felt himself drawn towards the great and venerable churches of the East. His chivalrous self-sacrifice and his eager zeal for truth deserve not to be forgotten.

It only remains on behalf of the Association to thank Mr. Birkbeck for the trouble that he has taken in editing the letters, and the many friends, both in England and in Russia, who have helped in the publication.

ARTHUR C. HEADLAM,
Secretary of the Eastern Church Association.

CONTENTS

CHAPTER I

MR. KHOMIAKOFF'S CORRESPONDENCE WITH MR. PALMER

Origin of Correspondence—'To my Children'—Mr. Palmer's translation, ... 1

CHAPTER II

MR. KHOMIAKOFF'S FIRST LETTER TO MR. PALMER. [1844]

The sign of the Cross—Communion of prayer between living and dead—Misrepresentations of Mr. Khomiakoff's opinions about England—Reunion of Christendom—Different views of Rome and the Orthodox Church—Obstacles to Reunion between Eastern and Western Communities—Mr. Palmer's eyesight—Report of Dr. Newman's secession, ... 4

CHAPTER III

MR. PALMER'S REPLY TO MR. KHOMIAKOFF'S FIRST LETTER

[1845]

Mr. Palmer's book of poems and hymns—Its contents and objects—Letter dedicatory—The English Church and the sign of the Cross—Invocation of Saints—Prospects of the Reunion of Christendom—Duty of the Russian Church in the matter—Reply to Mr. Khomiakoff's strictures upon Rome—Union of the English Church more possible with the East than with Rome—The question of *Filioque*, ... 12

CHAPTER IV

MR. KHOMIAKOFF'S SECOND LETTER TO MR. PALMER. [1845]

Obstacles to Reunion of Western and Eastern Churches, moral even more than doctrinal—Mr. Palmer's strictures upon the Eastern Church partly, but not entirely, fair—Invocation of Saints—Protestant objections to it due to inheritance of Roman traditions—The procession of the Holy Spirit—Western breach of the Church's unity—Mr. Khomiakoff's opinion of the English Church,   27

CHAPTER V

MR. PALMER'S REPLY TO MR. KHOMIAKOFF'S SECOND LETTER [1846]

Mr. Palmer's *Harmony of Anglican and Eastern Doctrine*—Question as to whether the West is still a part of the Catholic Church—Inconsistency of the Eastern Church in this matter—Agreement possible between the Eastern and English Churches upon the question of the Invocation of Saints—Remarks upon various points raised by Mr. Khomiakoff, ...   41

CHAPTER VI

MR. KHOMIAKOFF'S THIRD LETTER TO MR. PALMER. [1846]

Moral Obstacle to the West accepting Orthodoxy—The Eastern Church defended from the charge of lack of missionary zeal—And from charge of inconsistency with regard to *Filioque*—And with regard to the Re-baptism of Westerns—Replies to some further remarks of Mr. Palmer upon *Filioque* and the Inquisition—Difficult for Westerns, whether Latins or Protestants, to join the Orthodox Church—The Church cannot be a harmony of discords—Latent power and great future of the Orthodox Church, ...   55

CHAPTER VII

MR. KHOMIAKOFF'S VISIT TO ENGLAND. [1847]

Mr. Khomiakoff visits London and Oxford—His letter to the 'Moskvitjanin' about England—London and Moscow compared—An English Sunday, ...   73

CHAPTER VIII

MR. KHOMIAKOFF'S FOURTH LETTER TO MR. PALMER. [1847-1848]

The unity of the Church—Self-contented Individualism of Protestant Germany—Contrast with England—Count Protásoff upon reunion—The Metropolitan Philaret's conditions—Dr. Hampden's nomination as Bishop of Hereford—A call to join the Orthodox Eastern Church—The revolution in France and elsewhere, . . . 77

CHAPTER IX

MR. PALMER'S ANSWER TO MR. KHOMIAKOFF'S FOURTH LETTER [1849]

Mr. Palmer's 'Appeal to the Scottish Bishops'—Compulsory auricular Confession—Preparations for a book upon the Patriarch Nicon—Plans for the future—Mr. Allies's book upon the Papal Supremacy, 82

CHAPTER X

MR. KHOMIAKOFF'S FIFTH LETTER TO MR. PALMER. [1850]

Letter of Pius IX. to the Oriental Christians—Reply of the Orthodox Patriarchs—The Church consists of the totality of the ecclesiastical body, not merely of the hierarchy—Orthodox theory of the Church vindicated—Hopes for the future both in Russia and in England—Ecclesiastical news from Oxford, ... 91

CHAPTER XI

MR. KHOMIAKOFF'S SIXTH LETTER TO MR. PALMER. [1851]

The Gorham judgment—The Papal aggression—Their real significance—Anglican position defined—Only one solution, . . . 99

CHAPTER XII

MR. PALMER'S REPLY TO MR. KHOMIAKOFF'S FIFTH LETTER [1851]

Mr. Palmer's literary schemes—Outline of 'Dissertations upon the Orthodox Communion'—Journey to the East—In the South of Russia—Mr. Palmer applies for admission into the Greek Church—Question of Re-baptism—Question as to how far the laity have a voice in the teaching of the Church, ... 104

CHAPTER XIII

MR. KHOMIAKOFF'S SEVENTH LETTER TO MR. PALMER. [1852]

The Archbishop of Kazan on Mr. Palmer's case—Death of Mme. Khomiakoff, ... 112

CHAPTER XIV

MR. PALMER'S REPLY TO MR. KHOMIAKOFF'S SEVENTH LETTER.

Account of Mr. Palmer's 'Dissertations'—His present ecclesiastical position—Difficulty of joining either the Greek or the Russian Church—Claims of Rome, . . . 115

CHAPTER XV

MR. KHOMIAKOFF'S EIGHTH LETTER TO MR. PALMER. [1852]

Sympathy with Mr. Palmer—Difficulty concerning Re-baptism, not without precedent in the Early Church—Criticism of Mr. Palmer's attitude towards Rome and the East—Defence of the Greek Church, and of the Russian Church, against Mr. Palmer's strictures—Scheme for reconciling Anglicans to the Orthodox Church—A request—Communion with the departed—Proofs of the authenticity of the Gospels, ... 122

CHAPTER XVI

MR. KHOMIAKOFF'S NINTH LETTER TO MR. PALMER. [1852]

Mr. Khomiakoff's commission to Mr. Palmer—Further proofs of the authenticity of the Gospels, ... 135

CHAPTER XVII

MR. PALMER'S ANSWER TO KHOMIAKOFF'S EIGHTH LETTER. [1853]

Mr. Khomiakoff's commission—Mr. Palmer's plans—His literary work—Ecclesiastical movement in England—Mr. Palmer's own position—The question of Re-baptism—Reasons for turning towards Rome—Criticisms of an Essay by Mr. Khomiakoff—Communion with the departed, ... 142

CHAPTER XVIII

MR. KHOMIAKOFF'S TENTH LETTER TO MR. PALMER. [1853]

Mr. Palmer's objections inapplicable to the whole Orthodox Eastern Church—They refer to mere local and temporary defects—No books yet received from Mr. Palmer, ... 157

CHAPTER XIX

MR. KHOMIAKOFF'S ELEVENTH LETTER TO MR. PALMER. [1853]

Mr. Khomiakoff's commission—Mr. Palmer's book upon 'The Holy Places'—A Russian opinion upon Mr. Palmer's 'Dissertations,' . 161

CHAPTER XX

MR. KHOMIAKOFF'S TWELFTH LETTER TO MR. PALMER. [1854]

Mr. Khomiakoff upon the Eastern Question—His opinion of Mr. Palmer's 'Dissertations'—Distinction between the two higher Sacraments and the other five—Mr. Khomiakoff's letter upon the outbreak of the Crimean War, ... 164

CHAPTER XXI

MR. PALMER JOINS THE ROMAN COMMUNION. [1855]

Mr. Palmer's Profession of Faith upon joining the Roman Church, 177

CHAPTER XXII

MR. PALMER'S LETTER TO THE CHIEF PROCURATOR OF THE RUSSIAN HOLY SYNOD. [1858]

Mr. Palmer in the Roman Communion—Journey in Egypt and the Holy Land—Visit to Constantinople and Asia Minor—Last attempt at Philadelphia to join the Eastern Church—Starts for Rome—Stops at Corfu on the way—Makes his terms of submission to Rome with Fr. Passaglia—His present feelings with regard to the Eastern Church—Symbolical pictures—St. John Chrysostom, St. Thomas of Canterbury, and the Patriarch Nicon, . 182

CHAPTER XXIII

MR. KHOMIAKOFF'S ESSAY ON THE CHURCH. [*Circa* 1850]

Introduction—§ 1. The Church is one—§ 2. The Church on earth—§ 3. Her notes—§ 4. She is One, Holy, Catholic, and Apostolic —§ 5. Her Scripture, Tradition, and Works—§ 6. They are manifestations of the gifts of the Spirit; of faith, hope, and love —§ 7. The Church's Confession of Faith—The clause 'Filioque' not a part of it—§ 8. The Church—Her visible manifestation— Baptism—Other Sacraments—The Eucharist—Ordination—Confirmation—Marriage—Penance—Unction of the Sick—§ 9. Inward life of the Church—Gifts of the Holy Spirit—Faith— Justification by faith, and works—The Church, but no single individual within her, is necessarily infallible—Distinction between '*opus operans*' and '*opus operatum*' superfluous—The law of adoption of sons, and of love which is free—Communion of prayer—Invocation and worship of the Saints—Prayers for the living and the dead, and also for those as yet unborn—No presumption in praying even for the Saints—The worship of the Church an expression of her love—The use of images sanctioned by the Church—The Liturgy—§ 10. The Church's hope—The Resurrection of the body—The Last Judgment—Orthodox doctrine of grace—The distinction between 'sufficient' and 'effectual' grace superfluous—Faith, hope, and love are eternal, but love alone will preserve its name—§ 11. The Orthodox Eastern Church is the whole of the Catholic Church now living upon earth—The titles 'Orthodox' and 'Eastern' merely temporary—The whole world belongs to her, ... 192

PAGE

APPENDIX

TRANSLATIONS BY WILLIAM PALMER OF POEMS BY KHOMIAKOFF ON GREAT BRITAIN AND RUSSIA . . 223

INTRODUCTION

My original intention in undertaking to write a book upon the relations of the Russian and English Churches during the last fifty years was to give English readers the opportunity of forming some idea of the opinions concerning the English Church that I have come across during seven journeys in Russia, undertaken with the object of studying the ecclesiastical affairs of that interesting country. English Churchmen, although they have long taken an interest in the fortunes of the Eastern Church, and have always regarded her as an integral part of the One Holy Catholic and Apostolic Church, have had, as a rule, very few opportunities of acquainting themselves at first hand with the Russian Church, which in numbers constitutes four-fifths, and in learning represents at least nine-tenths, of the whole Eastern Orthodox Communion. If they know anything about her at all, their knowledge is derived from books, and these for the most part written by men who, however much they may sympathise with her, have had little practical experience of her methods of thought and action upon her native soil. Our chaplains at St. Petersburgh and Cronstadt, more than one of whom have conferred a lasting benefit upon Anglican readers by their excellent translations of Orthodox service-books, histories, and dogmatic writings, have nevertheless little time or opportunity for travelling about Russia, and acquainting themselves with the actual working of the Russian Church, which is certainly not seen to its greatest advantage in the cosmopolitan surroundings of the modern capital. Even Dr. Neale himself, who perhaps did more than any other writer, since the beginning of the great Anglican revival of the present century, to acquaint English Churchmen with the history, doctrines, and services of the Orthodox Church, never himself went to Russia; indeed, his whole personal experience of the Eastern Church was confined to a visit of a few days to the capital of the little principality of Montenegro. As a rule, English Churchmen have little idea either of what the Orthodox Church really is, or of the view that her theologians take of the English or of any other Western Communion. They are possessed with the notion that she lives in a state of semi-petrified stagnation, and that she cares little or nothing for what goes on outside of her own limits. They are hardly at all aware of the intelligent interest which is taken by Russian ecclesiastics and theologians in the religious phenomena of the West at the present day, still less have they any notion of the immense amount that has been written about the English Church herself, and the movements which have taken place within her during the present century. It was in order to give Englishmen some conception of what Russian Churchmen during the past half-century have thought and written about the English Church, and by the same means to throw some light upon the tendencies and principles of modern Russian theology, that I set out upon my task. Two limits in point of time naturally suggested themselves to me. The first was to begin where Dr. Newman's volume containing the account of Mr. Palmer's visit to the Russian Church ended, namely, in the year 1842: this constituted an obvious point of departure. The second was, the cordial reception afforded to the Archbishop of Canterbury's letter at the Festival of the ninth centenary of the first Conversion of the Russian Grand Duke Vladimir and his people, celebrated at Kieff in 1888. This, and the Metropolitan Plato's warm-hearted reply, expressing for the first time an explicit desire for the Reunion of the two Churches, seemed to suggest the closing of the old era of estrangement and misunderstandings, and at least provided a suitable termination to a book of the kind that I was contemplating.

I naturally first of all turned my attention to the letters of Mr. Khomiakoff to Mr. W. Palmer of Magdalen, published in a Russian translation in the second volume of his works. I had already begun to translate some of these back into English, when in the summer of 1893, while staying with some Russian friends in the neighbourhood of Moscow, I was informed that Mr. Khomiakoff's original letters in English had been returned by Mr. Palmer to his relations after his death, and were now preserved in the library of the Historical Museum at Moscow. With the assistance of my friends I obtained leave to copy them, and a few weeks later, in St. Petersburgh, came by chance upon a copy of Mr. Palmer's collection of hymns, in which one of his answers is contained in the shape of a letter dedicatory.[1] In the hopes of retrieving the rest of Mr. Palmer's answers, I obtained an introduction to Mr. Khomiakoff's son, Mr. Dmitri Khomiakoff; but although he was able to give me much valuable information concerning Mr. Palmer's relations with his father, and even remembered accompanying him on his visit to Oxford in his early childhood, no trace of the letters was to be found. In the course of the following year, however, three of them were discovered in an old writing-desk by Miss Khomiakoff, who now lives in Mr. Khomiakoff's former house in Moscow, and in the spring of the present year two more were found. These, together with other material which I collected, seemed sufficient for a volume in itself; while the outbreak of the Crimean War, which was the beginning of a new epoch, both in the relations between Russia and England, and in the internal history of Russia herself, seemed to suggest a natural point of division. I therefore decided to divide my subject into two volumes, and to devote the first entirely to the correspondence and relations between Mr. Palmer and Mr. Khomiakoff. The latter's name is not altogether unknown in England; his essays in the French language upon the Latin Church and Protestantism, which were published early in the sixties, are to be found on many of our theologians' bookshelves; but few Englishmen have any notion of the influence which his writings have had of late years in the Russian Church, and it seemed therefore all the more desirable that this volume should be confined to

---

[1] See chapter iii. of the present volume.

its present limits, in order that as much emphasis as possible should be laid upon his work, and the changes which his writings, and those of the Slavophile school to which he belonged, and of which he was to a great extent the pioneer, have brought about in the modern school of Russian Orthodox theology. I intend therefore to devote the greater part of this Introduction to a description of Mr. Khomiakoff himself, and to give special prominence to his views concerning England, and his influence upon Russian theology. Mr. Palmer's personality is already too well known in England from Cardinal Newman's description of him in his Introduction to his *Notes of a Visit to the Russian Church*, and from Sir William Palmer's *Narrative of Events*, to require any notice here.[1]

Alexis Stepanovich Khomiakoff was born on May 1st, 1804. Both on his father's and on his mother's side he was of the purest Russian descent. The ancient, noble family to which he belonged could boast of never having intermarried with foreigners, not even in the cosmopolitan days of the eighteenth century, when the conquests of the western provinces of Russia brought so much German, Swedish, and Polish blood into the ranks of the Russian nobility. His father traced his ancestry back through many generations of Russian history, and in their home were preserved numerous family relics and documents from the times of the Empress Elizabeth, her father Peter the Great, and his father, the Tzar Alexis Michaelovich. At the court

---

[1] An account of Mr. William Palmer, written by Lord Selborne, will shortly be published.

of the latter his ancestor, Peter Semenovich Khomiakoff held the post of Grand Falconer, and appears, from the letters preserved in the family archives, which the Tzar wrote to him, to have enjoyed that monarch's special favour. But it was not only memories of the past which contributed to the patriotism and deep religious feeling which formed the main features of Khomiakoff's life and work. The good old traditions of Russia were to him something more than a mere abstraction: all their best characteristics, a sober and perfectly sincere faith, an unostentatious and yet strict and ungrudging attention to the duties of religion, a sympathy for the Russian people and peasantry entirely unartificial and free from cant, and last, but not least, that sound common sense and healthy way of looking at things which Khomiakoff himself used to say (and I am quite inclined to agree with him), are to be seen nowhere to such advantage as in Russian and English families brought up in the true traditions of their country,[1] were all to be found at their very best in the home in which he was brought up. His father owned two estates in the country, one at Lipetzy, in the Government of Smolensk, in the west of Russia, and the other at Bogocharovo, in the Government of Tula, to the south of Moscow, and in one or other of these they used to pass their summer. But the greater part of the year they lived in Moscow, and it was the ancient capital, 'the heart of Russia,' which of all places was ever

---

[1] And not in those of *other* countries or civilisations, as, unfortunately for their country, has been the case with too many Russian families during the last two centuries.

nearest and dearest to Khomiakoff's heart. Moreover, the years of his childhood were among the most remarkable and stirring years of Russian history: and it is easy to realise what the effect upon his youthful imagination of the overthrow of Napoleon must have been. Indeed, ' the Deliverance of the Church and State of Russia from the attack of the Gauls, and of the twenty nations which accompanied them '—for this is how that event is described in the Church service-books—was in itself the commencement of the emancipation of Russia from the yoke of those foreign influences, which had so long hindered her true national development, and was the signal for the beginning of that great movement in favour of the intellectual independence and self-consciousness of the Russian nation, in which Khomiakoff was afterwards destined to take so prominent a part, and which has made Russia, both in Church and State, the great and influential power that she is at the present day.

Both his parents, and more especially his mother, were highly gifted and cultivated, and he received an excellent education at home, thoroughly mastering, amongst other things, the French, German, and English languages, as well as Latin, which he read with perfect ease. The latter language was taught him by the Abbé Boivin, a French priest who lived in their family: and it seems that even at this age he used occasionally to try his hand in those polemical discussions for which he afterwards became so famous; for there is an amusing story of how one day he discovered, in a book that he was reading, a solecism in the Latin of a Papal Bull, and immediately put the question to the good Abbé as to how after this he could ever again believe the Holy Father to be infallible! It is needless to say that the Abbé had little difficulty in escaping from the dilemma, but the episode is interesting as suggesting the possibility that the very fact of a man who belonged to a different religion from the rest of the household living in close intercourse with them for so many years, may have had something to do with inculcating in him a taste for the study of the various religious confessions of Christendom, and for the investigation of the principles which underlie their differences.

When he was eleven years of age the whole family moved to St. Petersburgh, where they spent two years. Two characteristic stories are told about him in respect to this event. It was the year 1815. All the world was talking about Napoleon's escape from Elba, and war was in the air; and accordingly Alexis and his elder brother, Theodore, during the whole journey to St. Petersburgh, talked of nothing else but of how they would go and fight Napoleon, until at last they came almost to believe that this was the object of their journey. On arriving at St. Petersburgh, however, they heard to their disappointment of the battle of Waterloo, and realised that their services would therefore not be required. 'Who is there now for us to go and fight with?' said the elder brother. 'I shall go and raise a revolt amongst the Slavonians,' answered the future leader of the Slavophile movement. Where he got this idea from at the age of eleven he himself never could make out, unless it was from the pictures of the

Servian leader, George the Black, which he remembered seeing posted up on the walls of the post-stations between Moscow and St. Petersburgh, and which may have suggested the first feelings of sympathy and enthusiasm for the Slavonic nations under Turkish and Austrian rule. But it probably, in reality, came from his home surroundings, as undoubtedly did the second point which is related concerning this journey, namely, the aversion with which the first sight of St. Petersburgh inspired him. On their arrival in the modern capital, with its wide streets and foreign, or rather cosmopolitan, appearance, so utterly unlike their beloved Moscow with her golden-domed Kremlin, her churches and monasteries, and everything which appeals most to the patriotism and faith of the Russian nation, it was quite impossible to get out of the boy's head that they had found their way into some *heathen* city, the inhabitants of which were certain to try sooner or later to force them to change *their religion*: and both boys made a firm resolve together that, rather than accept the religion of the foreigners, they would undergo every kind of torture, and even martyrdom itself.

After remaining two years in St. Petersburgh, the family returned to Moscow, where they remained for three years, until Khomiakoff had to return to St. Petersburgh in order to serve his time in a regiment of Horse Guards. During this period at Moscow he made great progress in his studies, and to the year 1818 or 1819 belongs his first printed work, namely, a translation of Tacitus's *Germania*, a selection which, in view of his future historical studies, was certainly very significant.

In 1825 he made his first journey abroad, spending some time in Paris, and returning to Russia through Austria, and thus making his first personal acquaintance with the Western Slavonic nationalities, whose cause afterwards interested him so much. Soon after this, the war of 1828, which the Emperor Nicholas undertook on behalf of the Orthodox populations in Turkey, broke out, and Khomiakoff immediately entered a regiment of White Russian Hussars, and served with distinction in Bulgaria throughout the campaign. In 1829 he returned straight from Adrianople to Moscow, and on the conclusion of peace resigned his commission and retired from the army. After this, with the exception of his journey to England, of which some account is given in Chapter VII. of this book, he never left Russia, but passed nearly the whole of his life either at Moscow or on one or other of his two country estates. His elder brother died in 1828 and his father in 1836, so that he inherited both, as well as his father's two houses in Moscow.

It is impossible to describe, in the short space afforded in an Introduction of this sort, the full scope and extent of Khomiakoff's many-sided activity. His literary labours, although they for the most part took the form of pamphlets or contributions to periodicals, are quite astonishing, now that we can see them collected together in the complete edition of his works, not only for their number and their originality, but also for the number of subjects upon which they treat. Philosophy, philology, history, law, art, and poetry, are all represented. Nor was his activity confined to purely literary or speculative pursuits. At the same time that he was elaborating new theories upon the origin of the Edda or the Buddhistic cosmogony, he was writing projects for the emancipation of the serfs in Russia, preparing schemes for the establishment of savings-banks in the country districts, and generally interesting himself in the movements and requirements of his surroundings. A friend of his thus describes him:[1]—

'At the very time when most busy with his literary work, he would be engaged over the invention of some machine or other which he was going to have patented in England, and exhibit in the London International Exhibition, or inventing a new sort of gun, or devising new methods for distilling brandy or refining sugar, or doctoring all the illnesses in the neighbourhood. Next day he would be out with his harriers on his country estate—for there was no better judge of horse or hound in the country than he—or winning the first prize in some shooting-match; and then in the evening he would come home and convulse us all with laughing over his stories, perhaps about some mad Bishop that had been caught in the forests of Kostroma, or else about the zeal of some petty official in the government of Perm for the spread of Christianity, who, when he was recommended for the Order of St. Vladimir in reward for his services, turned out after all to be a Mohammedan, and so was not allowed to receive it! Very few moments after Khomiakoff came into the room, every one in it was sure to be in peals of laughter, frowns would disappear from even the most morose and gloomy faces, all troubles would be forgotten, and then a discussion would begin, which, whether it were upon the most important or the most trifling subject in the world, was certain to be a lively one. For in discussion

---

[1] Mr. M. Pogodin : speech before the Russian Literary Society at Moscow, Nov. 6, 1860.

Khomiakoff was in his true element, and the more lively and exciting the argument became, the more his creative powers were aroused, and to follow him on one of these occasions when he was, so to speak, on his mettle, was a real psychological treat.

'In his arguments, as in his ordinary conversation and his writings, there was much that was paradoxical; his propositions were sometimes inaccurate, and even his conclusions, perhaps, contradictory, but his sallies were so original, so unexpected and fresh in their character, and were delivered with such kindliness, good-nature, and skill, that they always were suggestive and pleasant to listen to. He would often end his sentences with a simple merry laugh, accompanied by an inquiring pause, more especially after some clever retort or happy simile, or when he had detected a fault in his opponent's quotations. Sometimes for a moment he would exasperate you, so that you were ready to abuse him with all your might; but the next moment you would be laughing even more heartily than he himself at your own discomfiture.'

As far as his machine at the London Exhibition, which is mentioned more than once in the course of the correspondence with Mr. Palmer, was concerned, I cannot resist relating an amusing incident to which it gave rise. He had christened it 'the Silent Motor,' expecting that it would work in complete silence. However, when, on its arrival in London, it was put together by his friends and set in motion on trial before being sent to the Exhibition, it made such an appalling noise that the inhabitants of the neighbouring lodging-houses sent to know the reason for the unwonted and horrible sounds, and threatened legal proceedings if they did not cease. Khomiakoff, when he heard of these unexpected pranks on the part of his 'Silent Motor,' ordered it to be renamed 'the Moscow Motor.' It may easily be believed that he did not soon hear the end of this episode amongst his friends in Moscow!

Khomiakoff had from his earliest days the greatest regard and admiration for England. He was thoroughly well acquainted with our history and our literature, his works are full of references to them, while his friends tell me that he used to recite whole pages of Shakespeare and Byron by heart. A letter which he wrote to a Moscow journal when he came to England in 1847, giving his impressions of the country, is one long panegyric of almost all our customs and peculiarities. Foreigners might think little of us, but this was because, next to Russia, no country was so little known in Europe as England. And the reason of this was that Englishmen did not care to describe themselves, and as for other nations, they tried to imitate us, and imitators are the worst hands at describing that which they endeavour to copy. Englishmen were said to be inhospitable to foreigners, but this he had found by experience to be anything but true. It was merely that Englishmen did not go out of their way to court foreigners, and this for the reason that they could do without them, whereas some nations, not content with the traditions of their own country, ran after foreigners in order to learn from them, while the German liked foreigners because they came to him as pupils, and the Frenchman because they allowed him to show off before them. Foreigners might call the English stiff and ceremonious, and might laugh at their black coats and white shirt-fronts, but while it was true that those hideous appendages of modern civilisation were worn more in England than elsewhere, this was only because Englishmen like cleanliness and tidiness, and everything that witnesses to these qualities. If they were disinclined to talk on the railway, and were sometimes brusque in their manners to strangers, they were more ready than any other nation to help a foreigner if he was really in need of assistance, as he himself had once experienced in Switzerland, when he had run short of money, and an Englishman, whom he had only known for two days, had lent him enough to get back to Russia without any security except his note of hand. If Englishmen were less ceremonious than other nations, it was only because they were more natural. Where was such simplicity of life to be seen as in the London parks, where people rode, not for the sake of showing off, but for their own amusement, and whole families of grown-up people might be seen enjoying themselves as naturally as children? Compare, again, the simple but energetic and incisive oratory of an English member of Parliament with the stilted, artificial phraseology of the French deputy. Where else were men so practical, and where did they go so straight to the mark? You had a gathering of two or three hundred gentlemen lounging in their everlasting black coats in a large room, and some one or other amongst them just standing up in his place and saying what he had to say, and then sitting down again. And this was the English Parliament, the greatest motive power of modern history.

It was in this strain that Khomiakoff described

these and many more of our national idiosyncracies. And when he came to our more serious characteristics he was just as generous in his estimate of us. Foreigners might say that we were a nation of shop-keepers, and care about nothing but amassing wealth, but England did more for the spread of Christianity, and spent more of her wealth upon religion and philanthropy, than any other country in Europe. England had taken the lead in abolishing the slave trade, and had so earned the gratitude of the whole human race. He unreservedly maintained that she came nearest to Russia of all countries in her respect for religion, and no Englishman will deny that in this respect he did her full justice. His description of an English Sunday I have given in Chapter VII. Even the ranters in the Park on Sunday and the crowds that listened to them were to him an evidence of the deep religious feeling of the country, however contrary to Russian ideas their methods and doctrines might be.

He took a deep interest in the English party politics of that time, which it must be remembered was the period immediately following upon the first Reform Bill of 1832. He looked upon the Tory party as representing the true traditions of the country, tracing it from the time of the Reformation as being the national party in Church and State, whereas the Whigs he regarded as lineal descendants, through the Puritans, of the foreign Protestant elements then introduced. While recognising that the English party system was an integral part of the nation's life—indeed, he said that if he had to answer the question, 'What is England?'

in a single sentence, he should say: 'The land in which Tories fight with Whigs'—he was very far from taking the view which was usually accepted on the Continent at that time that Toryism represented nothing but reaction and class privilege, while Whiggism included all that is covered by the words 'freedom' and 'progress.' On the contrary, he maintained that 'to the intelligent observer, and certainly to any impartial Russian, the paralysing aridity of Whiggism when it is engaged in destroying the past, and its sterility, and, so to speak, lifeless lack of feeling when it attempts to construct, are only too evident.' Although perhaps we may here trace the influence of his Oxford friends and of conversations held upon 'green lawns' and under 'deep shades' in a certain English university, there is no doubt that such a view corresponded exactly with the principles and theories of the national or Slavophile school of thought then arising in Russia, of which Khomiakoff was one of the first and foremost leaders. His poem, 'The Island,' written ten years before his visit[1] to England or Oxford, shows that he had already made up his mind in this respect, while in this letter he applies the Slavophile theory to English religious and political history in the following words:—

---

[1] A translation of this poem, and another upon Russia, which was made by Mr. Palmer, was kindly copied out and sent to me by the late Lord Selborne, and is to be found in an appendix at the end of this volume. It was written in or about the year 1836, and was not improbably suggested by the events which led to Keble's famous sermon upon National Apostasy and to the Tractarian movement, and shows the interest which Khomiakoff took in England even at this early period of his life.

'Every community is of necessity in constant motion. This motion may be rapid enough to strike the eye even of an unexperienced observer; it may be so slow as almost to escape the most attentive and intelligent observation. But in any case complete stagnation is impossible; whether it be progress or decline, motion of some sort there must be. This is an universal law. Sound and progressive motion of a community of rational beings is constructed out of two powers or forces, differing indeed in their nature and origin, but capable of harmony and agreement. One of these is fundamental and rooted, belonging to the whole structure, the whole past history of the community; it is the power of life developing itself, of its own accord, from its own beginnings, from its own organic principles; the other, which is the reasoning power of individuals, being grounded upon the power of the community, and only deriving life from its life, is a power which of itself can neither construct nor attempt to construct anything, but being constantly at hand it watches the work of common development, and prevents it from passing over into the blindness of a lifeless instinct, or from surrendering itself to irrational one-sidedness. Both of these powers are necessary, but the second, which is that of the intelligence or intellect, ought to be bound by a living and loving faith to the former, which is the real power of life and creativeness. If the bond of faith and love between the two be broken, dissension and strife make their way in. England once was a Christian state in the fullest sense of the word, but the one-sidedness of Western Catholicism, after fully establishing its supremacy, necessitated and gave rise to Protestantism. The latter, which was born in Germany, passed over from there to England, and was received by her; but England in receiving Protestantism did not recognise its true character. The memories of a Church which once had been free, and of even recent struggles to preserve the remains of this freedom, deceived the English: they assured themselves that they had preserved their religion unchanged, whereas it was clear that they had changed or reformed it, and had abandoned or rejected that which, through the course of long ages, they had regarded as sacred and true; they believed in their own Catholicism even after they had become Protestants. Such is Anglicanism.[1] The other sects saw more clearly what they were about, and took a deeper plunge, and developed the freedom of Protestant scepticism with stricter logic. It was inevitable that the religious movement should soon convert itself into a movement of the whole community. The two intellectual forces of the nation were broken asunder, and entered into conflict with one another. The one, organic, living, historical, but weakened by the decline of village community life and by the scepticism of Protestantism, which it had unconsciously admitted, constituted Toryism. The other, individualistic and analytical, not believing in its past, prepared for long previously by the same decline of village community life, and reinforced by the whole of the disintegrating force of Protestantism, constituted Whiggism.

---

[1] Mr. Khomiakoff's final opinion concerning the Anglican Church is contained in his third Essay upon the Western Confessions, written in 1858, two years before his death. It is as follows:—'Ainsi le mensonge patent dans le monde romain, l'absence avouée de la Vérité dans la Réforme, voilà tout ce que nous trouvons hors de l'Eglise. L'incrédulité n'a qu'à se croiser les bras ; Rome et l'Allemagne travaillent pour elle avec une égale ardeur. Plus profondément, plus sincèrement religieuse que toutes les deux, l'Angleterre paraît faire exception dans le mouvement général des confessions occidentales ; et cependant, tout en rendant justice à ce pays, je trouve inutile d'en parler. En tant que romaine ou dissidente, l'Angleterre vogue dans le sillage de la pensée continentale ; en tant qu'anglicane elle est dépourvue de toute base qui puisse mériter un examen sérieux. L'anglicanisme est un contre-sens dans le monde réformé comme le gallicanisme dans le monde romain. Le gallicanisme est mort ; l'anglicanisme n'a pas de longs jours à vivre. Amas fortuit de principes conventionnels sans lien intime qui les unisse l'un à l'autre, ce n'est qu'une étroite jetée de terres sablonneuses, battues par les vagues puissantes de deux Océans ennemis et qui va s'éboulant des deux côtés dans le romanisme ou la dissidence. L'anglicanisme par ses représentants les plus distingués a condamné le schisme romain dans tous ses dogmes distinctifs (c'est à dire, dans la suprématie papale et dans

'... In reality every Englishman is a Tory at heart. There may be differences in the strength of convictions, in tendency of mind; but the inner feeling is the same in all. Exceptions are rare, and are as a rule found only in people who either are altogether carried away by some system of thought or beaten down with poverty or corrupted by the life of the large towns. The history of England is not a mere thing of the past to the Englishman; it lives in all his life, in all his customs, in almost all the details of his existence. And this historical element is Toryism. The Englishman loves to see the beafeaters guarding the Tower in their strange mediæval costume ... he likes the boys in Christ's Hospital still to wear the blue coats which they wore in the time of Edward VI. He walks through the long aisles of Westminster Abbey, not with the conceited vanity of the Frenchman, nor with the antiquarian delectation of the German, but with a deep, sincere, and ennobling affection. These graves belong to his family, and a great family it is;

l'addition du *filioque*, addition que les savants de l'Allemagne et entre autres M. Bunsen nomment également une falsification évidente). L'anglicanisme n'a pas une seule raison à donner et n'en a jamais donné une seule pour ne pas être orthodoxe. Il est dans l'Eglise par tous ses principes (j'entends par là ses principes réels et caractéristiques); il est hors de l'Eglise par son provincialisme historique, provincialisme qui lui impose un faux-air de protestantisme, qui le prive de toute tradition et de toute base logique, et dont il ne veut pourtant pas se défaire, en partie par orgueil national, en partie par suite du respect habituel de l'Angleterre pour le fait accompli. L'anglicanisme est en même temps la plus pure et la plus antilogique de toutes les confessions occidentales : ou plutôt plongé tout entier dans le sein de l'Eglise par tout ce qu'il a de religieux, il est tout ce qu'il y a de plus opposé à l'idée même de l'Eglise ; car il n'est ni une tradition, ni une doctrine, mais une simple institution nationale (an establishment), c'est à dire l'œuvre avouée des hommes. Il est jugé et il se meurt.'—(*L'Eglise Latine et le Protestantisme*, Lausanne et Vevey, 1872, p. 257-258). This was written soon after the secession of Mr. Palmer and others, and when it appeared as if the whole Catholic movement was likely to come to an end. It would be interesting to know what Mr. Khomiakoff would have thought on this subject at the present day.

and I am not speaking now merely of the peer or the professor, but about mechanics and cab-drivers; for there is just as much Toryism in the common people as there is in the upper ranks of society. True, this merchant or that artisan will give his vote to the Whigs, if he be convinced that either the public good or his private material interests require it of him; but in his heart he loves the Tories. He will vote perhaps for Russell or Cobden, but all his sympathies are with Wellington and Bentinck. Whiggism may be his daily bread; but Toryism is all his joy in life . . . his sports and games, his Christmas decorations and festivities, the calm and sacred peace of his family circle, all the poetry, all the sweetness of his daily existence. In England every old oak with its spreading branches is a Tory, and so is every ancient church-spire which shoots up into the sky. Under this oak many have enjoyed themselves, and in that ancient church many generations have prayed.'

Such were Mr. Khomiakoff's views about England. I have given them at great length in order that English Churchmen may see that, however unfavourable his views concerning Anglicanism, expressed both in the extract already quoted and in the letters which follow, may seem to be, they certainly were not inspired either by prejudice or by national antipathy. Some of his criticisms will be admitted by all candid Anglicans to have had their justification, others are the inevitable result of the attitude which Eastern theologians are almost logically obliged to assume towards all the Western confessions, whether Roman, Protestant, or Anglican. All will at least admit that the tone in which he conducted his case against the English Church was as free from bitterness and offence as it was, under the circumstances, possible to make it.

I have lately elsewhere[1] given some account of the Slavophile movement in Russia, and do not therefore propose to describe it here at any length. It was a great national movement, in many ways closely resembling the movements which in Italy and Germany has led during the present century to the re-establishment of national unity, and which in other countries have exercised so much influence upon literature and art. It was also a religious movement, a great revival of religious self-consciousness in many respects analogous to our Tractarian movement, and to the other religious revivals for which the nineteenth century has been so conspicuous. But it differed from these movements in other countries in that *it represented the national and religious movements in combination*: and that this was possible is entirely due to the fact that in Russia the relations between Church and State which existed in the first centuries after the conversion of the Roman Empire are still preserved intact, so far as the actual constitution of Church or State is concerned. In Italy the national movement has been carried forward in the teeth of the opposition of the Church, in Germany the Protestant Church of Prussia, being a mere department of the State, has had little influence either one way or the other with regard to the question of German unification. In Russia, on the contrary, the national and religious movements have gone hand in hand together, and have overcome all obstacles. What these

---

[1] *The Prospect of Reunion with Eastern Christendom, in special relation to the Russian Orthodox Church.*—London: English Church Union Office, 1894.

obstacles were may be easily seen from the correspondence contained in this book: but it only requires acquaintance with the Russia of the present day to see how almost completely they have now disappeared.

The great work of Khomiakoff's life was undoubtedly the definite direction which he gave to the Slavophile movement in Russia in its relation to the Orthodox Church. It is not an exaggeration to say that his theological writings have given a logical form to the idea of the Church which, although it has never received the sanction of an Œcumenical Council, nor even of a general Council of the Eastern Churches, nevertheless undoubtedly underlies the teaching of the Orthodox Church wherever she is met with. This is obviously a matter upon which a member of the Eastern Church can speak with more ease and accuracy than one who belongs to a branch of the Western Church, and I think, therefore, that in order to enable English readers to appreciate the services which Khomiakoff rendered to the Russian Church, and to understand the nature of the change which he was the means of introducing into her current theology, I cannot do better than translate a description of it written by his friend and disciple, Mr. George Samarin, in his introduction to the second volume of Mr. Khomiakoff's works, in which his principal theological writings are contained:[1]—

'According to our ordinary conceptions, the Church is an *institution*—an institution, it is true, of a special kind, and indeed unique, inasmuch as it is divine—but all the same an institution. This conception has the fault which characterises

---

[1] Khomiakoff's Works, vol. ii. ; Introduction, pp. xx-xxx.

almost all our current definitions and notions concerning religious matters. Although it does not in itself contain any direct contradiction to the truth, it is quite inadequate; it brings the idea of the Church down into too low and commonplace a sphere, and in consequence of this the idea itself becomes commonplace, by reason of its close association with a group of phenomena, with which, whatever may be their outward resemblance, she has essentially nothing whatsoever in common. An institution—we know what that word means; and to conceive of the Church as an institution, according to the analogy of other institutions, is easy enough—indeed, rather too easy. There is a volume which we call "the Criminal Code;" there is also a volume which we call "Holy Scripture"; the law has its doctrine and also its forms; the Church has her traditions and her rites; there is also a criminal court, where the criminal code is administered, and which has to bring it to life, to apply it, to administer it, etc.; and thus the Church appears to some of us to be something analogous, inasmuch as she, guided by the Scriptures, proclaims her doctrine, applies it, settles doubtful points, judges and decides. In the one case we have conditional truth, namely, the law, and along with it the legal body, the officials of the law, charged with its administration; in the other we have absolute truth—and here, of course, there is a difference —but, after all, a form of truth which, like the other, is contained either in a book or in a form of words, and she also has her officials and administrators, that is to say, the clergy.

'Now it is certainly true that the Church has a doctrine of her own, and that it constitutes one of her indefeasible manifestations; it is also true that, looking at her from another—that is to say, from the historical point of view—it is as an institution of her own particular kind that she comes into contact with other institutions. Nevertheless, the Church is not a doctrine, nor a system, nor an institution. She is a living organism, the organism of truth and love, or rather, *she is truth and love, as an organism.*

'From this definition, her attitude towards error of all kind follows as a natural consequence. Her bearing towards error is just that of every organism towards whatever is hostile to, and incompatible with, its own nature. She separates error off from herself, rejects it, and casts it away, and by the very act of drawing a line between herself and error she defines herself, that is to say, the truth; but she does not herself condescend to argue with error, neither does she refute, explain, or define it. Controversy, and the refutation, explanation, and definition of errors are the business, not of the Church herself, but of her theologians. It is the task of ecclesiastical science, or in other words, of theology.

'The heresies of the East gave occasion to an Orthodox school of theology, in order to work the Church's teaching concerning the essence of God, the Trinity and the God-Man, into a harmonious [system of] doctrine; and the cycle of this magnificent development of human thought enlightened by grace from on high was completed before Rome fell away from the Church. Shortly after this the historical destinies of the East underwent a change; her learning and enlightenment were no longer what they had previously been, and, accordingly, the intellectual productiveness of the Orthodox school of theologians necessarily underwent impoverishment. Meanwhile the stream of rationalism, which the Roman schism had admitted into the Church, gave birth to new theological questions in the West, of which the Orthodox East had no cognizance, and as this stream continued its course further, it became divided into two channels, and at length gave birth to two opposite systems of doctrine—Latinism and Protestantism.

'All these new formations arose out of local and exclusively Romano-German elements: Catholic tradition played in them the part of a passive material which was gradually transformed, mutilated, and adjusted to the notions and requirements of these nations; the whole of this intellectual movement, from Nicholas I. down to the Council of Trent, and from Luther and Calvin down to Schleiermacher and

Neander, went on entirely outside the Church, and she took no part whatever in it. Nor could it possibly have been otherwise. The Church remained what she had been before; the lamp which had been intrusted to her had not ceased to burn, nor was its light obscured. But the attacks upon her from the West, the formidable efforts of Western propaganda, its attempts, first to refute the Catholic tradition which the Eastern Church held and still holds, and next to make friends and enter into a bargain with her, necessitated the entry of an Orthodox school of theologians into the contest, drew them into controversy, and obliged them to take up some position or other in relation to Latinism and Protestantism.

And what was it that our school of theologians did? Its action may be described in one word, *it parried*;[1] in other words, it took up a position which was essentially defensive, and which consequently subordinated its form and manner of action to those of its adversaries. It took into consideration the questions which Latinism and Protestantism proposed to it, and took them in the same form as that into which Western controversy had shaped them, without even suspecting that error was to be found not only in the conclusions, but also in the very manner in which these questions were stated—indeed, perhaps even more in this than in the conclusions themselves. Accordingly, involuntarily and unconsciously, and without foreseeing the consequences, our school moved off from the *terra firma* of the Church and passed over on to that land of quagmires, pitfalls, and mines, whither the Western theologians had long been endeavouring to entice it. On advancing thither it was subjected to a cross fire, and was forced, almost of necessity, in order to defend itself against the attacks directed upon it from two opposite sides, to seize upon the weapon which had long before been prepared and adjusted to the work by the Western confessions in their own internecine, domestic

---

[1] Отбивалась, the imperfect tense of the reflexive form of the verb отбивать, *to parry*, or *to ward off*.

conflicts. The inevitable result of course was that, as step by step they entangled themselves more and more in Latino-Protestant antinomies, the Orthodox theologians themselves ended by becoming divided into two sections. They formed themselves into two schools, the one exclusively anti-Latin, the other exclusively anti-Protestant; an Orthodox school in the strict sense of the word ceased to exist. It is, of course, hardly necessary to say that they were unsuccessful in the conflict. A good deal of zeal, learning, and perseverance was no doubt displayed, and not a few individual successes were achieved, more particularly in exposing instances of Latin frauds, concealments, and trickery of all sorts. As far also as the final results were concerned, it is hardly necessary to say that Orthodoxy was not shaken; but for this no thanks are due to our theologians, and indeed we cannot but admit that the contest was conducted by them upon anything but the right lines.

'The mistake which they made at the very outset, in allowing themselves to be led over on to alien soil, entailed three inevitable consequences. In the first place, the anti-Latin school admitted into itself a Protestant, and the anti-Protestant school a Latin leaven; secondly, and as the result of this, each success of either of these schools in its conflict with its rival always resulted in injuring the other, and provided for the common enemy with which both had to deal a fresh weapon against themselves; and thirdly, and most important of all, *the rationalism of the West filtered through into Orthodox theology, and crystallised itself there in the form of a scientific setting to the dogmas of the faith*—in the shape of proofs, explanations, and deductions. For such of our readers as are unacquainted with the subject we will bring forward some examples of this in a shape which all can understand.

'"Which is the more important, and which serves as the ground to which: Scripture or Tradition?"

'This is how the question is put by Western theology. In this way of stating it Latins and Protestants are at one, and it is in this form that they submit it to our consideration. Our theologians, instead of rejecting it and pointing out the senselessness of opposing to one another two phenomena, each of which is devoid of meaning without the other, and which are both indivisibly intermingled in the living organism of the Church, accepts the question for investigation as it stands, and on this soil enters upon a disputation. Against some Martin Chemnitz or other an Orthodox theologian of the anti-Protestant school enters the lists and says: "It is from tradition that the Scriptures receive their definition, as revealed truth, as revelation; consequently it is from tradition that they receive their authority; moreover, in themselves the Scriptures are not complete, they are obscure and difficult to understand, they often give occasion to heresies, and therefore, taken by themselves, they are not only insufficient, but even dangerous." A Jesuit hears all this. He comes up to the Orthodox theologian, congratulates him on his victory over the Protestant, and whispers into his ear: "You are perfectly right, but you have not followed your argument up to its logical end; there yet remains for you one small step—take the Scriptures away from the laity altogether."

'But at the same time an Orthodox theologian of the anti Papal type appears on the scene and says: "You are quite wrong! The Scriptures contain within themselves both inward and outward signs of their divine origin; Scripture is the norm of truth, the measure of all tradition, and not tradition the measure of Scripture; the Scriptures were given to all Christians in order that all might read them; they are complete, and require no supplementing, for whatever is not found within them in actual words may be abstracted from them by accurate logical reasoning; and lastly, in every matter necessary to salvation they are clear and perfectly intelligible to the understanding of every man who searches them in good faith." "Excellent!" says the Protestant; "just so; the Bible as the object, the individual intellect investigating it in good faith as the subject, and nothing more is wanted!"

'Another question: "By what is a man justified? By faith alone, or by faith with the addition to it of works of satisfaction?" This is how the question is stated in the Latino-Protestant world, and our Orthodox theologians reiterate it, not perceiving that the very raising of such a question indicates a confusion between faith and irresponsible learning, and between works in the sense of a manifestation of faith, and works in the sense of a manifestation which has passed over into the domain of tangible and visible facts. And so a fresh dispute commences.

'The Jesuit hurries up to the Orthodox theologian of the anti-Protestant school, and enters into a conversation with him, somewhat as follows: "Of course you abhor the sophistries of the Lutherans when they assert that works are not necessary, and that a man may be saved by faith alone?" "Yes, we abhor them." "That is to say, besides faith works are also necessary?" "Yes, certainly." "And therefore, if it is impossible to be saved without works, works have a justificative power?" "Yes, so they have." "But then, suppose the case of the man who, on account of his faith, has repented and received absolution, but has none the less died without having succeeded in accomplishing works of satisfaction; what about him? For such an one we have purgatory, but what have you?" "We," replies our anti-Protestant Orthodox theologian, after talking it over a little bit, "we have something of the same sort: sufferings." "Quite so; that is to say, the place exists; we only differ about what to call it. But that is not all: there is another question besides that of whether there is such a place and what we are to call it. Inasmuch as in purgatory men can no longer perform works of satisfaction, while at the same time these are just what those who have been sent there require, we advance them to them out of the Church's treasury of good works and merits which have been left over to us as a reserve fund by the Saints. But how is it with you?" The anti-Protestant Orthodox theologian begins to get confused, and answers in a low voice: "We have also the same sort of capital; that is to say, the merits *of works of supererogation.*" "But how is it then," the Jesuit, catching him up, replies, "that you reject indulgences and their sale? For, after all, these are only acts of transference. We put our capital out to the exchangers, whereas you keep it hid under the earth. Is this right of you?"

'At the very same time, however, and at the other end of the theological arena, another disputation is being held. A learned Protestant pastor is putting questions to one of our Orthodox theologians of the anti-Latin school: "Of course you reject that nonsense of the Papists, which attributes to the works of men the significance of merits in the sight of God, and a justificative power?" "Of course we do." "And you know that men are saved by faith, and faith alone, without anything more in addition to it?" "Certainly." "Then be so good as to explain to me your reason for having all those penances of yours, and your so-called counsels of perfection, and your monasticism? What is the use of them all? And what value do you expect to receive for them? Moreover, I would ask you to prove to me that it is necessary to have recourse to the intercession of the Saints. What do you want it for? Or is it that you have no confidence in the power of redemption, made one's own by personal faith?" The Orthodox theologian thoughtfully takes out his text-books, and searches them for the necessary proofs and answers, and finds none. His opponent soon realises this, and proceeds to press the matter home, and asks him: "To pray of course means to ask God something in the hope of obtaining it?" "True." "And one can only pray, when one expects to obtain something in return for the prayer?" "That also is true." "And there is no intermediate state between hell and heaven, between damnation and salvation—for of course purgatory is nothing but a fable, invented by the Papists, which it is hardly necessary to say that you do not accept?" "Oh! of course not." "Very well then: why do you waste your prayers and expend them all to no purpose by praying for the dead? One thing or the other: either you are Papists, or else you are behind the times: you have not yet got so far in your religious development as we Protestants."

'Finally, a Jesuit (belonging to the *newest*[1] school) comes forward, and turning to the anti-Protestant Orthodox theologian begins to question him once more: "Surely you do not agree with those thrice accursed Protestants in thinking that an isolated individual with a book in his hands, but living outside the Church, is able to discover the truth and the way of salvation by himself!" "Of course not: we believe that there is no salvation outside the Church, which alone is holy and infallible." "Excellent! But if this be so, then the first object of every man's care must be not to forsake the Church, but to be at one with her in all things, both in faith and deed?" "Certainly." "But then, as you know, sophisms and flattery have often forced their way into the Church, and have led the faithful astray under the mask of ecclesiasticism." "Yes, we know that." "And this shows the necessity of a tangible outward *sign* by means of which every man may unmistakably distinguish the infallible Church?" "Yes, this is necessary," the Orthodox theologian replies, not seeing the trap into which he is being led. "This we have got,—namely, the Pope; but how about you?" "With us it is the full manifestation of the Church in her teaching, and the organ of her infallible faith is an Œcumenical Council." "Yes, and we also acknowledge the authority of an Œcumenical Council; but explain to me how an Œcumenical Council is to be distinguished from one that is not Œcumenical, or merely local? By what visible sign, I mean? Why not, for instance, acknowledge the Council of Florence as œcumenical? And do not tell me that you only admit that Council to be œcumenical in which the whole Church recognises her own voice, and her own faith,—that is to say, the inspiration of the Holy Ghost; for the very problem which we now have before us is to arrive at what and where the Church is." The anti-Protestant Orthodox theologian finds himself at a loss for

---

[1] This was written in 1867.

an answer, and the Jesuit, as a final farewell, says to him: "There is a great deal of good in you, and you and we are both on the same road; but we have arrived at the end, whereas you have not got there yet. We both agree in acknowledging the necessity of an outward mark of the truth, or, in other words, *a sign of what is and what is not the Church*,[1] but you are searching for one, and cannot find it, whereas we have got one—the Pope; that is the difference between us. You also are in essence Papists, only you do not follow the consequences of your own premises."

'It was on lines such as this that for nearly two centuries the controversy of our two Orthodox schools of theology with the Western confessions dragged along. It was accompanied, as was to be expected, by constant controversy at home between the two schools themselves. As the most complete, exact, and able expression in writing of the line taken by each of them, one has only to mention Theophanes Procopovich's *Latin Theology* [on the anti-Latin side], and Stephen Javorski's *Rock of the Faith* [on the anti-Protestant side];[2] all that was published afterwards grouped itself round one or other of these thoroughly representative works, and represented nothing more than extracts from them, more or less feebly restated. Let it be remembered, we are now speaking of our theologians, not of *the Church* herself. The fortress indeed withstood the assault, and was not shaken by it: but the reason that it was not shaken was that this fortress was the Church of God, and therefore could not fail to maintain

---

[1] Знамени церковности. These words, which in the original are in italics, are particularly difficult to translate on account of there being no English equivalent for the word церковность. 'Sign of *churchness*,' or '*churchity*,' would exactly render it, if either of these words existed in English.

[2] Stephen Javorski, Metropolitan of Riazan, on the death (A.D. 1700) of the Patriarch Adrian of Moscow, was appointed "Guardian of the Patriarchal Throne," until the establishment of the Holy Synod in 1721. Theophanes Prokopovich, Archbishop of Pskoff, a favourite of Peter the Great, author of the *Ecclesiastical Regulations* set forth by the Holy Synod, of which he was the presiding member.

her ground; as far as the defence itself was concerned, it is impossible not to admit that it was thoroughly weak and insufficient. The spectators who watched the conflict from outside (and all our cultivated society, with very few exceptions, maintained the attitude of disinterested spectators towards it), judged of the justice of the cause according to the quality of its defence, and were left in perplexity; doubt seized upon many of them, while many more actually took the side of the enemy, some in mysticism, others in Popery, the greater number of course in the latter, inasmuch as there the satisfaction hoped for in taking the step was more cheaply gained. People who considered themselves entirely impartial, that is to say, who imagined, that in having left one shore and not having reached the other, they had, from the lofty height of their religious indifferentism, acquired an aptitude for passing judgment upon the Church, arrived at the notion that Orthodoxy was nothing more than an antiquated and indifferent medium out of which, according to the laws of progress as seen in the West, which was far in advance of us in enlightenment, two tendencies, the one Latin and the other Protestant, had to apportion themselves, and that these, as more fully developed forms of Christianity, were destined in time to divide Orthodoxy between them and eventually to swallow her up. Others there were which said that Latinism and Protestantism, inasmuch as they were contradictory poles mutually excluding one another, could not be the final expressions of the Christian idea, and that, earlier or later, they would have to come to terms and themselves disappear, certainly not in Orthodoxy, which was obsolete and played out, but in some new form of religion which would regard the universe from a higher standpoint.[1] Popery, mysticism, and eclecticism—all three were very seriously preached in our midst, and each of them found followers, and met with hardly any resistance from the point

---

[1] 'Въ какой-нибудь новой, высшей формѣ религіознаго міросозерцанія,' literally, 'In some new, higher form of religious world-contemplation.'

of view of the Church. It is evident that our school of theology could not provide materials for a successful resistance. It continued to carry on its polemics on the treacherous soil already described without changing its position: in a word, it simply acted on the defensive. But to defend oneself is not the same thing as to repulse, still less is it the same thing as to gain the victory; in the domain of thought one can only regard as conquered that which has been finally understood and defined to be error. And our Orthodox school of theology was not in a position to define either Latinism or Protestantism, because that in departing from *its own Orthodox* standpoint, it had itself become divided into two, and that each of these halves had taken up a position *opposed* indeed to its opponent, Latin or Protestant, but not *above* him.

'It was Khomiakoff who first looked upon Latinism and Protestantism from *the Church's* point of view, and therefore from *a higher* standpoint:[1] and this is the reason that he was also able *to define* them.

'We have already said that foreign theologians were perplexed by his brochures. They felt that there was something in them which they had never met with before in their controversies with Orthodoxy; something quite unexpected and new to them. Very likely they were sometimes unable clearly to realise of what this new element consisted; but we at any rate understand what it was. They had at last heard the voice of a theologian not of the anti-Latin, nor the anti-Protestant, but of the Orthodox school. And having met with Orthodoxy in the region of ecclesiastical science for the first time, they began in a confused sort of way to feel that hitherto their whole controversy with the Church had turned upon certain misunderstandings; that their everlasting litigation with her, which had seemed to them almost on the point of completion, was in fact only now beginning, and upon entirely new ground, and that the very position of the two

---

[1] '*Изъ Церкви, слѣдовательно сверху,*' literally, '*out of the Church, consequently from above.*'

sides had changed, inasmuch as they, Papists and Protestants, had become the accused instead of the accusers, they were called upon for an answer, and it was they that had to justify themselves. . . .

'Not less striking in its novelty was the system upon which Khomiakoff conducted his controversial undertakings. Up to his time our learned theological disputes had lost themselves in particularism. Each position of our opponents, and each of their deductions, were analysed and refuted separately. We were engaged in detecting forged additions to texts or omissions, and in recovering the meaning of corrupted passages. We compared text with text, and witness with witness, and pelted one another with proofs from Scripture, tradition, and reason. When we succeeded in gaining our point the result was that the proposition of our adversaries was not proven, sometimes perhaps it was even shown to be contrary to Scripture and tradition, and therefore false and to be rejected, but nothing more. Of course this was sufficient in order to refute the error in the form in which it had presented itself: but this obviously was not all that was wanted. The questions, how, why, and from what inner motive causes it had sprung, and what exactly it was in these that was false, and wherein lay the root of the error, remained still unanswered. These questions they never solved, and hardly even touched upon, and consequently it sometimes happened that after having shaken off an error expressed in one form (as a dogma or decision), we did not recognise it in another form; it sometimes even happened that in the very refutation itself we appropriated it, by transferring over into our own point of view the very motive causes which had given rise to it; its root remained all the same in the earth, and the fresh shoots which it threw out often cumbered our ground. Khomiakoff sets to work in a very different manner. Passing from manifestations to their original causes, he reproduces, if one may so express it, a physical genealogy of each error, and brings them back together to their common starting-point, in which the error, on being exposed to view, reveals itself in its inner inconsistency. This is nothing less than to tear error up by the roots.

'If we go further into Khomiakoff's theological writings, and pass from his system to their contents, we shall find another distinguishing characteristic. They have the appearance of being primarily of a controversial nature; but in reality polemics occupy in them a secondary place, or, to put it more exactly, of polemics in the strict sense of the word, that is to say, of refutations of a purely negative character, there is hardly a trace. It is impossible to take the negative side of his controversies—namely, his objections and refutations, apart from the positive side—that is to say, his explanation of the teaching of Orthodoxy; and this is so, because the one cannot be separated from the other, for they always form one indissoluble whole. There is not a single argument to be found in his works which he has borrowed from the Protestants to use against the Latins, nor has he taken a single argument from the Latin arsenal to use against the Protestants; not one of his arguments but which will be found to be double-edged, that is to say, which is not just as good against the Latins as against the Protestants, and this is because each of his demonstrations is in its essence not a negation, but an affirmative proposition, although it be pointed with a view to controversy. . . .

'When a man stands in a cloud or a fog, he is conscious only of the absence or want of light, but whence the fog came, or how far it extends, or where the sun is, he neither knows, sees, nor can say.

'On the contrary when the sky is clear, and the sun is shining brightly, every passing vapour shows itself off against the sky in all its outlines and limits, as a cloud, as an object the opposite of light.

'Khomiakoff cleared the region of light, the atmosphere of the Church, and consequently false doctrine as it passed across it appeared of its own accord in the shape of a negation of the light, as a dark spot on the sky. The boundaries and outlines of false doctrine became evident and self-defined.

We speak of false doctrine in the singular and not in the plural number, although we include both Latinism and Protestantism under the term, because from henceforth these two confessions will constitute for us but one single form of error; and this their intrinsic unity can only be seen from one point of view, namely that of the Church, and it was just this that Khomiakoff pointed out to us. Before his time our theologians always took Latinism and Protestantism to be two contradictories, mutually excluding one another. And this is what they are actually represented to be in the West, because there religious consciousness is irrevocably divided into two parts, and has lost the very notion of the Church, that is to say, of that centre from which these two confessions separated themselves under the influences of the elements which they had imbibed from Rome and Germany. A similar view of them passed over from the West to us, and we adopted their definitions ready made, and looked upon Latinism with Protestant eyes, and *vice versâ*. At the present time, thanks to Khomiakoff, all this is changed. Formerly we saw before us the two clearly defined forms of Western Christianity, and Orthodoxy *between them*, having, as it were, pulled herself up at the parting of the ways, but now we see *the Church*, or, in other words, the living organism of truth, intrusted to mutual love; and outside the Church, logical knowledge cut off from a moral basis, that is to say, *Rationalism*, in two aspects of its development, namely, reason clutching at *a phantom* of the truth, and selling its freedom into bondage to an external authority—which is what Latinism is, and reason, trying to find out a self-made truth for itself and sacrificing unity to subjective sincerity—or, in other words, Protestantism.'

Such was the change brought about in the current theology of the Russian Church by Khomiakoff's theological writings. Illustrations of his method will be found both in the present volume and in his three Essays in the French language upon the Latin Church and Protestantism which have been already referred to. Its great importance consists in the fact that whatever may be thought of its intrinsic merits—and of course no Western can accept Khomiakoff's views without certain very considerable limitations—it has undoubtedly given logical form and expression to what has been implicitly held by the whole of the Orthodox Eastern Church from the time of the Great Schism downwards.

The great fact to remember about Russia is that she has not in Church or State gone through either a feudal or a scholastic period; and this she owes to the fact of her belonging to the Eastern Orthodox Church. The theology borrowed from the West, which was partly adopted in the seventeenth and eighteenth centuries in the Eastern Church, has never sunk very deeply into Eastern religious consciousness. Even documents such as the Articles of the Synod of Bethlehem, which received the approval of the four Patriarchs, are now looked upon as to a great extent obsolete; indeed, in Russia they were never accepted except in a modified form—and this because they were from the first felt not to be in accordance with the true spirit and tradition of the Eastern Church.

If any one wishes to estimate what Khomiakoff has done for Orthodox theology, let him first read the *Notes of Mr. Palmer's Visit to the Orthodox Church*, published by Cardinal Newman, and in the conversations of those with whom Mr. Palmer had his first discussions recognise the results of the schools of theology which Mr. Samarin has described as existing before Khomiakoff's time in Russia, and then, after reading Khomiakoff's

d

theological treatises, let him go to Russia and study the Church there as she exists at the present day. He will not be long in realising how completely the channel into which the Slavophiles led contemporary Russian theological thought corresponds with actual facts. Mr. Khomiakoff always regarded the declaration of the Eastern Patriarchs given in reply to the encyclical of Pius IX. to the Oriental Christians as the point of departure from which the modern school of Orthodox theology should start. And indeed, just as the Vatican decrees may be said to be the logical outcome of the line taken by Rome at the Great Schism, so when the Eastern Patriarchs declared, 'We have no sort of worldly inspectorship, or, as his Holiness calls it, sacred direction, but are united only by the bond of love and zeal for our common Mother in the unity of the faith. . . . With us neither Patriarchs nor Councils could ever introduce anything new, inasmuch as with us the body itself of the Church is the guardian of her Orthodoxy,' they were for the first time formulating a definition of the principle which underlies the whole teaching of the Orthodox Church. Khomiakoff seized upon this declaration of the Patriarchs, applied it in every imaginable way to Orthodox tradition and practice, and found that it always corresponded with them. It will be found to underlie the whole of his essay upon the Unity of the Church at the end of this volume; while in the second of his Essays upon the Latin Church and Protestantism, after maintaining that it was clearly indicated on the day of Pentecost, for the Holy Spirit, Who was sent to lead the disciples into all truth, came down not only upon the Apostles, but *upon all the disciples*, he thus defines the difference between the East and West upon this point:[1]—

'When, after having overcome death, the Saviour of men withdrew His visible presence from them, He did not leave them comfortless, but consoled them with the promise that He would be with them to the end of the world. This promise was fulfilled. The Spirit of God descended on the heads of the disciples gathered together in the unanimity of prayer, and restored to them the presence of their Saviour, no longer a presence indeed such as could be apprehended by the senses, but an invisible presence, a presence no longer external, but dwelling within them. From that time forward, notwithstanding the trials that awaited them, their joy was full. And we also have this full and perfect joy, for we know that the Church has not, like the Protestants, to search for Christ, for she already possesses Him, and that she possesses and obtains Him constantly by the inward action of love, without requiring an external phantom of Christ, such as the Romans believe in. The invisible Head of the Church had no need to bequeath her with an image of Himself in order to pronounce oracles, but has inspired the whole of her with His love in order that she may have the unchangeable truth within herself.

'Such is our faith. The Church, even on earth, is a thing of heaven; but both the Roman and the Protestant judge of heavenly things as if they were earthly. "There will be disunion," says the Roman, "unless there is an authority to decide questions of dogma." "There will be intellectual servitude," says the Protestant, "if everybody is obliged to agree with all the others." Is this way of speaking in accordance with the principles of heaven or with those of the earth ? . . . Catholicism, or rather the universality of known truth, and Protestantism, or rather seeking for the truth, are as a matter of fact elements which have always co-existed

---

[1] *L'Eglise Latin et le Protestantisme*, pp. 111-116.

together in the Church. The first belongs to the totality of the Church, the second to each of her members. We call the Church universal, but we do not call ourselves Catholics —when this word (or the word Orthodox) is used in speaking of an individual it is only an elliptical form of language—for this word implies a perfection to which we are very far from pretending. When the Spirit of God permitted that the holy Apostle of the Jews should deserve the blame of the Apostle of the Gentiles, He gave us this sublime truth to understand, that the highest intellect and the mind most illuminated from heaven ought to humble itself before the catholicity of the Church, which is the voice of God Himself. Each of us is constantly seeking that which the Church ever possesses. Ignorant, we seek to understand; evil, we seek to unite ourselves to the sanctity of her inward life; ever imperfect in all things, we press forward towards that perfection which is to be found fully displayed only in the manifestations of the Church herself, in her writings, which are the sacred Scriptures, in her dogmatic traditions, in her sacraments, in her prayers, in her decisions, and which, in short, make themselves heard every time that there is an error to refute, a difficulty to solve, or a truth to proclaim within her bosom, in order to sustain the trembling steps of her children. Each one of us is of the earth, the Church alone is of heaven.'

And here we will take leave of Khomiakoff's theological works and opinions. The reason that I have tried to present them as far as possible in his own words, or in those of his disciples, must by this time be obvious. If I had attempted to describe them in my own words, I must, of necessity, have presented them to English readers in a modified form. My object in writing about the Russian Church has ever been to represent her as being not necessarily what I should like her to be, but what she is; and if my readers will forgive a personal reminiscence, I may say that I think that one of the proudest moments of my life was when, in a criticism of one of my articles in *The Guardian* upon Russia, which appeared in a Protestant journal, published at Leipzig, and which was anything but friendly towards the line which I took, the writer began his final sentence by the words: 'Birkbeck bemüht sich doch objectiv zu sein'! The time for telling half-truths about the Russian Church, even if it ever existed, has certainly now quite passed away; the question of the Reunion of Christendom is ever coming more and more to the front, and the Russian Church, quite apart from the other Orthodox Eastern Churches which are in full communion with her, is by far the most important national Church now existing, and indeed, next to the Roman Church, is the largest Christian body on the world's surface at the present time. It must be patent to all intelligent observers—and it is well known that no one appreciates the fact better than Leo XIII. himself —that the Reunion of Christendom will not be brought about without her. As Eugenius IV. said of Mark of Ephesus, when he heard that he had not signed the Act of Union at the Council of Florence, so we may say with regard to Russia: 'Without her, all our labours are lost.' And therefore the first object of those who are interested in, and who long for, the Reunion of Christendom, should be, to get really to know her, and to see things from her own point of view. This preliminary step is absolutely indispensable. Whether the views of her theologians are absolutely true, or whether they are only relatively so, is comparatively an unimportant matter, and may be discussed hereafter. There is much in Mr. Khomiakoff's writings, both in this correspondence and in his other works, which no Anglican can unreservedly accept. While we can readily admit that, there was much in the development of Western theology after the Great Schism which was one-sided, and much that was even altogether erroneous, we can never admit that the West ceased to be part of the Church, or that the whole truth has been committed to the East alone since that unhappy event. We can of course allow that, inasmuch as the East has never admitted the principle of development, and as a matter of fact has obviously hardly changed, even outwardly, since the division between East and West, she is a perfectly faithful representative of the Eastern Church before that unhappy event, while those who really know her, and have seen her practical working, her services, her missions, her monasteries, her guilds, her charities, and all the daily evidences of her vitality in the vast Empire of the Tzars, will certainly allow that she has been wise in adhering to her traditions, that in this lies her great strength, and that that good part which she has chosen is extremely unlikely to be taken from her. But the object for which this book has been published will be very much mistaken, if it is thought that it is intended to throw away doubt upon the claims, both of the English and the Roman Churches, to be considered true members of the Catholic Church. No English Churchman could wish to do this. To return once more to Mr. Khomiakoff: he repeatedly expresses his admiration for the English system of education, and gives the warmest praise to our public schools and universities. Yet at the end of his account of his visit to England he relates how, when he was at Oxford, a clergyman belonging to the Tractarian School said to him: 'How are we to arrest the pernicious effects of Protestantism?' Khomiakoff's ready reply was: 'Shake off your Roman Catholicism!' He seemed hardly to realise that to do this would be to bury the English university and public school system and all that it represents under the earth, and if this conversation took place at the high table of Magdalen, which, as he was Mr. Palmer's guest during his stay at Oxford, is not improbable, it must have been almost enough to make the portraits of Waynflete, Wolsey, and Pole over his head weep from their frames! That it was difficult for an Anglican to join the Church of Rome when once he had realised what the Eastern Church is, even in the discouraging times of the Secession of Dr. Newman and of the Gorham Judgment, is made abundantly clear by the latter part of this correspondence, and at the present day such a thing would be quite impossible. On the other hand, even now that the difficulty about Baptism exists no longer, Eastern writers admit that Reunion of East and West is not in the least likely, even if desirable, to be brought about by individual conversions to Orthodoxy.[1]

Mr. Khomiakoff died in the year 1860. He had been staying for about a month, towards the end of the summer, on a small property which he owned in the government of Riazan, looking after its affairs. His eldest son had been with him most of the time, but he

---

[1] *Cf.* an article upon W. Palmer published last month (August) in Moscow in the *Ruskij Archiv.*

had sent him home to Bogocharovo, intending to finish off some literary work which he had on hand, and to follow him in three days. On the night before his death his bailiff had been with him arranging about the affairs of the estate, and left him at two o'clock in the morning of 23rd September in perfect health. He then sat down to write, and continued to do so until about five o'clock, when he felt the first symptoms of cholera. The suddenness of the attack is best illustrated by the fact that his manuscript ended abruptly in the middle of a sentence, at the word 'in.' At seven o'clock, feeling himself getting worse and worse, he sent for the priest, who arrived at eight o'clock, and after confessing and communicating him, administered to him the Sacrament of Unction. During the whole of this service, which in the Eastern Church is extremely long, he retained his consciousness, holding a candle in his hand, at times repeating the prayers with the priest in a whisper, and making the sign of the cross. At three o'clock he became unconscious, and the priest, thinking that the end had come, began reading the commendatory prayers. However, afterwards he recovered consciousness, and the village doctor told him that his pulse was improving. 'Are you not ashamed of yourself,' answered Khomiakoff, 'after having seen so much sickness, not to know the pulse of a dying man?' About twenty minutes before the end, his neighbour, Mr. Muromtzeff, who was the only person with him besides the priest and doctor, said to him: 'You are getting better; the warmth is returning to your limbs, and your eyes are brighter.' 'But to-morrow how bright they will be!' replied Khomiakoff. These were his last words. He died at a quarter to eight in the evening. His body was removed to his beloved Moscow, where it now lies in peace in the cemetery of the great Danileffski Monastery on the outskirts of the city. Со святыми упокой, Хрісте, душу раба Твоего!

. . . .

The letters of Mr. Khomiakoff throughout this volume have been given in almost exactly the same words as they were written. Any addition which I have made I have put into square brackets, and any alteration which could in any possible manner alter the sense, I have indicated in a footnote. The alterations which I have made without noticing them are extremely small in number, and consist merely of such details as the occasional transference of the position of an adverb, or the alteration of 'will' into 'shall' where the English idiom seemed to require it. I have been careful to initial my own footnotes, and, for the rest, to indicate whether they were those of Mr. Khomiakoff himself or of his Russian translator.

With regard to the orthography of Russian names spelt in English letters, I have throughout reduced them to one system, in order to avoid confusion. The only exception I have made is in the case of Mr. Khomiakoff's own name, which I have left in every case as he spelt it at the end of his letters. The diversity in spelling comes from the very fugitive character of the sounds of unaccented Russian vowels. The name in Russian is spelt Хомяковъ, and the first two syllables being short, may very easily be represented by letters other than *o* and *ja*. The *ŏ* sound in Russian, however, resembles rather the sound of the English *o* in

c

the word 'testimŏny' than the broad sound of *a*. The *Kh* at the beginning is equivalent to the German *Ch*. Perhaps the best way of indicating the true sound of the name would be to spell it 'Hŏmiăkoff.'

In conclusion, I would express my gratitude for the assistance I have had in preparing this work for the press. It would be difficult to say how much I owe to the late Lord Selborne, not only for providing me with his brother's Confession of Faith upon joining the Church of Rome, and the two poems at the end of the volume, but also for his kind assistance throughout the whole undertaking. All my MSS. of Mr. Palmer's letters were looked over and corrected by him, and the punctuation in them was added by him in pencil. The assistance of the Very Rev. Archpriest E. Smirnoff, Chaplain to the Russian Embassy in London, has also been invaluable: it would be impossible to exaggerate how much I owe to him, not only for helping me in the biographical details in the footnotes, but also for his constant readiness to help me to clear up any difficulty which occurred in the course of the work. I have also to thank many friends in Russia, especially Mr. Dmitri and Miss Mary Khomiakoff, for their assistance throughout, Mme. Bachmetieff for relieving me of much of the labour of copying Mr. Khomiakoff's letters, Mr. Peter Bartenieff for furnishing me with the original text of Mr. Palmer's letters in 1858 to the Chief Procurator of the Holy Synod, and to Canon Bramley of Lincoln for his valuable help with the theological terms in my translation of Khomiakoff's Essay on the Church.

W. J. BIRKBECK.

THROPE, *September 23rd*, 1895.

CORRESPONDENCE

BETWEEN

MR. WILLIAM PALMER

AND

M. KHOMIAKOFF

1851-1853

CHAPTER I

MR. KHOMIAKOFF'S CORRESPONDENCE WITH MR. PALMER

Origin of correspondence—'To my Children'—Mr. Palmer's translation.

The correspondence between Mr. William Palmer and Mr. Alexis Khomiakoff commenced in the year 1844. On neither of his two visits to Russia had Mr. Palmer made the acquaintance of the great Slavophil leader. This was probably because that up till then none of Mr. Khomiakoff's theological treatises had been published. Such of his writings as had appeared in Russia were either of a philosophical or of a historical complexion, and only indirectly touched upon questions such as Mr. Palmer went to Russia to study. The reasons for this will be perfectly clear from what has been already said in the Introduction, and it is therefore unnecessary to repeat them here. It was through their mutual friend, Mr. Redkin, that the correspondence which we are publishing in this volume commenced, and which led to their subsequent friendship. Upon the death of his two eldest children, Mr. Khomiakoff had written in the year 1839 his touching and beautiful poem upon the death of his two eldest children, which at the present day is known wherever the Russian language is spoken. Mr. Palmer translated it into English, and sent a copy of his translation to Mr. Redkin. The following is Mr. Palmer's translation; and to it we append Khomiakoff's Russian text, the exquisite grace and pathos of which it is impossible adequately to render in any language but in the original.

A

TO MY CHILDREN

(Translated from the Russ of A. S. Khomiakoff
by W. Palmer of Magdalen.)

Time was, when I loved at still midnight to come,
My children, to see you asleep in your room;
The Cross' holy sign on your foreheads to trace,
And commend you in prayer to the love and the grace
    Of our gracious and merciful God.

To keep gentle guard, and watch over your rest,
To think how your spirits were sinless and blest,
In hope to look forward to long happy years
Of blithe merry youth, without sorrows or fears,
    Oh how sweet, how delicious it was!

But now, if I go, all is silence, all gloom;
None sleep in that crib, nothing breathes in that room;
The light that should burn at the image[1] is gone:
Alas! so it is, children now I have none,
    And my heart how it painfully throbs!

Dear children, at that same still midnight do ye,
As I once prayed for you, now in turn pray for me;
Me who loved well the Cross on your foreheads to trace;
Now commend me in turn to the mercy and grace
    Of our gracious and merciful God.

---

[1] That is to say, the *Eikon*, or sacred picture placed in the corner of every Russian room, before which a lamp often hangs, which is kept burning when the room is occupied, more especially on Sundays and Festivals.—[W. J. B.]

КЪ ДѢТЯМЪ.

Бывало, въ глубокій полуночный часъ,
Малютки, приду любоваться на васъ;
Бывало, люблю васъ крестомъ знаменать,
Молиться, да будетъ на васъ благодать,
    Любовь Вседержителя Бога.

Стеречь умиленно вашъ дѣтскій покой,
Подумать о томъ, какъ вы чисты душой,
Надѣяться долгихъ и счастливыхъ дней,
Для васъ, безваботныхъ и милыхъ дѣтей,
    Какъ сладко, какъ радостно было!

Теперь прихожу я: вездѣ темнота,
Нѣтъ въ комнатѣ жизни, кроватка пуста,
Въ лампадѣ погасъ предъ иконою свѣтъ....
Мнѣ грустно, малютокъ моихъ уже нѣтъ!
    И сердце такъ больно сожмется!

О дѣти, въ глубокій полуночный часъ,
Молитесь о томъ, кто молился о васъ,
О томъ, кто любилъ васъ крестомъ знаменать;
Молитесь, да будетъ и съ нимъ благодать,
    Любовь Вседержителя Бога.

CHAPTER II

MR. KHOMIAKOFF'S FIRST LETTER TO MR. PALMER

[1844]

The sign of the Cross—Communion of prayer between living and dead—Misrepresentations of Mr. Khomiakoff's opinions about England—Reunion of Christendom—Different views of Rome and the Orthodox Church—Obstacles to Reunion between Eastern and Western Communities—Mr. Palmer's eyesight—Report of Dr. Newman's secession.

As has been already stated, Professor Redkin had received from Mr. Palmer a copy of his translation of Mr. Khomiakoff's poem, and showed it to the latter. The result was the following letter, which proved to be the commencement of a theological correspondence which lasted for ten years, and which forms the greater part of the present volume:—

Sir,—The elegant and faithful translation of some stanzas written on the death of my first children, which you have had the goodness to include in your letter to Mr. Redkin, has been received by me with the utmost gratitude and pleasure. Yet give me leave to say, that, highly as I value the honour conferred on my poetry, I rejoice still more in the consciousness that it has been paid rather to the human feeling which has inspired my verses than to the merit of the expression.[1] It is indeed a great joy for me to have met with your sympathy, and the more so as I have met with it in the highest of all regions, in the communion of religious sentiments and convictions. In one respect it is even more than I could have anticipated, [inasmuch] as the sign of the Cross and

---

[1] 'to their poetical deserts.'—[R. T.]

the belief in a communion of prayers between living and dead are generally rejected by the over-cautious spirit of the Reformation.

You are, methinks, very right in approving of them. Those who believe that the Holy Cross has been indeed the instrument of our salvation cannot but consider it as the natural symbol of Christian love; and if they reject a most natural and holy sign for fear of idolatry, they seem to be almost as inconsistent as a man who should condemn himself to voluntary dumbness for fear of idle words. In the like manner I think [it] rather reasonable [than otherwise] to believe that no bond of Christian love can be rent asunder by death in the spiritual world, whose only law is love. The Episcopal Church of England seems in the last times to have adopted that principle.[1]

Perhaps I should [here] add a few words for my own justification, as some ridiculous calumnies have been circulated in Germany about my having expressed sentiments of hate towards your noble and highly enlightened country, and may have found their way to England. These calumnies originated in the writings of an Oratorian (Theyner), and were repeated by Jesuits and reprinted in some newspapers. It was a strange thing to see England's cause defended by unlooked-for champions seldom considered as her friends. But a deep and implacable hatred towards Russia and the Oriental Church had inspired them suddenly with a fervent love towards England. Yet I will not attempt a justification; I am sure that English good sense and justice will always prove a sufficient defence against the brazen-faced hypocrisy of an Oratorian or a Jesuit. Permit me rather to add some few observations on the last passage of your letter to Mr. Redkin, which he has communicated to some of his friends.

You say: 'Those who desire to be *true patriots* and *true*

---

[1] 'This principle, it appears, has begun to be admitted of late by the Episcopal Church of England.'—[R. T.]

cosmopolites should repeat, not with their lips only, but from their inmost heart, the words "о соединéнiи всѣхъ"[1] whenever they occur in the services of the Church.' Indeed, sir, I think that many are the cultivated Russians who repeat that part of the Liturgy not only with their lips and breath but with their heart and soul. I, for my part, having been educated in a very religious family, and particularly by a pious mother, still living, have been taught to join sincerely in that beautiful prayer of the Church. When very young, almost a child, my imagination was often delighted by a hope of seeing all the Christian world united under one banner of truth. Later, that became less vivid as the obstacles grew more and more visible. At last, I must confess it, what was a hope has dwindled into a desire relieved from despair by nothing but a faint glimmering of a possible success after many and many ages. The South of Europe, in its dark ignorance, is out of the question for a long while. Germany has in reality no religion at all but the idolatry of science; France has no serious longings for truth, and little sincerity. England with its modest science[2] and its serious love of religious truth might [seem to] give some hopes; but—permit the frank expression of my thoughts—England is held by the iron chain of traditionary custom.

You add that 'most serious people in England think only of union with Rome.'

This conclusion seems to me very natural. Union cannot

---

[1] 'For the union of them all,' taken from the third clause of the Great Ectene : ' For the peace of the whole world, for the welfare of the holy Churches of God, *and for the union of them all*, let us make our supplications to the Lord. *Kyrie eleison.*' The Great Ectene is said at the Liturgy, Vespers and Matins, and many other offices of the Eastern Church.—[W. J. B.]

[2] In the original MS., as also in his reply when he quotes this passage (see page 17), Mr. Palmer has inserted a question mark after the word 'modest.' But Mr. Khomiakoff obviously intended, in using this expression, to show that he appreciated the more humble tone of Anglican theological literature, as contrasted with that of Protestant Germany.—[W. J. B.]

be understood by any Orthodox otherwise than as the consequence of a complete harmony, or of *a perfect Unity of Doctrine*. (I do not speak of rites, excepting in the case when they are symbols of a dogma.)

The Church has in itself nothing of a state,[1] and can admit of nothing like a conditional Union. It is quite a different case with the Church of Rome. She is a state. She admits easily of the possibility of an alliance even with a deep discordance of doctrine. Great is the difference between the logical slavery of Ultramontanism and the illogical half-liberty of Gallicanism, and yet they stand both under the same banner and head.[2] The union of the Nicene Symbol and Roman obedience in the United Church of Poland was a thing most absurd,[3] and yet that Church was admitted by

---

[1] 'The Church in her structure [состав = σύστημα] is not a state.' [R. T.]

[2] It must be remembered that this letter was written before the suppression of Gallicanism during the pontificate of Pius IX.— [W. J. B.]

[3] That is to say, the Nicene Creed in its original form, without the Western addition. The Easterns will never admit that the Creed with the addition *Filioque* is the Niceno-Constantinopolitan Creed at all. On the other hand, when the *Unia* was effected in 1596, by the terms of which the Metropolitan of Kieff and several other Orthodox bishops in the Russian and Lithuanian provinces of Poland submitted to the supremacy of Rome on condition that they were allowed to retain the Oriental Rite, the Uniats were not required to bring the Nicene Creed into conformity with the Latin form, but only to acknowledge the supremacy of the Pope. This of course implied the formal acceptance of the Florentine decree in favour of the Latin doctrine, but practically this did not affect the rank and file of the Uniats, who together with the Eastern form retained the Eastern belief. Indeed, in Austria I have come across uninstructed Uniats who to this day are entirely unaware that they are not still in full communion with the Russian Orthodox Church. To understand Khomiakoff's argument, it must be remembered that Eastern theologians maintain that the insertion of *Filioque* fundamentally alters the meaning of the whole clause of the Creed, and that, as they stand, the Eastern and Western formulæ contradict one another, inasmuch as the first implies one ἀρχή, but the second two ἀρχαί, in the Godhead. Accordingly he

Rome very naturally, because the Church of Rome is a state, and has a right to act as a state. The Union with Rome seems to me the more natural for England, [inasmuch] as England in truth has never rejected the authority of the Roman doctrine. Why should those who admit the validity of the Pope's decree in the most vital part of Faith—in the Symbol —reject it in secondary questions or in matters of discipline ?

Union is possible with Rome. Unity alone is possible with Orthodoxy. It is now more than a thousand years since Spanish bishops invented Inquisition[1] (in the time of the Goths), and an addition to the Symbol. It is almost as much since the Pope confirmed that addition by his word of might.[2] Since that time the Western communities have nurtured a deep enmity and an incurable disdain for the unchanging East. These feelings have become traditional

---

argues, that while it is of course possible for *a state* to recognise and accept the two forms, and the difference of doctrine which they involve, in two different parts of its dominions, just as with us the State recognises Anglicanism in England and Presbyterianism in Scotland, it is impossible that contradictions in a vital clause of the Symbol of the Faith should co-exist together in *the same Church*. And therefore he concludes that Rome is not a Church, but a state. —[W. J. B.]

[1] These words are given exactly as Mr. Khomiakoff wrote them. In the MS. Mr. Palmer has underlined the word 'invented,' and has written over it in pencil: 'advanced the principle of.' He then erased the word 'advanced' and substituted for it 'decreed.' This is written tolerably clearly, but the last word might possibly be intended for 'devised,' and this would correspond better with the Russian translation, 'изобрѣтили инквизицию,' which literally means 'invented' (or 'contrived') 'the Inquisition.' On the whole passage, and the historical objections which may be raised to it, it will be best to refer the reader to Mr. Khomiakoff's own explanation on page 65.— [W. J. B.]

[2] In the original MS. Mr. Palmer has underlined the word 'might' in pencil, but what he has written above it is now illegible. It may be 'authority.' The Russian translation gives: *властью и словомъ своимъ*, 'by his own *authority* and *words*.' The italics are those of Russian version.—[W. J. B.]

and, as it were, innate,[1] to the Roman-German world, and England has all the time partaken of that spiritual life. Can it tear itself away from the past? There stands, in my opinion, the great and invincible obstacle to Unity. There is the reason why so many individual attempts have met with no sympathy and no success at all, and why communications on points of theological science not unknown to many of your divines (as for example to the [Scottish] Bishop of Paris,[2] to Dr. Pusey and others), have not even been brought forward to the knowledge of the public. It is an easy thing to say: 'We have ever been Catholics; but the Church being sullied by abuses, we have protested against them, and have gone too far in our protest. Now we retrace our steps.' This is easy, but to say: 'We have been schismatical for ages and ages, even since the dawn of our intellectual life,' is next to impossible. It would require in a man an almost superhuman courage to say it, and in a nation an almost incredible humility to adopt that declaration.

These, sir, are the reasons why, in Russia, the most ardent wishes for universal unity are so little mixed with hope, or why hope (where it exists) turns itself rather to the Eastern communities, Nestorians, Eutychians, and so forth.

---

[1] The word in the MS. is 'innated.' Mr. Palmer has written 'natural' over it in pencil. 'Innate' seems however to be the best word. The Russian translation renders it сроотиоъ съ.—[W. J. B.]

[2] Bishop Luscombe, consecrated at the request of some of the British residents in France, and with the consent of the heads of the English hierarchy, by Bishop Gleig, Primus of the Scottish Church, assisted by Bishops Low and Sandford, on Sunday, March 20, 1825, on which occasion Dr. Hook preached the sermon. In the letters of Collation delivered to him by his consecrators, it was stated that his administrations were to be confined to members of the Churches of England and Ireland, and of the Scottish and American Episcopal Churches on the Continent, and that he was 'not to disturb the peace of any Christian society established as a national Church in whatever nation he may chance to sojourn.' He resided at Paris, where he built the English Church in the Rue d'Aguesseau. He died in 1846. —[W. J. B.]

They are certainly further from Orthodoxy than the Churches of the West, but are not withheld from a return by feelings of proud disdain.

Now, my dear sir, permit me to turn to a question more individual, but extremely interesting for me, as it concerns a man for whom I feel the sincerest esteem, and who has had the goodness to give me a never-to-be-forgotten proof of sympathy and goodwill. You complain of the weakness and irritation of your eyes, a terrible complaint for one who loves study as you do. I am somewhat of a physician (a quack doctor, if you like it), and though I am sure you have had the counsels of men by far more able than I am, I will take the liberty of proposing to you a remedy of which I have made many experiences with the best and most astonishing effects. The remedy is simply a dilution of one part of alum with one hundred and fifty parts of water, to be applied to the eyes on very fine linen three or four times a day. If you find it worth trying, I hope it will do you good; if you do not, I am sure my good intention will excuse the absurdity of the proposition. I forgot to say that the first application is a little irritating, but generally the amelioration is very remarkable in the space of a few days.

I pray you, my dear sir, to excuse the barbarous style of a foreigner and the indiscretion of a man who has taken the liberty of addressing himself to you without having the honour of a personal acquaintance, and to accept the assurance of the most sincere respect and gratitude of, your most humble and obedient servant, ALEXIS KHAMEKOFF.

P.S.—Since this letter was written, I have seen in the newspapers the conversion of Mr. Newman and many others to Romanism,[1] and must confess that I think a critical moment very near at hand for the Church of England. My

---

[1] The writer is probably referring to the premature reports which found their way into the London papers of November 2, 1844. (*Vide* Liddon's *Life of Pusey*, vol. ii. p. 444.) As a matter of fact, Newman did not join the Roman Communion until October 9, 1845.—[W. J. B.]

address is: Въ Москвѣ: Алексѣю Степановичу Хомякову, въ собственномъ домѣ на Собачьей площадѣ возлѣ Арбата.[1] Perhaps the way indicated by yourself, through the medium of Mr. Law, will yet be the surest and best. Knowing the interest you take in Russian literature, I take the liberty to send you a little selection of verses by Yazikoff.

The 10th of December 1844.

---

[1] *To Moscow: To Alexis Stepanovich Khomiakoff, In his own house in Hounds' Place, beside the Arbat.* In Moscow the houses in the same street are not, as with us, distinguished by numbers, but by the names of their owners, so that if a man lives on his own freehold, his letters are directed to 'his own house,' but if he hires a house, 'to the house of N.,' the name of his landlord. Mr. Khomiakoff's house in 'Hounds' Place' (so called after the kennels of the Tzar John the Terrible which in the sixteenth century stood on this site) is still owned by the family, and is at present occupied by his daughter Miss Mary Khomiakoff. The Arbat is one of the principal streets of Moscow.—[W. J. B.]

CHAPTER III

MR. PALMER'S REPLY TO MR. KHOMIAKOFF'S FIRST LETTER

[1845]

Mr. Palmer's book of poems and hymns—Its contents and objects—Letter dedicatory—The English Church and the sign of the Cross—Invocation of Saints—Prospects of the Reunion of Christendom—Duty of the Russian Church in the matter—Reply to Mr. Khomiakoff's strictures upon Rome—Union of the English Church more possible with the East than with Rome—The question of *Filioque*.

MR. PALMER'S reply took the form of a small volume, privately printed, entitled 'Short Poems and Hymns, the latter mostly Translations,' printed by T. Shrimpton at Oxford, 1845.[1] On the English title-page occurs the following quotation from the great Ectene of Eastern Liturgies:—

'For the peace that is from above,
For the welfare of the holy Churches of God,
And for the union of all,
Let us pray unto the Lord.'

Upon the outside paper cover a Russian title is printed in an amusing combination of English, Russian, and Greek capital letters—

СТИХОТВОРЕНІЯ.
ΔΙΑΚΟΗΑ
В. В. ПААМЕРА.
ОКСФОРДЪ.[2]
1845.

---

[1] Not 1843, as is erroneously stated in the list of Mr. Palmer's works given at the end of his *Visit to the Russian Church*, edited by Cardinal Newman.

[2] 'Poems of the deacon V. V. Palmer, Oxford.' The initials V. V. stand for 'Vassíli Vassílievich,' or 'Basil, the son of Basil,' 'Basil' being always used in Russia as the nearest equivalent for 'William' to be found in the Calendar of the Eastern Church.

This shows that Russian type was at this time not so accessible at Oxford as it has since become. The volume commences with five poems by Mr. Palmer himself, the first of which is entitled 'Anticipations, on hearing of the events of the three so-called Glorious Days at Paris, in July 1830,' while the last is his translation of Mr. Khomiakoff's poem as already given in the first chapter. A collection of hymns follow, which are mostly translations from the Latin made by Mr. Palmer himself or others. It also contains some well-known English hymns, including Bishop Ken's for the Morning and Evening. Mr. Palmer's first object was to show how much nearer Anglicanism was to Eastern Christianity than the ordinary Protestantism of Germany, with which at that time the English Church was usually identified by uninstructed people in Russia. Although it cannot be denied that Mr. Palmer's collection was in considerable advance of the hymnals in ordinary use at that time, they would not now be thought so; indeed, they contain no expression for which a parallel may not be found in *Hymns Ancient and Modern*, and many other popular collections at the present time. But the main object of this book was to give expression to Mr. Palmer's longing for the Reunion of Christendom. This is apparent from cover to cover. That he realised that the task was not an easy one is evident from the heading which precedes the metrical paraphrase of the psalm *Qui regis Israel* with which the volume concludes. Besides the passage from the Liturgy already quoted, this heading contains the following sentences: 'Ask those things that be great, and the lesser shall be added unto you'; 'The things which are impossible with men are possible with God: for with God nothing is impossible'; and, in Slavonic, Богъ идѣже хощетъ, побѣждается естества чинъ (God, wheresoever He willeth it, overcometh the order of nature). But the chief interest in this little volume undoubtedly lies in the 'Letter Dedicatory' to Mr. Khomiakoff with which it commences, which is, in fact, his reply to Mr. Khomiakoff's first letter, which we now reprint.

A LETTER DEDICATORY TO MR. A. S. KHOMIAKOFF

[1845]

MY DEAR SIR,—While I thank you for your letter of the 10th of December last, and for the poems of M. Yazikoff which accompanied it, you must allow me to offer you a small return in kind in the following pages, and at the same time to add a few reflections of my own on ecclesiastical matters, partly suggested by what you have been pleased to write to me.

1. You say that the sympathy of an Anglican with the feelings which inspired those verses of yours, which I translated, and which you will find again printed below at p. 6 of these present sheets, 'was in one respect a pleasure greater than you could have anticipated, as the sign of the Cross and the belief of a communion of prayers between living and dead are generally rejected by the over-cautious spirit of the Reformation. You are, methinks,' you continue, 'very right in approving of them. Those who believe that the Holy Cross has been indeed the instrument of our salvation cannot but consider it as the natural symbol of Christian love; and if they reject a most natural and holy sign for fear of idolatry, they seem to be almost as inconsistent as a man who should condemn himself to voluntary dumbness for fear of idle words. In the like manner, I think it reasonable to believe that no bond of Christian love can be rent asunder by death in the spiritual world, whose only law is love. The Episcopal Church of England seems in our own times to have admitted this principle.'

Upon this passage I need not say anything for myself, as the contents of the following pages will sufficiently show how cordially I agree both with your belief and your feelings; but I wish to draw your attention to a point of some interest and importance as regards the character of the Anglican or British Church, of which I am a member. It is unhappily but too true, and too notorious to all the world, that Anglicans have practically laid aside that salutary use of the sign of the Cross by which Christians have ever been distinguished from Jews and heathens; also that they have now no Invocations of the Blessed Virgin or of the Saints in the public Offices of their Church; while in their private opinions they commonly reject all such things as tending to separate us from Christ, *in* Whom alone, and not *apart from* Whom, they ought properly to be viewed and considered. However, you may not, perhaps, be aware, and I am sure you will be pleased to learn, that the Anglican Church *in herself* is not nearly so corrupt on either of these two points as she is *in the prejudices of her members*, and so is quite capable of a very great improvement, whenever it may please God to turn our hearts from our own deep spiritual and intellectual idolatries to Himself. She actually *requires* the use of the sign of the Cross in Baptism, which, you will agree with me, is the root and germ of all other subsequent use of it, whether in the worship of the Church or in daily life; and in one of her canons she defends at length its frequent use on all occasions against the objections of the Puritans or Calvinists, and signifies her own sympathy with the Primitive Church in regarding those who revile this most holy sign as the enemies of the Cross itself and of Christ crucified.

On the other point, of addresses to spirits and souls departed, I will only remark here, that even those Anglican Bishops who are least inclined to favour the spiritual movement called Puseyism do not fail, nevertheless, to acknowledge that their Church has never in any way condemned *apostrophes* and *poetical addresses* to Saints and Angels; for in truth it would be most absurd to retain the Psalms and Hymns of the Old Testament, in which holy David and others speak spiritually both to Angels and to the souls of the righteous, and to their own souls too, and to all things, absent or present, animate or inanimate, and remind God of His departed servants, in order to give efficacy to their own prayers; it would, I say, be most absurd to retain all these addresses from the Church of the Old Testament, as we do still in the Offices of the Anglican Church, and yet refuse to the Church of the New Testament the like liberty of speaking spiritually and *in Christ* to all Angels and spirits, to all persons and things, in all such manners as may be natural and suitable under the new dispensation. But the truth is, the real objection of intelligent and well-disposed Anglicans is not against such poetical addresses as are to be found in your verses, or in the Hymns of your Church, or in those which I now send you, and which are mostly translations, but against *prayers in prose seriously addressed to spirits or souls not present in the body, as a service of homage and devotion.* This is a subject into which I will not now enter; nor indeed is it necessary, for if we Anglicans would only practically re-admit and appreciate that most beautiful and touching sacred poetry, which is common both to the Greek and Latin Churches, and even to the long-separated Nestorian and Eutychian communities, and which our own Anglican Church has never condemned, there would be no fear of any great difficulty remaining afterwards on this point in the way of peace.

You complain of some calumnious reports which originated, as you say, in the writings of an Oratorian, Theyner, and were repeated by Jesuits, whom you charge, not unjustly, I fear, with a deep and implacable hatred against Russia and the Oriental Church. It is indeed true that almost everything relating to Russia comes to us doubly dyed in the religious and political gall of the Poles and of the German and French democrats. Still, setting politics aside, I must confess that I think both we in England and you in Russia will do well to say as little as possible about the faults of the Roman Catholics, at least till such time as we ourselves shall set them a better example, either by a general spirit of prayer and intercession for their improvement and *reconciliation*, or else, if we really think them external to the true Church, by an *active* zeal for their *conversion*.

In allusion to what I had written about the duty of praying for unity, you tell me you 'are convinced that there are very many in Russia who repeat those words in the Offices of their Church, to which I referred, "*for the union of all,*" not only with their lips and breath, but from their inmost heart and soul.' You say of yourself that you 'were taught to join sincerely in that beautiful prayer of the Church; and that while very young, almost a child, your imagination was often delighted by the hope of seeing all the Christian world united under one banner of Truth; that later, however, this hope became less vivid, as the obstacles grew more and more visible. At last,' you conclude, 'I must confess it, what was a hope has dwindled into a desire relieved from despair by nothing but a faint glimmering of a possible success after many and many ages. The south of Europe in its dark ignorance is out of the question for a long while; Germany has in reality no religion at all but the idolatry of Science; France has no serious longings for truth, and but little sincerity; England, with its modest (?) science and its serious love of Religious Truth, might have offered some hope; but, permit the frank expression of my thoughts, *England is held by the iron yoke of Traditionary Custom.*'

In answer to this passage, I must say, that nothing can be more thankfully received by us, nothing can be more consolatory and refreshing, than to be assured that there are in the Eastern Church some hearts, at least, which beat for unity and peace, some, at least, that pray not vaguely and mechanically, but intelligently and fervently for the reunion of the West. Would to God that this were more distinctly known and felt among us here in England! Would to God that you in Russia knew and felt more distinctly how many thousands, both of clergy and laity, there are in England who day and night most earnestly implore God for the reconciliation of Christendom! Such mutual knowledge might do much to increase our zeal, and prevent that despondency which, as it is, you are obliged to confess has crept over many. Now, that there are difficulties in the way of a general reconciliation I well know; that these difficulties should become more and more visible and seem insuperable, as we advance in years and experience, is no wonder at all; but, still, my dear sir, you must allow me to say that even if there were no such counterbalance of encouraging circumstances as I think there is in our days, I should feel it a duty to entreat you never to give way as long as you live to that evil despair of which you speak. Even supposing that the thing desired seems impossible, still, 'What is impossible with men is possible with God'; 'With God nothing is impossible.' *'If ye have faith as a grain of mustard seed,'* says our Saviour, *'ye shall remove mountains'*; and *'Whatsoever two of you shall agree to ask here upon earth, it shall be done for you in heaven.'* *'Whatsoever two of you,'* He says: how much more, then, if *many of us* agree now to ask together upon earth that which our Saviour Himself asked for us beforehand so earnestly on the night of His agony? The very thought of Christians ever despairing in such a cause should be an intolerable thorn to Christian souls.

This, I say, even on the supposition that all appears absolutely dead and stiff,—that to recall Christians in the divided Churches to the practice of earnest prayer for re-union is as hopeless, humanly speaking, as to attempt to raise the Dead,—and yet even the Dead *might* be raised *by Faith*. But in truth things are not so; there are several plain grounds for hope in the prospect before us; I will notice one or two on different sides. First, *if* you in Russia sincerely and heartily believe that the Eastern Catholic, or Orthodox, or Greek Church is really, as it has pretended to be since the Schism, *the whole of the true Church*, that it alone and exclusively is the depository of the True Faith, the Ark of Salvation, this of itself ought always and under all conceivable disadvantages to be a sufficient motive for the most unwearied energy, both in prayer and action, and for the most confident and unbounded hope of success in the work of evangelising the unbelieving world, and bringing back all heretics or schismatics, whether Romanists, Anglicans, Lutherans, or Calvinists, into the true Fold. On the other hand, *if you do not feel quite sure* of this theoretical position of the Eastern Church, or if your eyes and senses tell you, that, whatever she may say upon paper, she herself does not practically believe her own pretensions, then, I grant, you would have among yourselves some reason at first for perplexity and dejection. But, still, the very circumstances of the world and of the present age, circumstances which are daily bringing all men into closer communication, which are popularising all questions and all knowledge, and unchristianising and demoralising all Governments and all nations, especially the higher classes,—this gigantic development, I say, of general sensualism and infidelity, horrible though it be, and a plain sign of the last days, has still an element of hope in it for those whose hearts seek Christ and the Unity of His Church. '*Then lift up your heads,*' He says Himself, '*for your redemption draweth nigh*': and indeed this may be true, in some sense, even before the end, even in our own time. If steam-communication and railroads go on multiplying, if what is called civilisation and education, and with them sensualism in practice and liberalism in belief, go on spreading in all countries from the higher classes to the lower, then neither in England, nor in Rome, nor in Russia, can the well-disposed minority remain exactly where they now are. They have been fixed and crystallised, perhaps, by influences partly political and partly religious for generations: but now all is broken up; and as for you, in Russia, either the Eastern Church must evolve from herself a new spirit, to stem the torrent of evil flowing in from the West, to convert and heal, not the 'heretical' and 'schismatical' Latins only *without*, but too often also her own people *within*,—or she must eventually submit to Rome,—or else, for these are the only three alternatives, she must come to think of a fair reconciliation, on whatever terms it may be effected. Thus the very development of evil in society all around us both suggests grounds of hope and will also afford some considerable facilities for the pressing and fusing together of the divided elements of good.

As regards England more particularly, there is at the present moment a very striking promise of future good. Nowhere, perhaps, is the development of evil more tremendous, both in a religious and in a social point of view; and yet nowhere is there more ground for hope. Only, we may fear lest, while all the world is beginning to be inquisitive about the Religious Movement in England called Puseyism, the Eastern Church should present to Englishmen nothing to engage towards herself any share of those sympathies, which are returning towards Rome. It matters comparatively little whether you seek our *conversion*, as of heretics or schismatics, or our *reconciliation*, as of brethren, who may perhaps be able to explain their seeming heresies, and show that they have never absolutely denied the Orthodox Faith. It matters little, I say, whether you take the one line or the other, either with Anglicans, or with Roman Catholics; only, pray, do one or the other; show something like Christian zeal and energy; either such as may become the whole, if you are *the whole*, of the true Church, or else such as may become a part, if indeed you are so much as *a part*: only do one or the other; and that 'proud disdain' of which you accuse us will be at an end,—we shall be drawn towards you by any sign of life, even though its first energy may seem to be directed against ourselves. Not only France, but North America also, and England, are quite open to all religions. Why does not then the sole true Orthodox Greek Church send *at least one* Missionary to England ?—to Oxford ? which now, all the world knows, is the centre of an important religious movement. Seek whichever you please, I repeat, it matters little,—either our conversion or our reconciliation: but do one or the other. Do not go on for ever folding your hands in a shocking self-complacency, outwardly showing not tolerance only, but something very like fraternal recognition to worse heretics than either Romanists or Anglicans, while you inwardly say in your heart, 'We alone are the true Church, and *they* are all heretics in the way of darkness and destruction,'—*they*, whom you do not so much as move a finger to bring into your exclusive Ark of salvation!

You say 'it seems to you very natural that serious people in England should think only of *union* with Rome: because a *union* cannot be understood by any Orthodox Christian,' (*i.e.* by Christians of the Greek or Eastern Church) 'otherwise than as the consequence of a complete harmony, or *perfect unity of doctrine*, (you do not speak, you say, of rites, excepting so far as they may be symbols of any dogma). The true Church has in itself nothing of a state, and can admit nothing like a conditional union. It is quite a different case,' you proceed, 'with the Church of Rome. That Church *is* a State. It admits easily the possibility of an *alliance* even with a deep discordance of doctrine. Great is the difference between the logical slavery of Ultramontanism and the illogical half-liberty of Gallicanism; and yet they both stand under the same banner and the same head. The union of Nicene Creed and Roman obedience in the Uniat Church of the Polish provinces was a thing most absurd; and yet that Church was admitted into Communion by Rome very naturally, because the Church of Rome is a state and has a right to act as a state. *Union* is possible with Rome, *unity* alone is possible with Orthodoxy.'

Upon this passage I must remark, that we in England, and the Pope too, and all Roman theologians entirely agree with you and with the Eastern Church in holding that the true Church can never admit any political or conditional union, nor anything short of absolute *unity* in doctrine; but the Roman Catholics would think your remarks upon their admission of the Uniats and upon their toleration of Gallicanism unjust. For the Uniats by communicating with the Pope and his Churches, in which the Creed is sung with the addition, and that not as equals with equals, but as inferiors with their superior, virtually submitted to the Latin doctrine, although the Pope tolerated the prejudice or weakness, as he would think it, in the merely external point of form. And as for Gallicanism, that again is viewed as an evil tendency in an inferior and particular Church, by no means recognised as of right, but distinctly condemned by the superior authority, and only tolerated *de facto* within certain limits, so long as not fully developed to its consequences; just as in every society, and in the Eastern Church herself no less than in the rest, many particular opinions contrary to the ruling spirit have ever been, and ever will be, tolerated, until they are so developed or rise to such practical importance, as to force the supreme authority either to add to its authoritative decrees, or to require submission to those which exist already with more minute and strict vigilance. Thus, in the Eastern Church, it was at one time free for a bishop, say for Epiphanius, to reject pictures; but when the controversy in later times was developed, such toleration ceased. And now[1] in the Latin Church it is free to deny that the Blessed Virgin Mary was conceived without sin, while in the Eastern it is free to assert the contrary proposition, though the general sentiment in the Latin Church is in favour of the Immaculate Conception, and in the Eastern perhaps against it. But, to dwell no more on this, it is enough to say that you greatly mistake the present religious movement in England, if you think it has been characterised by any desire of a hollow, political, or conditional *union*, or that any such desire has prompted that inclination which now shows itself in many towards Rome. It began in a spirit of the most loyal Anglicanism evoked by the successful attacks of the Protestant sectaries and the Roman Catholics, aided by a Liberalist Government, upon the Established Church; it proceeded, up to a certain point, in a spirit of resolute hostility to Popery no less than to Sectarianism; and it was only as increased knowledge and continued efforts after self-improve-

---

[1] That is to say, in the year 1845. The Immaculate Conception of the Blessed Virgin Mary was declared to be a dogma of the Roman Church on December 8, 1854. The Greeks have long kept upon December 9 the festival of the 'conception of St. Anne, the Mother of the Mother of God,' and the Canon for the day was written by St. Andrew of Crete (A.D. 660-732), but nothing which either this Canon or any other part of the service for the day contains refers in any way to the doctrine of the Immaculate Conception. Indeed the whole service is, as was the mediæval office in the English service books for that day, merely a complement to the offices for the Nativity of B. V. M. on September 8.—[W. J. B.]

ment and certain unhappy signs of the dominancy of evil among ourselves, revealed more and more the inconceivable mass of traditionary prejudice and ignorance under which we are all buried, that some of the most earnest and influential minds were carried on to doubt even of the Spiritual existence of the Anglican Church, and to desire reconciliation with Rome not conditionally, but simply, and with feelings of the most abject self-abasement and self-renunciation.

For myself, I do not profess to go all lengths with this feeling in favour of simple and absolute submission to Rome; not, I hope, from any unwillingness to confess myself or my Church heretical or schismatical, if truth require it; but because as a matter of fact I have not come to the conviction either that the Anglican Church has lost the continuity of her spiritual life, or that simple and absolute submission to Rome is at present either possible or desirable for her as a body. So far as my studies have gone, I am persuaded that the declaration of *unity*, not the negotiation of any political or conditional *union*, with the Eastern Church is much more possible and much more desirable at present than with the Roman: though God forbid that I should ever think or speak of any such thing otherwise than as a step both for us and for the Easterns towards ultimate union with Rome. I repeat it, I think that unity (not *union*) with the Eastern Church is a thing both desirable and possible for the Anglican Church: not immediately indeed, nor even soon, but eventually: and that, by no organic or violent change on either side, but by a natural and gradual development of what exists at present. I do not suppose that the Eastern Church ought either now or at any future time to alter one jot of her doctrine in favour of any prejudices or reasonings of Anglican bishops, nor that she should admit the Anglican Church in her present state, or any of her members to her communion: for that would only be to introduce anarchy among her own members, and to declare it free to admit or reject upon private judgment the greater part, or at least a very great part, of what are now rightly held in her for holy and inviolable traditions. Still less do I suppose that the Anglican Church or her members could ever gain any good thing by becoming professors of Græco-Russicism or Orientalism :—not that they should be withheld by feelings of pride or of disdain : but the thing is in itself impossible, that any man of understanding, whatever his opinion may be of the particular character of the particular *Eastern* Church, should ever come to be drawn to her as a convert upon the general ground of *Catholicity*. Without any such vain anticipations, I declare to you seriously, as one who has passed some years of his life in Ecclesiastical studies, that I am perfectly sure of the existence in the Anglican Church of an element of faith and doctrine not only *like*, but *identical* with, the faith and doctrine of the Eastern Church : so that though union with the present Anglican Church, which is made up of conflicting and undeveloped tendencies, partly orthodox and partly heretical, is out of the question, union with the orthodox element of the Anglican Church, whenever it shall have asserted its own exclusive ascendency, and expelled its heretical antagonist, will be perfectly natural and easy, and scarcely need any negotiation or conference, except for merely subordinate matters of discipline and ritual. To illustrate what I mean, I may mention the Armenian Church, which seems, in like manner with the Anglican, to have had a double existence from a very remote period. Now, though union with the Armenians without explanation or change on their part would be union with heresy, still, if that Church were to do again what she has already done more than once, that is to say, explain her heretical language in an orthodox sense, and formally reject and disuse the language as well as the spirit of heresy for the future, *Unity* being thus declared and received, *Union* would be no longer objectionable.

But what I have here said needs some reservation ; for there is certainly one point on which, though I have a very strong opinion of my own that your faith virtually agrees with ours, yet I cannot speak with such absolute certainty as I can on questions relating to my own personal Faith, or the Faith of that Church of which I am a member, and which so

I contemplate from within, while I know the Eastern Church only by external evidence. And this brings me to the last part of your letter, in which you speak of the great difference between the Western and Éastern Churches, the question of the addition of the words '*Filioque*' to the Creed. This difference you judge 'to be the greatest obstacle not only to union, but even to the thought of union.' I fully admit that this is indeed so; and, far from inviting a member of the Greek or Eastern Church to underrate this difficulty, I agree with him in thinking that it is right and natural, and even his duty, *in the first instance*, to think the Latins heretics (not schismatics merely) upon this point, just as it is right and natural for us on our side also, *in the first instance*, to think the Greeks schismatics at least, or, as I should rather say, heretics, upon the same. Still, this should not be done on either side by an ignorant and bigoted tradition, which neither seeks to understand its own faith aright, nor to estimate rightly the error of the heretics, nor sighs with charity for their return to the truth, nor seeks diligently to remove all unnecessary obstacles, whether on the one side or the other; but rather, I contend, if this point of the 'Filioque' is really the wall of separation which causes our distinct Churches to regard each other as heretical, then surely the minds and prayers of all Christians on both sides, according to their ability, should be constantly turned upon this point, seeking not from any foreign conferences, or even from Synods, but from the Holy Ghost Himself, the Bond of union between Father and Son in the Holy Trinity, and the Giver of all truth, peace and concord upon earth, that this also may be revealed to us. We should be constantly trying to make progress in the knowledge and appreciation of our own faith on this point, constantly trying to discover what stumbling-block there may be in the way of our separated brethren, which prevents them from agreeing with us; while, on the other hand, we should be jealously fair and charitable in ascertaining that we do not misrepresent or calumniate their belief, and so wilfully make a difference where there need be none, or, where there is one, make the difference greater than it really is. Michael the Archangel, it is written, feared to bring a railing accusation, even against the Devil. How much more, then, should we be cautious how we speak bitterly even against heretics! And if even civil judges are careful to give all prisoners who are brought before them every possible allowance, and every fair advantage toward . their defence, how much more should the members of Christ be careful in judging *two-thirds of the Christian world, and the first Bishop*, as when you accuse the Latins, or *one-third of the Christian world, and five patriarchs*, as when they accuse you? But I will not attempt now to go deeply into this question. I do not desire, even if I were able, to suggest the thought that all difficulties can be overcome at once, even theoretically; but rather I would entreat you to sympathise yourself and bring others to sympathise with that moral and spiritual yearning for unity, which, with all our faults, we certainly have now in some degree in the Anglican Church, and which, if it showed itself among you also, would sooner or later obtain from God all that may be necessary to enable us to arrive at the desired end. For the present it will be enough if you on your side seek daily to realise more and more within yourselves that faith, which is indisputably the tradition of your Church, that *the Holy* SPIRIT *is from all eternity truly and properly the* SPIRIT *of the Son, even as He is the* SPIRIT *of the Father* ; while it is heresy to say that *the* SON *is the* SON *of the Spirit* : and seeing that there are many among us in England who certainly desire unity, and you assure us that there are some at least in the Eastern Church who desire the same, let us strive henceforth with one another in our prayers, each asking, both for ourselves and for the others, that we may grow ever more and more in the truth which we have, and that whatever is lacking to us on either side may be supplied. And so I conclude my letter, begging you to believe me to be, my dear Sir, yours most sincerely and respectfully,

W. PALMER (*Deacon*),
Fellow of St. Mary Magdalene College,

OXFORD, *June* 4, 1845. *in the University of Oxford.*

CHAPTER IV

MR. KHOMIAKOFF'S SECOND LETTER TO MR. PALMER

[1845]

Obstacles to Reunion of Western and Eastern Churches, moral even more than doctrinal—Mr. Palmer's strictures upon the Eastern Church partly, but not entirely, fair—Invocation of Saints—Protestant objections to it due to inheritance of Roman traditions—The procession of the Holy Spirit—Western breach of the Church's unity—Mr. Khomiakoff's opinion of the English Church.

MOST REVEREND SIR,—Accept my sincerest thanks for your friendly letter and the copies of your short Poems and Hymns, which I have received by post, and the expressions of my gratitude for the Letter Dedicatory which is printed at the head of that instructive and elegant edition. The honour you have conferred on me in affixing my name to your Poems, unforeseen and unmerited as it was, is deeply appreciated, and shall always be cherished by me as a proof of a dear and never-to-be-forgotten sympathy. I should be happy indeed if I could by work or word show myself not unworthy of it.

The reflections you have been pleased to address to me on ecclesiastical matters call for a reply. They have not been inspired by a cold spirit of scholastic dispute, but by a warm and Christian desire of universal unity; and deficient as I think myself in many points of theological knowledge, I feel that I have no right to evade the duty of answering the questions you have proposed and the opinions you have stated about Church and doctrine.

Both your letters contain some friendly reproaches directed to me personally, and some which seem addressed to all our Eastern communities. There is in them much of truth which I will not attempt to extenuate, but I will take the liberty to say a few words of justification, as I think you are not quite right in the point of view which you have chosen.

In the first place I readily admit that the hopelessness with which I consider the obstacles that oppose the return of the Western communities to Orthodoxy may prove and proves me indeed but of little faith and of a faintness in my desires for that return. Warmer feelings and a more Christian disposition would probably have shown me things in a different light, or at least would have turned my eyes from the calculations of worldly probabilities to the thoughts of divine Providence and its inscrutable ways. This fact being once admitted, I may be allowed to say that I think myself right in the statement of things as they stand at present (the future being in the hands of a merciful God), and in the opinion that the greatest obstacles to Unity are not in the visible and formal difference of doctrine (as theologians are apt to suppose), but in the spirit which pervades the Western communities, in their customs, prejudices, and passions, but, more than all, in a feeling of pride which hinders a confession of past errors, and a feeling of disdain which would not admit that divine truth has been preserved and guarded for many ages by the long-despised and darkened East. My words have not been, perhaps, quite useless, if they have turned your attention to the latent feelings which widen the chasm between the Eastern and Western communities.

The reproach you seem to address to all Eastern communities, and particularly to Russia, for want of Christian zeal and energy, and for evident indifference about the diffusion of true doctrine is a bitter one, and yet I will not deny its justice. Perhaps we could find some excuses in the long sufferings of our country, and of Greece, in the Mahometan yoke, in political causes and in the spiritual battle which is unceasingly to be fought within the precincts of our own country against errors, schisms, and the continual attacks of modern scepticism; but all such excuses are insufficient. More than half of the world is still in complete darkness; our nearest neighbours in the East live still in utter ignorance of the Word and Doctrine of Christ; and that could not have happened if we had inherited the burning zeal of the Apostles. We have nothing to say against these proofs. We stand convicted, and should be quite unworthy of the grace and mercy that have been shown to us if we did not confess how worthless indeed we are. Humility is a duty not only for individuals, but also for nations and communities. In Christians it is not even a virtue; it is simply obedience to the voice of reasonable conviction. We can only request and expect that the Faith which we hold may not be judged by our actions. The justice of your reproach being confessed in its full extent, I think I may add that it cannot at least be inferred from our seeming indifference for the reconciliation or conversion of our Western brothers. Apostles brought to the world new tidings of joy and truth; our missionaries could do the same in the pagan or Mahometan East; but what can we do in the West? What new tidings have we to bring? What new sources of information can we open to Europe, and particularly to England? Is not the Holy Scripture as well and (to our shame be it said) better known to the majority of your nation than to ours? Is not your clergy, and even a part of your laymen, as conversant with the Fathers and Ecclesiastical history as our most learned Divines? Is not Oxford a centre of Science which we cannot rival? What can a missionary bring to you except unavailing eloquence and, perhaps, some individual errors from which no man is sure to be free, though the Church is? There was a time when Christian society preached by example even more than by word. The individual example of a missionary would prove nothing at all; and as for national example, what shall we say? Our only request should be that your eyes may be turned away from us; for our good qualities are hid and our vices are audaciously brought to view, particularly in that capital and in that part of society which are foremost to meet the observation of a foreigner. The rites and ordinances of our

Church are despised and trampled on by those who should set the example of obedience. The only way left for us (though it may subject us to seemingly just accusations), is, perhaps, to wait with anxious expectation for the result of the struggle which is going on everywhere (and in England certainly with more earnestness than anywhere else), and to express our sympathy by prayers to God that He may give victory to the better part of human nature.

Now, to return to your reflections on matters of ecclesiastical doctrine. I am well aware that Luther himself was inclined to re-admit the sign of the Cross and the communion of prayer between living and dead (which he has attacked many times), and that the Anglican Church has never formally rejected them; but a practical rejection seemed to prove that Anglicans had gone further on in the way of Protestantism than in earlier ages, and I could not but rejoice in seeing signs of return to good and Christian doctrines. Yet allow me a remark which, though directed to a single point, seems to me extremely important, as it brings on conclusions about the whole spirit of the Western Churches.

You say that 'even those Anglican bishops who are least inclined to favour the spiritual movement called Puseyism, do not fail nevertheless to acknowledge that their Church has never in any way condemned apostrophes and poetical addresses to saints and angels, but that the real objection of intelligent and well-disposed Anglicans is against prayers in prose seriously addressed to Spirits and Souls not present in the body as a *service* of homage and devotion.' I think the word *service*, though certainly often used in the acceptation you give to it, throws some confusion on the question. The song of triumph which meets the victorious warrior on his return to his native land has never been called a service, though it is assuredly joyful homage and an expression of gratitude and devotion. In the like manner, the homage paid by Christians to the noble warriors who have fought the Spiritual battle of the Lord through ages and ages, and have held aright the tradition of the Church, should not perhaps be called a service, but an expression of joy and humble love. We cannot properly be said to serve our fellow-servants, though their station be infinitely exalted above our own. The objection of Anglicans and other Protestants has truth in it if directed against the word, none if against the thing itself. No enlightened member of the Orthodox Church could indeed understand it unless he was acquainted with the Roman definitions [1] and theories which have in fact given birth to almost all the errors of Protestantism. But another objection remains. We address to created Spirits not only the homage of our praises, but very earnest requests (as this expression would in this case perhaps be more correct than the expression 'prayers'), asking for their intercession and prayers before the Majesty of our Saviour. 'Where is the use of such requests? Where is our right to them? Do we want any other advocate but Christ our Lord? There can be no serious meaning in our addresses to created beings, and we may as well reject all those useless and idle forms.' There is the question. I will answer it with another. Was the Apostle serious when he asked for the prayers of the Church? Are the Protestants serious when they request their brethren (as they often do) to pray for them? Where is, if you please, the logic of the distinction? A doubt about the possibility or reality of a communication between living and dead through Christ and in Christ is too un-Christian to want an answer. To ascribe to the prayers of living Christians a power of intercession which is refused to the Christians admitted into heavenly glory would be a glaring absurdity.

---

[1] That is to say, the word 'service (*Servitium beatae Mariae*, etc.) used in connection with the worship of the Saints. The Eastern Church does not employ the Western terms *dulia* or *hyperdulia*, but retains the more ancient terminology of the Seventh Œcumenical Council, describing the relative and secondary worship which the Church offers to the Saints, the holy images, the book of the Gospels, etc., by the term τιμητικὴ προσκύνησις as contrasted with λατρεία, or the absolute and primary worship which is due to God alone.— [W. J. B.]

If Protestantism was true to logic, as it pretends to be, I may boldly affirm, that not only Anglicans, but all Protestant sects (even the worst) would either admit serious and earnest addresses to saints and angels, or reject the mutual prayers of Christians on earth. Why, then, are they rejected, nay, often condemned? Simply because Protestantism is for ever and ever protesting. Because the semi-pelagianism of Popery and its doctrine about merits and, as it were, self-worthiness of the Saints is ever present to Protestantism. Because Protestantism is not, nor ever can be, free. In short, because with its unceasing cry, 'No Popery,' it stands on Popish ground and lives on Popish definitions, and is as much a slave to the doctrine of utilitarianism (which is the ground-work of Popery) as the most fanatical Ultramontanist. Now we are free, and, though well aware that we want no intercessor but Christ, we give vent to our feelings of love and to our earnest longings for mutual prayer and spiritual communion not only with the living, but with the dead, who have not been saved by their own worthiness (for none, even of the best, was worthy, save Christ alone), but by the grace and mercy of the Lord, which, we hope, will be extended to us likewise.

I readily concur with you in the opinion that if Anglicans would only practically admit and appreciate the beautiful poetry of hymns addressed to saints and angels, there would be no fear of any great difficulty remaining afterwards on this point in the way of peace; nor would I have spoken on the matter if I had not considered it as an example and a proof of the constant subjection of all the Western communities to the doctrines and spirit of Romanism. This subject is as evident in the negations as in the affirmations of Protestants, and the illustration of it which I find in their rejection of prayers addressed to the Church invisible could be corroborated by many other examples; such as the dispute about Faith and Works, about Transubstantiation, about the number of the Sacraments, or the authority of Holy Scripture and Tradition; and, in short, by every question about ecclesiastical matters and every Protestant decision concerning them.[1] But it is certainly most evident in that all-decisive point which you agreed with me in considering as the greatest obstacle not only to Unity between Orthodoxy and Anglican communities, but even to the thought of Union.

I will not enter upon the question [of the *Filioque*] itself nor attempt to defend the Nicene Creed in its original form; I will not say that the Western has no authorities for it [*i.e.* the addition *Filioque*] excepting falsified passages of the Fathers, or texts from them which prove nothing, as regarding only the Mission *ad extra*, or even texts which, rightly understood, would prove the contrary of the Roman doctrine. Such is the passage of St. Augustine (if my memory fails me not), where he says, *principaliter autem a Patre* (that is, *quoad principium*), which if

---

[1] This point is further worked out in the author's first Essay upon the Latin Church and Protestantism. 'Il serait bien facile de montrer que l'empreinte romaine a marqué de son caractère indélébile les doctrines réformées, et que le même esprit de rationalisme utilitaire, qui était celui de la papauté, est encore celui de la Réforme. Les conclusions sont constamment différentes, mais les prémisses et les définitions qu'elles contiennent implicitement restent toujours les mêmes. La papauté dit : " L'Eglise a toujours prié pour les morts ; mais cette prière serait *inutile* s'il n'y avait pas d'état intermédiaire : *donc* le purgatoire existe." La Réforme répond : " Il n'y a pas trace de purgatoire dans les saintes Ecritures et dans l'Eglise primitive : *donc* il est *inutile* de prier pour les morts, et je ne prierai pas." La papauté dit : " L'intercession des saints a été invoquée par l'Eglise : *donc* elle est *utile* : *donc* elle complète les *mérites* de la prière et de l'expiation." La Réforme répond : " L'expiation par le sang du Christ, acceptée par la foi dans le baptême et dans la prière est suffisante pour racheter non seulement l'homme, mais tous les mondes possibles : *donc* l'intercession des saints est *inutile*, et nous ne leur adresserons plus de prières." La sainteté de la communion des âmes reste inconnue aux deux adversaires. La papauté dit : " La foi selon saint Jacques est insuffisante : *donc* elle ne peut pas nous sauver, et les œuvres sont *utiles* et constituent un *mérite*." Le protestantisme répond : " La foi seule peut sauver selon saint Paul, et les œuvres ne constituent pas le mérite : *donc* elles sont *inutiles*," etc., etc. C'est ainsi que la lutte a continué et continue pendant des siècles à coup de syllogisme, mais le terrain sur lequel elle a lieu reste le même : c'est toujours celui du rationalisme, et aucun des deux adversaires n'en peut choisir d'autre.'—*L'Eglise Latine et la Protestantisme*, p. 42.—[W. J. P.]

rightly translated means: 'the Spirit comes (i.e. *ad extra*) from the Father and Son, but originates from the Father.'[1] I will not recall the decisive approval given by an Oecumenical Synod to the anathema of Theodoretus against the doctrine of Procession from Father and Son. (The absurd explanation given by Jäger in his life of Photius and by other Roman writers who pretend that the anathema was directed against Monophysite tendencies looks like anything rather than fair and Christian discussion of a theological question.) All this I leave aside. I could add nothing to promote knowledge, or to the strong attacks of the illustrious Zernikoff and Theophanes. I will only add an observation of my own. The Protestant world has been torn asunder by all sorts of errors; it has given birth to most strange sects which differ widely the one from the other in almost every point of doctrine. Now this point [of the *Filioque*] every candid Protestant will admit to be at least a doubtful one (though in my opinion there is not even place for a doubt). How does it happen, if you please, that not one of these numerous sects has re-admitted the Nicene Symbol?[2] How happens it that some of them (evidently feeling doubts) have preferred excluding the words about the Procession altogether to the necessity of using the orthodox form, though it is literally transcribed from the words of our Saviour? Does not that circumstance go far to prove undoubted though unconfessed subjection to

---

[1] The passage of which A. S. Khomiakoff is here speaking is to be found in Augustine's treatise upon the Trinity, lib. xv. cap. 12, and is as follows: 'Et tamen non frustra in hac Trinitate non dicitur verbum nisi Filius, nec donum Dei nisi Spiritus Sanctus, nec de quo genitum est verbum et de quo procedit *principaliter* Spiritus Sanctus, nisi Deus Pater. Ideo autem addidi *principaliter*, quia et de Filio Spiritus Sanctus procedere reperitur.' Adam Zernikoff in his well-known work proved, and after him Protestant theologians have maintained, that the word *principaliter* in the first sentence, and the whole of the second sentence (Ideo autem etc.), are nothing but a later insertion—'stercus falsatoris,' as one learned writer of the seventeenth century expressed it.—[*Note of the Editor of the Russian Translation.*]

[2] That is to say, the Nicene Creed without the *Filioque*.—[W. J. B.]

Roman precedents, and a deep-rooted feeling of repulsion against anything that could seem to confirm the truth of Orthodoxy? I hope you will not accuse me of judging our ecclesiastical adversaries unfairly.

The matter is most important in two respects, as it is not only a question of doctrine, but a question of morality. Leaving aside the first point, I will consider only the second. In the seventh century, the Catholic Church was one in full communion of love, and prayer, from the depth of Syria and Egypt to the distant shores of Britain and Ireland. About the middle of that century (perhaps even at the end of the preceding one) a change was introduced in the Symbol by the Spanish clergy. In the first letter I had the honour to address you, I added, that this change was made at the same time when the Inquisition was first introduced in its worst forms,[1] and by the same provincial Synods, with the intention to recall to your memory that the first step towards schism was taken by the worst, most corrupted and most un-Christian clergy, swollen with the pride of exorbitant political rights. The innovation was left unnoticed, as having been made in a distant country which was soon overrun and conquered by Mohammedans. Still, unnoticed as it was in the East and even in Italy, the new doctrine crept on further and further through the Western communities. About the end of the eighth and beginning of the ninth centuries, the new Symbol was admitted by most of them as a thing of course. We have no right on that occasion to accuse the Roman See. The Popes felt the unlawfulness of the proceeding, they foresaw its dreadful consequences, they tried to stem the flood, but could not. Their only fault (and a great one it was) was to have shown a want of energy in their resistance. The West felt itself of age; it could speak for itself; it had no want of anybody's opinion or assent in things of faith. The innovation was solemnly adopted without a general Synod being held, without the Eastern Bishops being invited to give

---

[1] For this statement, see p. 65.—[W. J. B.]

their assent, without even so much as a notice being given to them. The bonds of love were torn, the communion of faith (which cannot exist with different symbols) was rejected in fact. I will not say, 'Was that lawful?' The idea of law and lawfulness may do for casuists and disciples of the *jus Romanum*, but cannot do for Christians. But I will ask: 'Was that moral? Was it brotherly? Was it Christian?' The rights of the Catholic Church were usurped by a part of it. An unmerited offence was given to unsuspecting brothers, who till that time had fought with the greatest perseverance and certainly the greatest ability for Orthodoxy. This action was certainly a most heinous sin, and a most shocking display of pride and disdain. The bad inheritance has been accepted and held till now. Must it be held for ever?

Let worldly societies deviate from moral law; let them sin and glory in their sins, and in the temporary advantages they have gained by them. I am not, nor can ever be, a political man; therefore, I will not judge political communities, though I do indeed suspect that every bad action of the fathers is or shall be visited on their children by the logic of providential history. But I know for certain that every man must answer for his sins and be punished for them until he confesses and repents. Still more assuredly do I know that there can be no sin in the Church of God, in the holy elect and perfect vessel of His heavenly truth and grace; and that therefore no community which accepts the inheritance of sin can be considered as a real part of it.

You may remark, most Reverend Sir, that I have not entered on the dogmatic part of the question, and only considered the moral part of it. I may add that, left alone and rejected as we were by our usurping brethren, we have had a right to decide all sorts of questions by ourselves and by the authority of our own clergy and laymen; yet we have not used that right. We are unchanged; we are still the same as we were in the eighth century, before the West had rudely spurned its Eastern brethren. Let us be brought to the test. Oh that you could only consent to be again what you were at that time when we were united by Unity of Faith and communion of spiritual love and prayer!

Some words more must be said in answer to the last part of your printed letter. You are right in giving the following rule: 'We should be jealously fair and charitable in ascertaining that we do not misrepresent or calumniate the belief of our separated brethren, and so wilfully make a difference when there would be none, or, when there is one, make the difference greater than it really is.' I do not think that we are much inclined to fall into the said error, and, by the knowledge I have of my countrymen, I should rather suppose that they lean to the opposite extreme; yet if the thing be disputed, I will readily admit that no man can be impartial either in his own cause or in the cause of his nation or community. In the present case, I confess that I do not clearly see the possibility of an error. Either the addition has the meaning generally ascribed to it by the Romans as concerning the original[1] Procession of the Spirit, which cannot be considered by us in any other light than as an heretical proposition; or it expresses only the procession *ad extra*, which no Orthodox can or dare dispute. In the first supposition the difference is immense, and the question must be solved by scriptural and moral proofs, viz.: by considering whether the Western communities have any authorities for them in the Holy Scriptures, or in their early commentators, or in the decisions of Œcumenical Synods, and whether there is any probability that the grace of the Holy Ghost may have dictated a change, which was accompanied by such an open

---

[1] In Khomiakoff's MS. the world used is 'originary.' The word used in the Russian translation is начальный, which corresponds exactly to the Greek ἀρχικὸs and the Latin *principalis*. The following is the Definition of the Council of Florence :—*Definimus quod Spiritus Sanctus a Patre et Filio eternaliter est . . . declarantes quod id quod sancti doctores et patres dicunt ex Patre per Filium procedere Spiritum Sanctum, ad hanc intelligentiam tendit, ut per hoc significetur, Filium esse, secundum Graecos quidem causam, secundum Latinos verò principium subsistentiae Spiritûs Sancti sicut et Patrem.* This of course the Easterns reject.—[W. J. B.]

usurpation of rights, and such an evident and un-Christian disdain shown to a considerable part of the Church. I think that both propositions would easily be negatived. In the second case there is indeed no difference at all. But the duty of rejecting the addition becomes still more imperative. Who can continue to use equivocal expressions when this double meaning has had, and has even now, such dreadful consequences? Who can hold up the standard of ancient usurpation condemning at the same time in his heart the usurpation itself? The line of moral duty seems in this case to be quite evident.

My real opinion of the Anglican Church is, in many respects, very near to your own. I believe seriously, that it contains many orthodox tendencies, perhaps not quite developed, but growing to maturity; that it contains many elements of unity with Orthodoxy, obscured, perhaps, by nothing but unhappy habits of Roman scholasticism, and that the time is at hand when a better understanding will be followed by real union between long separated brethren. The seemingly heretical, or at least equivocal, language should only be explained in an orthodox sense, and the language and spirit of heresy should be formally rejected *and disused* for the future. These are your own expressions. In the first point the power usurped in the change of the Symbol should be frankly condemned as offensive to charity and love; but there stands the great moral obstacle; for such a condemnation would seem, and indeed would be, a confession and an act of penitence; and, sweet as penitence is in its consequences, it is at first bitter and repulsive to the pride from which no man is free. And yet what good can be done without moral renovation, when every good consequence is sure to be derived from it, as it brings with itself the perfect grace of the Father of lights? But it is indeed no easy thing; and there is the reason why, with so many apparent causes for hope, my hopes are so faint and null. I know I am not right in giving way to my fears, and yet I should be still more wrong if, entertaining such thoughts, I should not express them frankly. Certainly my greatest joy would be to be convicted of error and pusillanimity by the event.

Having gone thus far, I will take the liberty to observe that, in my opinion, many, even of the best disposed amongst English divines, are apt to fall into a strange and dangerous delusion. This delusion is to suppose that not only every particular Church can run into partial errors without ceasing to belong to Catholicity, but that the whole of the Catholic Church can likewise be obscured by temporary errors, either the same in every part of it, or different in the different communities, so that Truth is to be distilled out of the corrupt mass by the rule of 'quod semper, quod omnes, quod ubique.' I have lately had the pleasure of reading a book, which you are probably acquainted with, of Mr. Dewar about German Rationalism.[1] I consider it a masterpiece of fair and sound logic, free from passions and prejudices. The sharp intelligence of the author has not only perfectly found out the reasons of the inevitable development of Rationalism in Protestant Germany, but has found its traces in Roman Catholicism, notwithstanding its continual pretensions to the contrary. This is certainly a great truth which could be corroborated by many other and even stronger proofs; but, strange to say, Mr. Dewar excepts the Anglican Church from the general accusation, as if a Church which confesses to a reform did not stand self-convicted of Rationalism! Indeed if the totality of the Church could ever have fallen into errors of doctrine, individual criticism would have become not only a right, but an unavoidable necessity; and that is nothing but Rationalism, though it may hide itself behind the well-sounding words of 'Testimony of the Fathers,' whose writings are nothing but heaps of written pages; or, 'Authority of the Catholic Church,' which has no meaning at all if it could not escape error; or, 'Tradition,' which, once interrupted, ceases to exist; or even 'Inspiration from heaven,' which every man can pretend to be favoured with,

---

[1] Dewar: *German Protestantism*; Oxford, 1844.—[W. J. B.]

though no other believes his pretensions. The continual presence of the Holy Ghost is a promise given to us by Truth Itself; and if this promise is believed, the light of pure doctrine must burn and shine brightly, through all ages, seeking our eyes, even when unsought for. If it is once bedimmed, it is obscured for ever, and the Church must become a mere word without a meaning in it, or must be considered, as many German Protestants indeed do consider it, as a society of good men differing in all their opinions, but earnestly seeking for Truth with a total certainty that it has not yet been found, and with no hope at all ever to find it. These consequences are unavoidable, though some of your worthiest divines do not seem to admit them, and this is certainly a dangerous self-delusion.

If you find some expressions of this letter rather harsh, I beg of you not to judge them too severely. It is perhaps in my turn of mind to see obstacles rather than the means by which they may be avoided; and I hope I have been actuated by no desire of giving offence; but by an earnest wish that every difficulty may be rightly understood so as to be the better solved with the help of Him whose blessing is sure to illuminate hearts that are honestly and humbly longing for Truth and moral perfection. Such hearts are certainly no rarity in your country.

Accept, most reverend sir, the assurances of the sincere and perfect esteem with which I have the honour to call myself your most humble and obedient servant,

ALEXIS KHAMECOFF.

SMOLENSK, *August* 18, 1845.

CHAPTER V

MR. PALMER'S REPLY TO MR. KHOMIAKOFF'S SECOND LETTER

[1846]

Mr. Palmer's *Harmony of Anglican and Eastern Doctrine.*—Question as to whether the West is still a part of the Catholic Church—Inconsistency of the Eastern Church in this matter—Agreement possible between the English Church upon the question of the Invocation of Saints—Remarks upon various points raised by Mr. Khomiakoff.

ST. MARY MAGDALENE·COLLEGE,
OXFORD, *July* 1, N.S., 1846.

MY DEAR SIR,—I am ashamed when I look at the date of your letter to me (August 18, 1845) to reflect that it is now nearly a year ago since I received it. My only apology for not acknowledging and replying to it sooner is this, that my eyes being still weak and unfit for much work, though getting better, and your letter being of considerable length, and deserving, as I felt, a full answer, and my eyes being generally tasked from day to day by business which I could not avoid, I was tempted or forced to procrastination. Besides this, I was employed during all my spare time on a work which is by no means irrelevant to the subject of our correspondence, entitled *A Harmony of Anglican Doctrine with the Doctrine of the Catholic and Apostolic Church of the East.*[1] This work is at length finished, and I have requested my friend, Mr. Blackmore, our Chaplain at Cronstadt, for whom I have edited it, to send a parcel containing several copies of it to you in our joint names; you will perhaps do me

---

Printed at Aberdeen, 1846.—[W. J. B.

the favour to dispose of the contents of this parcel in the following manner, according as you may find opportunities without putting yourself to any inconvenience. First, there will be a parcel enclosed for the Metropolitan [Philaret] of Moscow, containing six or seven copies, two for himself, one for the library of the Academy, one for the library of the Seminary, one for Mr. Kyriakoff and one for his colleague, Mr. Netzaeff, Professor of the Academy, and last, one for the Bishop Aaron, who I believe reads English. These I have mentioned in a separate letter to the Metropolitan, and I make no doubt he will be ready to take charge of them. Besides these, I must depend upon your kindness to let the following persons of my acquaintance have each a copy with my regards and remembrances, viz., the Princess Dolgorouky, née Davidoff, or her aunt, Mme. de Novotsittsova (which will be the same thing), the Countess Potemkin, the younger Princess Meshchersky (her mother-in-law also should have one, if she is yet alive), and Professor Redkin. Besides these, you can at any time obtain from Mr. Blackmore other copies for any persons who you may think would like to have them, and upon whom they would not be thrown away. I will only observe further on this subject, that I shall hope in due time to receive your criticisms or reflections upon this work, to which I shall attach great interest; also I may as well anticipate one just animadversion which you might otherwise make, by requesting you to make one correction in the book at p. 158, the seventh line from the bottom: Insert 'as' before the words 'from St. Augustine.' I am quite aware that the words are not from St. Augustine, but an interpolation; they express, however, very well the Latin doctrine. In the same way I have myself no doubt at all that the Letter of Pope Leo at p. 160 is interpolated, and should never have admitted it, if I had not thought it worth while to draw attention to that part of Le Quien's Dissertations on St. John Damascene, from which it is taken.

Now to return to your most interesting and valuable letter. I will begin by saying that I am very glad to find that you have avoided almost entirely entering upon any particular Doctrinal discussions, which I quite agree with you in thinking ought to have no place in such a correspondence as ours. On the other hand, all that relates to Christian morality, mutual edification, and to those first principles which common sense and common feeling tell us lie at the very foundation of Catholic or Orthodox Christianity —and about which all ecclesiastical authorities are agreed— all such topics as these may very well and very profitably be treated of even between private individuals. It was in this spirit that I addressed to you my short Poems and Hymns and the Prefatory Letter which accompanied them, and whatever ecclesiastical or doctrinal reflections were to be found in that letter, whether relating to the Anglican Church or to the Eastern, were not meant to involve anything like discussion, but only to excite good feelings by the application of principles already admitted. In the same spirit, I am happy to find, you have answered me; and in the same I now propose to continue our correspondence.

First then, so far as regards my 'amicable reproaches' of the Easterns. You very frankly admit their justice so far as concerns the relations of your Church to heathens, Mohammedans, etc., and thus my whole object is answered if only your confession goes on to practice, and tends in any way to produce a change. But as regards the West, you excuse that want of zeal which you do not deny to exist. I also can find excuses for you, both those that you mention, and one greater than any of these (which you do not mention) and which alone makes them available. And this is the following, viz., that you know in your own consciences —that the Eastern Church herself knows in her own conscience—that yours is only a particular Church, not exclusively the Catholic Church; and that the West, though it may have erred, yet has not vitally and essentially apostatised from the Faith. On this being allowed, it is very natural and very reasonable that the Eastern Church should have little zeal or charity to convert the Latins—nay, that she even, as a particular Church, should be deficient in energy towards the heathens. But on any other supposition her present attitude as regards the whole world of those that are without her is wholly inconceivable. You, indeed, like most other members of the Eastern Church, do not see this, and are far from being ready to admit it: you are fully convinced that your Church has exclusively the truth, that the Latin Doctrine on the Procession, taken in its proper sense, is heresy; that we originally made the interpolation (when we 'felt that we were come to our full youth and could act for ourselves') in a spirit of immoral pride and lawlessness, and have been ever since kept only by the same evil spirit of pride and disdain from opening our eyes to see that the East alone has preserved the true faith, and from returning to that faith by confession and repentance. Now, in answer to this, I will only say that I allow and confess most freely that the West did act in a lawless and immoral manner in making the interpolation; and that this is so far, no doubt, a prejudice against the doctrine itself which was interpolated. Whether the Latin doctrine be in fact a heresy or not, I will not examine now, at least not on theological grounds; for that would be to do the very thing which I have already said neither I nor you ought to do in such a correspondence as the present. But this I will say, that if you think common people, laymen, or even priests, nay, if you think that even learned Bishops and Divines will for ever be content to rest their convictions upon such a point as the Controversy of the Procession upon their own private judgment concerning the intrinsic merits of the question alone—you are, I think, very much mistaken. To illustrate what I mean—the Nestorians, a community of perhaps 100,000 individuals in the mountains of Kurdistan, pretend that they have alone preserved the true faith, and that the Greek and Latin Church has apostatised in a vital point: I say that, under the circumstances of the case, a reasonable man, so far from allowing himself to test the controversy by theological arguments *alone*, would be only showing his good sense, and his piety, if he utterly refused even to enter upon the question: and this, even if he were competent and learned; and much more should all common and simple people perceive the voice of God Himself in the relative circumstances of the two contending parties. In exactly the same way, I say that the man who (not being bred in the Eastern Communion) could for one moment suppose it possible that the Eastern Church alone was the true, and had alone preserved the true faith, and that the Latin Church had erred fatally and essentially, I say that such a man would seem to me at least to be wanting in common-sense—to be not far short of a madman. Now do not think that this comes of a spirit of pride or disdain. I am conscious of no such spirit; and can contemplate without any sense of absurdity the admission that the Anglican Church should have erred even fatally—nay, I even think that the *prima facie* probability runs that way— and I should be quite ready to deny my own spiritual existence, or that of my particular Church, if I were fully convinced that this was indeed so. Further, I am separated from the Roman or Latin, which is bitterly hostile to us; and in my individual sympathies and convictions on particular points, I greatly prefer the Eastern Church to the Latin, and so would not be likely without cause to give any advantage to the Roman side over the Greek. And yet, I assure you, I could more easily conceive myself to doubt of the very spiritual existence of the Eastern Church on account of her exclusive pretensions viewed together with the general comparative phenomena of the two rival Communions, than I could conceive myself tempted to acknowledge her as the sole true Church, on account of any conviction of my private judgment (if I could arrive at such a conviction), that she was right in taxing the Latin Church with essential heresy on the point of the Procession. You have said indeed that you account for such feelings existing in all classes of Protestants as well as in Roman Catholics by the hypothesis that the Protestants are still all Crypto-Papists, either as having inherited the Papal pride and disdain, or else from some other traditionary prejudice which influences them in spite of themselves. About pride and disdain, so far as I myself am concerned, I have spoken already, and will now say further, that though my conscience witnesses to me no such feelings, but rather a very lively interest and zeal for the Eastern Church, and a desire to see her have her due influence on the world and on other Churches, still it is contrary to my principles ever to justify myself when accused, and therefore I will promise you both to seek myself and to try and induce others to cultivate especially the very contrary feelings to that pride and disdain towards the Eastern Church of which you accuse us. This being said, I must go on to give some reasons to show that pride and disdain are not the only motives (even if they exist) which forbid all the Westerns (may I not add, all the separated Easterns too ?) to think for one moment that the Greek Church can be the sole true and Catholic Church. The great argument and motive, as I have said above, lies in the general comparative circumstances, history, and attitude of the Greek Church as compared with the Latin, since the division. This you and others bred up within the Greek Church tell me that you cannot see nor understand. Tell me then, can you understand the following ? I assert that I have never yet met with a single member of the Eastern Church herself, whether layman, priest, or Bishop, who evinced the faintest sign of real conviction that his own Church was the whole Church. I have never found one who did not, on being pressed, allow the true spiritual existence of the Roman and Latin Church ; I have never found one who so much as invited me to conversion from the spontaneous movement of his own faith, far less who used zealous arguments and prayers, as is common even among the poorest and simplest Roman Catholics, to bring all whom they consider wanderers to their Fold. You claim indeed that you should not be judged by your conduct or habits of mind, but only by a candid examination of the point of the Procession, etc. ; but you yourself must see that certain habits of mind (as well as certain circumstances) when they are very general or universal, impress a character on the Body, and are no longer mere individual defects. Individual members of the One True Church may be wanting in zeal to teach and convert the nations—but the Body as a whole, and very many of its members, will always and necessarily have and show forth, even in the eyes of the world, the spirit of its mission. And if any body, as such, is felt and seen by the world at large not to have such a spirit, this alone, without seeking for other arguments, is a sufficient refutation of its claim to be alone the True Church. Would you not even laugh if a Nestorian, or an Abyssinian, or Armenian, on your remarking that their universal absence of zeal to proselyte the world and the other Apostate Churches (as they consider them) gives the lie to their miserable pretensions—if they, I say, were to answer by excuses and explanations, drawn from the local and other particular circumstances of their history? Such excuses might be true and reasonable enough for heretical or schismatical Bodies, or even for *particular* Churches which are not heretical or schismatical, but being only *parts* are not bound to exhibit all the necessary marks and notes of the *whole*: but such excuses, joined with exclusive pretensions to be the whole, only make the error more apparent, and the madness, because unconscious, the more pitiable. You must not judge us by the conduct or habits of our individual members, says the Nestorian: you must think only of the point of theology. You must not demand impossibilities. You see how we have been hemmed up in the mountains of Kurdistan; how we are poor and oppressed, only 70,000 or 100,000 souls: how the sword of the Turk and the Persian is ever hanging over our heads: how we are without learning, without means of communication, in all respects at a disadvantage when compared with those Greeks and Latins whom we rightly call heretics, and whom we are bound by our principles to wish to see converted; though circumstanced as we mutually are, we cannot pretend to act upon them; our only hope is that they may act upon themselves, and of themselves return to the truth which now we alone hold. Now this is, I know, a caricature; because the argument is exaggerated; but still it is the very same argument as is used in defence of the Greek Church. Who is there that does not see that it is at once and of itself an absurdity to suppose that the One True Church could ever come to be so circumstanced? Even if the Nestorians were alone in the world, and no other Christian communities to confront them, it would seem that Christianity has been a failure, that the promises had come to nought, if the true Church had ever come to such a state—or indeed if she had ever come to want any of her essential marks. But when there is, side by side with that Body, which pretends to be alone the true Church, and yet is wanting in some essential characteristic, another greater Body in full possession of that which the first wants, it is no longer merely the defect of the one which proves that it is not what it pretends, but also the comparative contrast presented by the other. Now the Latin Church presents not one only, but many and notable points of such superiority, when contrasted with the Eastern. Her own children, in common with all other Christians, disbelieve her *exclusive* claims; even when they most try to do otherwise, they still in some way or other show this. You will be surprised perhaps when I say that I can find this disbelief even in your own letter. 'What can we do in the West?' you ask, etc., etc. 'The only way left to us is to wait with anxious expectation for the result of the struggle which is going on everywhere, and to express our sympathy by prayers to God that He may give victory to the better part of' —what? Of the nominally Christian world? *i.e.* to the true Church and her representatives, for they are 'the better part' of nominal Christianity? no—'to the better part of human Nature.' Far different from this must ever be the language and feeling of the one true Church and her members, no matter how numerous, how great, how powerful, how learned, the Nation's Bishops or Churches, heretical or schismatical, with which she may have to contend. This sentence alone, from you, even when you are most inclined to Orientalise, is a confession that you are either a nullity, or at best only a particular Church. How different is the language and attitude of Rome—of Rome, do I say? nay, even of the simplest and poorest old woman among the Papists, of such, that is, as have any piety. But it is not enough that there should be this contrast, and that its force should be added to the common sense and conscience of all Christians, your own Easterns included. In the very public acts and documents of the Eastern Church these have ever been used, and are still the most abundant avowals of her own inconsistency. I need only refer you to p. 161 of the volume which I have now sent you, and to the two following pages under the heads V., VI., VII., VIII., IX., X., XI.: from which it is clear, that the Eastern Church has all along been willing to drop the whole question of the sense of the Latin Doctrine on the Procession, and to leave the Latins in full possession of their own opinion, and to communicate with them, if only they would consent to restore the Creed in its canonical form. But if the Latin Doctrine were really intrinsically and necessarily a heresy subverting the true Faith, is it not blasphemy and absurdity even to suggest or think for a moment, that the True Church could communicate with its professors without exacting from them a full and unequivocal retractation and denial? Can you conceive Athanasius, even when all the world (and perhaps the Pope too) were against him, offering to communicate with the Arians or Semi-Arians, provided that they would only abstain from interpolating their heresy into the Creed? You cannot even imagine anything of the sort: nor can you conceive it possible that the True Church should at many different times, and often for many years together, have communicated with vast Bodies publicly professing Nestorianism or Eutychianism, and even adding it to their own particular Creed; certainly never retracting or condemning it. And yet this is what you well know, and all the world knows, the Eastern Church has repeatedly done with the so called Heretical Latin

Church. Surely it is the greatest of all unrealities to persevere in this untenable and inconsistent language. You must see—you must feel—that whatever vehemence of language may have been used, even by Synods, against the Latin Church, such language must be modified and corrected, so as to make the Eastern Church consistent with herself. This, you may say, is[1] difficult. I know it is so. It is difficult to correct any bad habit, or excessive feeling, even in an individual character, however inconsistent it may be with other parts of the same character; much more certainly must it be difficult to correct so deep-rooted a fault in such a Body as the Eastern Church. Still, it seems to me, it cannot remain for ever as it is: you must change eventually, either in one way or the other. You must eventually either say: 'We have done wrong in so often communicating or offering to communicate with the heretical Latin Church without ever insisting upon an essential abjuration; we have done wrong, too, in showing so little faith in our own œcumenicity and consequent superiority, and so little energy or zeal for the conversion of the Latins; but now we will change, and attempt for the future to behave as becomes our exclusive pretensions.' Either you must say this, or else you must say: 'We have done wrong and inconsistently in pretending so long to be the whole, when we have not the necessary attributes of the whole, and know very well that we are only a part: we have done wrong in calling the Latins heretics, and their doctrine Heresy, when we knew all the time that they were not, strictly speaking, heretics, and that if they corrected themselves in a point of form, we might communicate with them freely: for the future we will do so no longer: we confess that the Latin Church is a living part of the same Universal Church with ourselves; that it has preserved the same faith essentially with our own. We accuse it indeed of certain acts of lawlessness and even perhaps of certain

---

[1] The bottom of the page of the original letter is cut away, so that the top only of the word 'is' is visible, and another short word ('very' or 'most'?) before 'difficult' is illegible.—[W. J. B.]

secondary errors in doctrine or ritual; we refuse to communicate with it till it returns to obedience to the Œcumenical law: we support by our authority and recognition all those Churches and Christians in the West, who contend for such a return; but we do not, as before, pretend that either they or the Churches to which they belong have ever so fallen away from the Faith itself as to need reconversion or reconciliation.' This, in my opinion, is the alternative before you. Which of the two lines of conduct you adopt in the first instance matters, I think, but little: I care not which you think right and which you think wrong, provided you only are serious and zealous enough to do either the one or the other. The only thing which I do really dread for you is the continuance of the present apparent insensibility and inaction. If you *seem* dead, you may be sure that you will exercise no influence upon us: we shall look more and more to Rome, which is evidently active and alive. If, on the contrary, you show signs of life, signs, I mean, of a returning sense of duties (of some kind or other) due to the whole Church, to the whole world, then we shall at any rate begin to feel an interest in you—we shall respect you, even though your energies seem to be directed against us. And you yourselves, even if you attempted to be Œcumenical (which seems to me impracticable) would yet assuredly be led on by the very effort to see your error, and correct yourselves if you were attempting an impossibility.

There remains only one other point in your letter on which I will say a few words: that is on the subject of addresses or Invocations to Saints and Angels. I agree with you that Anglicans as well as the Protestants generally are held in bondage on very many points by their habit of seeing all things through Roman phraseology and scholasticism, or rather through their own mistaken ideas of both these. I also agree with you in what you say of the word 'service,' and of 'very earnest requests'; but in going into this question to the extent you have done, I think you must have failed to notice, that I had expressed beforehand, by implication at least, my agreement with you on the whole subject: my remarks tended to show that the Anglican Church certainly admits all that is necessary in this matter for unity. It is true that the opinion held by many Anglicans against 'serious addresses' to Saints or Angels would be intolerable, if imposed by them upon others; but as a private opinion they might hold it without breach of unity themselves. Neither the Latin nor the Greek Church has decided anything formally on this point: and the Eastern Patriarchs in particular distinctly offered their Communion to certain British Bishops in the last century, even though these latter should, through a mistaken caution, refuse to admit any *direct* addresses to Saints or Angels at all. See p. 174 of the book I have sent you. But as we are fully agreed upon this subject, I need say no more upon it.

In conclusion, I have one or two desultory remarks to make. (1) The passage from St. Augustine with 'principaliter' is not St. Augustine, but an interpolation, as Zernikoff has shown. It is the same as that which I have already referred to in a former part of this letter, as requiring correction in the book that I have sent you. (2) Theodoret never argued at all against the *Latin* doctrine of the Procession from the Father and the Son, but against a very different doctrine of a procession from the Son alone, either absolutely or (by delegation) intermediately. This also you will find acknowledged by Zernikoff in his great work. At the same time I fully acknowledge that Theodoret clearly shows that he knew not nor received either the language or the idea of the modern Latins. (3) I quite agree that M. Jäger's hypothesis is unworthy of notice. (4) What are the precise facts relating to the origin of the Inquisition which you allude to ? Roman Catholic writers do not ascribe to it anything like the antiquity which you do; nor do I remember anything which can fairly be identified with the Inquisition at that early period to which you refer. (5) I do not myself feel at all sure that the Symbol was really interpolated in Spain so early as you allow, *i.e.* in the middle of the seventh or end

INFALLIBILITY OF THE CHURCH

of the sixth century. However, this is generally affirmed. (6) Also Zernikoff and others have shown that it was by no means allowed as a matter of course, even in the West, at the beginning of the ninth century. (7) You will see from the book I send you, that I fully admit that the interpolation ought to be taken out of the Creed. I will say more; I fully admit that the Eastern phraseology is that of the Primitive and Universal Church, and, when rightly understood, and taken altogether, is fully sufficient for faith and piety. The Latin language can claim no more than to be a variety in the expression without difference of sense. (See p. 156 (*sic*), 159, and 156 (*sic*) of the volume.) (8) Lastly, I must express my entire concurrence in your excellent remarks upon an error very common among Anglicans as well as Protestants generally: viz., that of supposing that not only every particular Church can run into partial errors without ceasing to belong to Catholicity, but that the whole of the Catholic Church can likewise be obscured by temporary errors, either the same in every part or different in the different communities, so that truth is to be distilled out of the corrupt mass by private reason following the rule *Quod semper, quod ubique, quod ab omnibus*. This is certainly a very common notion and a very false one—indeed heretical: that is, if the errors spoken of be supposed to be essential, whether in doctrine or practice. Otherwise, if you distinctly draw the line, and declare that you mean only secondary errors or abuses which do not subvert the faith, or amount to heresy; in this limited sense I cannot deny but that particular Churches, or even the whole Church, may at times be more or less infected with such abuses and errors; although, even so, piety will ever shrink from supposing any the least error or abuse to be prevalent even in a particular Church, without being absolutely forced to see that it is so. Thus, in the Roman Communion the sale of Indulgences—and thus, in your own Russian Church the uncanonical rebaptizing of Christians already baptized, was for many years prevalent, and even sanctioned by local Canons. Thus, for a time even great heresies (as Arianism) have infected the whole Church and seemed on the point of arriving at dominancy—for even this also is possible, so long as you do not suppose heresy to be established and taught by the public law of the Church; for that would indeed be inconsistent with Christ's promise. (9) A 'Reformed' Church (if the word 'reformed' be understood of any essential point of faith), must certainly be heretical.

I hope you will make my best remembrances to Professor Redkin. I saw the other day at Paris a friend of yours, M. Moukhanoff. I was very much obliged for the books sent me through Mr. Williams, and exceedingly sorry to hear of the death of Mr. Voronieff.—Pray believe me to be always, my dear Sir, yours most sincerely,

W. PALMER.

CHAPTER VI

MR. KHOMIAKOFF'S THIRD LETTER TO MR. PALMER

[1846]

Moral obstacle to the West accepting Orthodoxy—The Eastern Church defended from the charge of lack of missionary zeal—And from charge of inconsistency with regard to *Filioque*—And with regard to the Rebaptism of Westerns—Replies to some further remarks of Mr. Palmer upon *Filioque* and the Inquisition—Difficult for Westerns, whether Latins or Protestants, to join the Orthodox Church—The Church cannot be a harmony of discords—Latent power and great future of the Orthodox Church.

MOST REVEREND SIR,—Accept my heartiest thanks for your friendly letter, and my excuses for having been rather slow in answering it. I cannot but call your letter a friendly one, though it contains some very severe attacks on us; but a truly friendly disposition lies in my opinion at the bottom of them, and is manifested by the honest frankness of their expression. I think your attacks generally wrong, but they are sincere, and show a serious desire to find out truth, and to come to a satisfactory conclusion in the debated question. Every doubt, every difficulty, and every accusation, let it be ever so hard for the accused party, should be candidly and clearly stated; this is the only way for establishing the difference between right and wrong. Truth must never be evaded; it should not even be veiled in truly serious questions.

Permit me to resume briefly your accusations. First: ' If we pretend (as indeed we do) to be the only Orthodox or Catholic Church, we should be more zealous for the conversion of erring communities, as the Spirit of apostleship, which is the true spirit of Love, can never be extinct in the true

Church; and yet we are manifestly deficient in that respect. Secondly: 'Our pretensions are evidently contradicted by the admission (proposed by some of our most important divines) of a communion with the Latin Church on very easy conditions.' Thirdly: 'Slight errors (proved by a change of[1] rites) have been admitted by our own Church, and therefore we cannot logically uphold the principle that the true Church can never have fallen into a dogmatical error (be it ever so slight), or have undergone any change, be it ever so unimportant.'

I have fairly admitted our deficiency in Christian zeal, though at the same time I exculpated our Church from that accusation with respect to the Western communities. You explain that same faintness by a latent conviction of our Church, which, you suppose, feels herself to be no more than a part of the whole Church notwithstanding her pretensions to the contrary. This explanation seems to me quite arbitrary, and has no right to admission till it be proved that no other explains the case quite sufficiently. But the question stands differently. The distinction I made between our relations to the heathen and our relations to Europe you consider rather as an evasive than as a direct answer, yet I think it is easily maintained by a very high authority. I had said, 'What new tidings can we bring to the Christian West? What new source of information to countries more enlightened than we are? What new and unknown doctrine to men to whom the true Doctrine is known though disregarded?' These expressions imply no fear of a contention which indeed would show weakness and doubt, no distrust of the strength of our arguments and authorities, perhaps even no great want of zeal and love. They simply imply a deep conviction that the reluctance of the West to admit the simple truth of the Church arises neither from ignorance nor from rational objections, but from a *moral obstacle* which no human efforts

---

[1] Mr. Palmer has underlined the words 'change of,' and has written in pencil over the top 'variations in some.'—[W. J. B.]

can conquer, if it is not conquered by the better feelings of the better part of human nature, in those who can know the truth but do not wish to confess it. Such a disposition can exist, though the question is whether it exists in the case I am speaking of. Did not the Father of Light and Source of Love say in the parable by the lips of Abraham: 'Have they not Moses and the Prophets? If they do not listen to them, they will not listen to Lazarus, even if he was to rise from the dead.' Do not, I pray, consider this quotation as being made with an intention of offence. I would not make injurious accusations; and, having once confessed a want of zeal in our country and people, I would confess it again; but my conviction is, that indeed in the present case the words of Christ may fairly be applied, and that you are separated from us by a moral obstacle, the origin of which I have tried in my former letter to trace to its historical beginning.

But does not this faintness of zeal—which I admit (with regard to the heathen nations)—imply a defect in the Eastern Church herself, and prove her to be no more than a part, perhaps even not so much as a part of the whole true Church? This I cannot admit. It may be considered as a defect of the nations to whom the destiny of the Church is temporarily confided (be they Russians or Greeks), but can nowise be considered as a stain to the Church itself. The ways of God are inscrutable. A few hundreds of disciples in the space of about two centuries brought to the flock of Christ more millions of individuals than there were hundreds in the beginning. If that burning zeal had continued to warm the hearts of the Christians, in how short a space of time must not all the human race have heard and believed the saving Word? Sixteen centuries have elapsed since that epoch; and we are obliged to confess with an unwilling humility that the greater and by far greater majority of mankind is still in the slavery of darkness and ignorance. Where then is the zeal of the Apostle? Where is the Church? That would prove too much if it proved anything at all. Many centuries, particularly in the middle ages, and at the beginning of modern history, have hardly seen some few examples of solitary conversions and not one national, and not one remarkable effort at Proselytism. This seems to inculpate the whole Church. The spirit of missions is now most gloriously awakened in England, and I hope that that merit will not be forgotten by the Almighty in the days of trial and danger which England has perhaps to meet; but this noble tendency is a new one, or at least has become apparent only very lately. Is it a sign that the Church of England is now nearer to truth than it was before? Is it a proof of greater energies or purity? No one can admit the fact. Or let us take the Nestorian community, which you hold out as a parallel to us. I do not consider the parallel as a caricature, though you have added that word, probably with an intention to avoid offence. The Nestorians are generally ignorant, but ignorance (in point of Arts and Sciences) was our own lot not more than a century ago. The Nestorians are generally speaking poor; but that is no great blemish for any man and particularly for a Christian. They are few, but the truth of a doctrine is not to be measured by the number of its votaries. The Nestorians have been richer and more learned and more numerous than they are at present. They have had the spirit of Proselytism. Their missionaries have extended their activity over all the east as far as the inner India and the centre of China, and that Proselytism was not ineffectual. Millions and millions had embraced Nestorianism (Marco Polo's testimony is not the only one to prove their success). Was Nestorianism nearer to truth in the time of its triumph than in our time? Mohammedanism and Buddhism would give us the same conclusion. Truth and error have had equally their time of ardent zeal or comparative coldness, and the characters of nations may certainly produce the same effects as the characters of epochs. Therefore I see no reason for accusing the Orthodox Church in herself of a defect or weakness which may, and in my opinion evidently does, belong to the nations that compose her communities.

Having thus distinguished the notes of the Church herself

from the national qualities or defects of the Eastern community which alone represents it temporarily, permit me to add that the comparison which you institute between the zeal of the Romanists and the seeming indifference of the Eastern World is not quite fair. I do not deny the fact itself, nor do I express any doubt concerning the apparent superiority of the Latins in that respect; but I cannot admit their spirit of proselytism to be anything like a Christian feeling. I think it should be left quite out of the question, as being the necessary result of a particular national or ecclesiastical organisation, nearly akin to the proselytising spirit of Mohammedanism in the days of its pride. I will not condemn the zeal of the Romanists; it is in some respects too praiseworthy to be ill or even lightly spoken of; I can neither praise nor envy it. It is in many respects too un-Christian to be admired, as having produced and being always ready to produce more persecutors than martyrs. It is, in short, a mixed feeling not dishonourable for nations which belong to Romanism, but quite unworthy of the Church, and not to be mentioned in questions of ecclesiastical truth. I am, I trust, very far from having the disposition to boast, and yet I cannot but call your attention to a strange and generally unnoticed fact, viz., that notwithstanding the apparent ardour of Romanism and seeming coldness of Orthodoxy as to proselytism, yet that since the time of the Papal Schism (which certainly begins not with the quarrels of Photius and Nicolas, but with the interpolation of the Symbol when the West declared itself *de facto* sole judge of Christian doctrine) it has been the destiny of Orthodoxy to be happier in its conquests than its rival community. No one will doubt the fact if he considers the numerical superiority of Russian Orthodox Christians over the inhabitants of Scandinavia and about a third part of Germany, which were called to the knowledge of Christ after the time of Charles the Great. To this comparison you must add that even of that lesser number more, and by far more, than a half was not converted, but driven into the Latin Communion by cudgel, sword, and fire.

I repeat that I am rather ashamed of our having done so little, than proud of our success; but in the unaccountable ways of Providence it is perhaps a particular dispensation of the Eternal Goodness to show that the Treasury of Truth must and shall thrive though confided to seemingly careless hands. No Anscar or Wilfried, no Willbrod or Columban came to instruct Russia. We met truth more than half-way, impelled by the grace of God. In after-times we have had our martyrs, we have had and still have our missionaries, whose labour has not been quite fruitless. I admit they are few in numbers;[1] but is not the voice of truth which calls upon you, the voice of the whole Church? You have as yet seen no Russian or Greek missionary. But did Cornelius reject the Angel's voice and declare that he would not believe till the Apostle came? He believed, and the Apostle came only as a material instrument of Christian confirmation; and shall the message of God, the emanation of the whole Church, the voice of truth, be the less powerful or the less acceptable because no single individual has been found worthy of bringing it to you? The Church may have and has undoubtedly many different forms of preaching.

The second point of accusation concerning the easy conditions on which Communion was proposed to the Latin Community may equally be answered without difficulty. Firstly, I readily admit that Mark of Ephesus went too far in his concessions; but in a fair trial of that great man and eminent divine we should, I think, rather admire his undaunted firmness than condemn his moments of human weakness. His was a terrible task. He felt, and could not but feel, that in rejecting the alliance of the mighty West he was literally condemning his country to death. This was

---

[1] This is anything but the case at the present time. The mission work which has been done during the last forty years and is still going forward amongst the Mohammedan and other non-Christian populations within the Russian Empire need fear comparison with no other mission work in the world either for zeal or for success.— [W. J. B.]

more than martyrdom for a noble spirit, and yet he stood the trial. Are we not to be indulgent in our judgment over an unwilling error inspired by the wish of saving his country, and are we not to bless the memory of his glorious opposition? Other divines of a later period [may have] consented to a communion with Latins requiring nothing but a restitution of the Symbol to its ancient form and other less material changes in doctrine. These you consider as too easy conditions. 'Would Athanasius' [you ask] 'have admitted Arius to communion, and allowed him the liberty of teaching Arianism everywhere excepting [in] the Symbol?' Very certainly he would not; but there is an immense difference between the heresy of Arius and the false doctrine of the Latins. The first rejects the true doctrine; the second admits it, and is only guilty of adding an opinion of its own (certainly a false one) to the holy truth. That opinion in itself has not been condemned by the Church, not being directly contrary to the holy Scriptures, and therefore does not constitute a heresy. The heresy consists in calumniating the Church and in giving out as her tradition a human and arbitrary opinion. Throw the interpolation out of the Symbol, and tradition is vindicated; opinion is separated from Faith; the keystone is torn out of the vault of Romanism, and the whole fabric falls to ruins with all its proud pretensions to infallibility, as if Romanism were the sole judge of Christian truth; the rebel spirit is hewed down and broken. In short, all is obtained that need be obtained. A deeper insight into the question would show (and that observation did not probably escape our divines) that the [human] opinion which is [merely] added to [the true] traditionary doctrine and implied in the *Filioque* has indeed no other support but the decision of ignorant Synods, and the declarations of the Roman See. Being once rejected out of the Symbol, and consequently out of Faith and Tradition, it could not stand by itself, and would be sure to fall and be forgotten like many other partial and local errors, such as, for instance, the error of considering Melchizedek as an apparition (though no incarnation) of Christ. The high majesty of the Church, most reverend sir, has nothing to do with individual opinions, though false, when they do not run directly against her own doctrine. They may, and do, constitute a heresy only when they dare to give themselves out as her doctrine, her tradition, and her faith. This seems to me a sufficient justification of the conditions proposed to the Romans and a proof that they did not imply the slightest doubt of the Eastern Orthodoxy and of her doctrine being the only true one.

Your third accusation is not positively stated; it is rather insinuated by a comparison with the sale of Indulgences than directly expressed; but I cannot leave it without an answer. Your own expressions that 'the re-baptizing of Christians was prevalent for many years and even sanctioned by local canons' would be sufficient for our justification; for local errors are not errors of the Church, but errors into which individuals can fall by ignorance of the ecclesiastical rule. The blame falls on the individuals (whether they be Bishops or laymen signifies nothing). But the Church herself stands blameless and pure, reforming the local error, but never in need of a reform. I could add that in my opinion even in this case the Church has never changed her doctrine, and that there has only been a change of rites without any alteration in their meaning. All Sacraments are completed [1] only in the bosom of the true Church, and it matters not whether they be completed in one form or another. Reconciliation renovates the Sacraments or completes [2] them, giving a full and Orthodox meaning to the rite that was before either insufficient or heterodox, and the repetition of the preceding Sacraments is virtually contained in the rite or fact of reconciliation. Therefore the visible repetition of

---

[1] Mr. Khomiakoff uses the expression 'are completed' in the sense of the Russian 'совершаются,' which is equivalent to the Latin 'conficiuntur.'—[W. J. B.]

[2] Here he used the word 'completes' in the sense of the Russian 'довершается,' which is equivalent to the ordinary English term, 'completes.'—[W. J. B.]

Baptism or Confirmation, though unnecessary, cannot be considered as erroneous, and establishes only a ritual difference without any difference of opinion. You will understand my meaning more clearly still by a comparison with another fact in ecclesiastical history. The Church considers Marriage as a Sacrament, and yet admits married heathens into her community without re-marrying them. The conversion itself gives the sacramental quality to the preceding union without any repetition of the rite. This you must admit, unless you admit an impossibility, viz., that the Sacrament of Marriage was by itself complete in the lawful union of a heathen pair. The Church does not re-marry heathens or Jews. Now, would it be an error to re-marry them ? Certainly not, though the rite would seem altered. This is my view of the question. The re-baptizing of Christians did not contain any error, but the admission of the error (if error it be) having been a local one is quite sufficient for the justification of the Eastern Church.[1] The case is quite different with the sale of

[1] There has never been a period when the whole of the Eastern Church re-baptized Westerns. A Synod held at Constantinople in the 13th century after the expulsion of the Latins in 1260, and also another Synod held in 1484 after the failure of the Council of Florence, decreed that Westerns on joining the Church were to be anointed with Chrism, but not re-baptized. The Russian Church was the first to depart from this rule. A Synod held in 1629 under the Patriarch Philaret Nikitich Romanoff (the father of the Tzar Michael Romanoff, the founder of the present Russian dynasty) ordered the rebaptism of all Westerns. This however was reversed in the case of the Latins by a Synod held at Moscow under the Patriarch Nicon in 1655, and the reversal was confirmed in 1667 by his successor Joasaph, as well as by all four Eastern Patriarchs. The baptism of Lutherans and Calvinists was first acknowledged by the Russian Church in 1718, on the receipt of a letter from the Patriarch Jeremiah III. of Constantinople giving his assent. It was at a Council in 1756 that the four Eastern Patriarchs first instituted the rebaptizing of Westerns, on the ground that baptism without immersion was not $βάπτισμα$. It was only during the last twenty-five years that first the Church of the modern kingdom of Greece, and soon afterwards the Patriarchate of Constantinople, conformed to the Russian Church and their own earlier practice in this matter.—[W. J. B.]

Indulgences. It was an error of the whole Roman Church, being not only sanctioned by her infallible head, but emanating directly from him. But I will be content to leave that argument aside, decisive though it be for a true Romanist, and will admit that the sale of Indulgences was attacked by some divines who were never condemned as heretics. It matters little whether it be so or not. The error remains the same. The sale of Indulgences cannot be condemned from a Roman point of view. As soon as Salvation is considered as capable of being obtained by external means, it is evident that the Church has a right to choose the means, considering the different circumstances of the community. Charity to the poor may be reasonably changed into charity to the whole body of the visible Church or to her head, the See of Rome. The form is rather comical; but the doctrinal error does not lie in the casual form; it lies in the doctrine itself of Romanism, a doctrine which is fatal to Christian freedom, and changes the adopted sons of God into hirelings and slaves.

I have thought it necessary to answer the accusation hinted at by the comparison you institute between two errors of Romanism and Orthodoxy, yet I do not much insist on accusing Rome in that particular case. The only thing I wanted was to show that we have a right to uphold the doctrine that no error, even the slightest, can ever be detected in the whole Eastern Church (I neither speak of individuals nor of local communities); and permit me to add that without this doctrine the idea itself of a Church becomes an illogical fiction, by the evident reason that, the possibility of an error being once admitted, human reason stands alone as a lawful judge over the holy work of God, and unbounded rationalism undermines the foundations of faith.

I must add some observations concerning the remarks that conclude your letter.

1. I have no doubts about the passage of St. Augustine (*principaliter autem*, etc.) being an interpolation. The proofs given by Zernikoff seem conclusive; but I am inclined to

consider it as an ancient interpolation and no wilful falsification, and therefore thought it not quite useless to show that it contained nothing in favour of the Latin doctrine.

2. I am quite aware that the doctrine attacked by Theodoret was not the Latin one, which was quite unknown at that early period; but the expressions of Theodoret are directly opposed to the addition in the Symbol, and this is quite sufficient to show that such an addition would have been utterly impossible at the time of the Ephesian Synod, and is contrary to the doctrine then admitted as Orthodox.

3. The Inquisition of the Gothic period in Spain is not known under that name, and is not united by any visible historical link with the later one; that is the reason why no historian has ever sought for the origin of that dark institution in those remote centuries; but the bloody and iniquitous laws which were so fiercely urged against Arians and Jews in the time of the predecessors of Roderick have all the character of [a] religious Inquisition in its most abominable form, and originated, as did the later Inquisition, from the will of the Clergy. That is the reason why I have given them a well-known name, though that name was not yet used in the Gothic epoch. It is to be remarked that neither the Mohammedan conquest, nor a struggle of seven centuries, nor all the changes of manners, habits, and civilisation which must have taken place during such a long space of time, could alter the national character of the Spanish Clergy. No sooner was Spain free and triumphant but it renewed its old institutions, a terrible and [hitherto] unnoticed example of the vitality of errors and passions and of their hereditary transmission to the remotest generations.

4. There is no doubt that at the end of the eighth, and at the beginning of the ninth century, the *Filioque* was not yet generally admitted by the Western Communities. Zernikoff is right in that respect, and a decisive argument may be derived from Alcuin's testimony; but the Spanish origin of the addition is an undoubted fact, and I see as yet no conclusive reason to suppose that the Acts of the Spanish

Synods have been falsified. The addition itself may be easily explained by the struggle between Arians and Catholics at the time of the Goths, and by a desire of attributing all possible qualifications of the Father to the Son, whose divinity was denied by the Arians. This indeed is, I think, the only reasonable explanation of the arbitrary change in the Western Symbol. After the Arian struggle, and at the time of the Arabs, I can see no reason nor occasion to suggest such a change, and therefore have not the least doubt that the error originated from one of the Gothic Synods, though I am not quite sure whether it was from one of the earliest. At all events, it must have begun no later than the end of the seventh century.

Having thus answered your remarks, I will take the liberty, most reverend sir, to add some observations on the whole tenor of your friendly letter. It is a friendly one, not to me alone, but to all of us children of the Orthodox Church. We could not have asked for larger concessions, nor for a greater agreement in points of doctrine. That yours is not a solitary instance may be inferred not only from your quotations in your most valuable book about the Russian Catechism, but still more from the letters and professions of the Reverend Bishop of [the Scottish Church at] Paris. Believe me, this assurance is a source of great and heartfelt joy for all who feel an interest in truth and unity; and yet, sad to say, what have we gained? Nothing. We have been tried in our doctrine and found blameless; but now we are again tried in our morals (for zeal and love, which are the impelling motives of the Apostle, are nothing but a part of Christian morality), and we are found defective, as indeed we are, and our doctrine is to be condemned for our vices. The conclusion is not fair. You would not admit it if a Mohammedan was to bring it as an objection against Christianity itself, and yet you urge it against Orthodoxy.

Permit me to search into the latent causes of this fact, and excuse me if you find something harsh or seemingly offensive in my words. A very weak conviction in points of doctrine can bring over a Romanist to Protestantism, or a Protestant to Romanism. A Frenchman, a German, an Englishman, will go over to Presbyterianism, to Lutheranism, to the Independents, to the Cameronians, and indeed to almost every form of belief or misbelief; he will not go over to Orthodoxy. As long as he does not step out of the circles of doctrines which have taken their origin in the Western world, he feels himself at home; notwithstanding his apparent change, he does not feel that dread of apostasy which renders sometimes the passage from error to faith as difficult as from truth to error. He will be condemned by his former brethren, who will call his action a rash one, perhaps a bad one; but it will not be an utter madness, depriving him, as it were, of his rights of citizenship in the civilised world of the West. And that is natural. All the Western doctrine is born out of Romanism; it feels (though unconsciously) its solidarity with the past; it feels its dependence from one science, from one creed, from one line of life; and that creed, that science, that life was the Latin one. This is what I hinted at, and what you understand very rightly, viz., that all Protestants are Crypto-Papists; and indeed it would be a very easy task to show that in their Theology (as well as philosophy) all the definitions of all the objects of creed or understanding are merely taken out of the old Latin System, though often negatived in the application. In short, if it was to be expressed in the concise language of algebra, all the West knows but one datum, a; whether it be preceded by the positive sign $+$, as with the Romanists, or with the negative, — as with the Protestants, the a remains the same. Now a passage to Orthodoxy seems indeed like an apostasy from the past, from its science, creed, and life. It is rushing into a new and unknown world, a bold step to take, or even to advise.[1]

---

[1] Cp. Khomiakoff: *L'Eglise Latine et le Protestantisme*, p. 106-108:—
'En toutes choses la lutte de la vérité contre l'erreur est remplie de difficultés, quoique le triomphe lui soit finalement assuré. Combien

This, most reverend sir, is the moral obstacle I have been speaking about; this, the pride and disdain which I attribute to all the Western communities. As you see, it is no individual feeling voluntarily bred or consciously held in the heart; it is no vice of the mind, but an involuntary submission to the tendencies and direction of the past. When the Unity of the Church was lawlessly and unlovingly rent by the Western clergy, the more so inasmuch as at the same time the East was continuing its former friendly intercourse, and submitting to the opinion of the Western Synods the Canons of the second Council of Nicæa, each half of Christianity began a life apart, becoming from day to day more estranged from the other. There was an evident self-complacent triumph on the side of the Latins; there was sorrow on the side of the East, which had seen the dear ties of Christian brotherhood torn asunder, — which had been spurned and rejected, and felt itself innocent. All these feelings have been transmitted by hereditary succession to our time, and more or less, either willingly or unwillingly, we

n'est elle pas plus difficile quand les obstacles à la reception de la vérité se trouvent non seulement dans la raison, mais encore dans la volonté et les passions. Ceci est particulièrement le cas dans les rapports de l'Église envers les communautés qui s'en sont séparées. Quelles que soient les haines et les défiances entre les différentes confessions occidentales, les peuples qu'elles renferment dans leur sein sont plus ou moins sur un pied d'égalité entre eux. Ils ne forment, pour ainsi dire, qu'une seule famille.

'C'est leur vie commune qui a fait l'histoire de l'Europe; ce sont leurs communs efforts qui ont fait la civilisation contemporaine. Enfin, à l'exception de l'Italie et de l'Espagne, il n'est pas un seul de ces peuples qui ne compte parmi ses citoyens des membres de presque toutes les confessions occidentales. Le passage d'une croyance à une autre n'offre rien d'insolite, rien qui blesse les deux formes, peut-être les plus invincibles de l'orgueil humain, celui de la race et de la civilisation. Il en est tout autrement dans les rapports de ces mêmes peuples avec l'Église. Ils ont à recevoir les vérités de la foi d'une société que leur dédain a autrefois rejetée, et qui depuis lors s'est trouvée étrangère à leur vie intérieure et à leur développement. Ils ont à écouter en disciples la voix d'une race qui leur est étrangère par le sang, et qu'une vie historique, pleine de souffrances et de luttes

are still under their power. Our time has awakened better feelings; in England, perhaps, more than anywhere else, you are seeking for the past brotherhood, for the past sympathy and communion. It would be a shame for us not to answer your proffered friendship, it would be a crime not to cultivate in our hearts an intense desire to renovate the Unity of the Church; but let us consider the question coolly, even when our sympathies are most awakened.

The Church cannot be a harmony of discords; it cannot be a numerical sum of Orthodox, Latins, and Protestants. It is nothing if it is not perfect inward harmony of creed and outward harmony of expression (notwithstanding local differences in the rite). The question is, not whether Latins and Protestants have erred so fatally as to deprive individuals of salvation, which seems to be often the subject of debate;— surely a narrow and unworthy one, inasmuch as it throws a suspicion on the mercy of the Almighty. The question is whether they have the truth, and whether they have retained the ecclesiastical tradition unimpaired. If they have not, where is the possibility of unity?

---

inégales, a indubitablement retardée dans la carrière de la civilisation.

'Ils ont à condamner ce qu'ils considèrent comme la gloire de leur passé, et beaucoup de ce qui fait l'orgueil de leur présent. Pour les nations c'est un sacrifice bien pénible; pour les individus c'est une expatriation intellectuelle. Plus la voix de la vérité deviendra claire et son accent impérieux, plus le cœur révolté se roidira contre sa puissance, et plus l'esprit, complice des mauvaises passions du cœur, inventera de subterfuges, des sophismes et même de mensonges directs pour se dérober à l'inévitable conviction. C'est à quoi doit s'attendre tout homme, qui a étudié l'homme et l'histoire de l'intelligence humaine, et c'est en effet ce que nous voyons arriver à l'époque présente. N'osant aborder de front aucun des enseignements dogmatiques proclamés par l'Eglise, n'osant attaquer en face aucune des positions avancées par ses organes, on lui invente des schismes, dont elle ne se doute pas, pour nier son unité; on lui invente des chefs temporels qu'elle ignore, pour nier sa liberté spirituelle; et cela dans le moment où se manifeste le plus vivement la puissance de sa communion vitale et où elle proteste le plus énergiquement contre tout soupçon d'Erastianisme.'—[W. J. B.]

Now permit me to add some observations not only on your letters, but on your book (which I have received with the greatest gratitude, and perused with unmixed pleasure), and on all the mode of action of those Anglicans who seem, and are indeed, nearest to us. You would show that all our doctrine is yours, and indeed at first sight you seem quite right. Many Bishops and divines of your communion are and have been quite orthodox. But what of that? Their opinion is only *an individual opinion*, it is not *the Faith of the Community*. The Calvinist[1] Ussher is an Anglican no less than the bishops (whom you quote) who hold quite Orthodox language. We may and do sympathise with the individuals; we cannot and dare not sympathise with a Church which interpolates the Symbol and doubts her right to that interpolation, or which gives Communion to those *who declare* the Bread and Wine of the High Sacrifice to be mere bread and wine, as well as to those who declare it to be the Body and Blood of Christ. This for an example—and I could find hundreds more—but I go further. Suppose an impossibility—suppose all the Anglicans to be quite Orthodox; suppose their Creed and Faith quite concordant with ours; the mode and process by which that creed is or has been attained is a Protestant one; a simple logical act of the understanding, by which the tradition and writings of the Fathers have been distilled to something very near Truth. If we admit this, all is lost, and Rationalism is the supreme judge of every question. Protestantism, most reverend sir, is the admission of an unknown [quantity] to be sought by reason; and that unknown

---

[1] Mr. Khomiakoff wrote: 'The almost Calvinist Ussher': Mr. Palmer has erased the word 'almost.' In the Russian translation the word has, however, been restored. The whole passage is rendered thus: Ушеръ—почти совершенный Кальвинистъ; но и онъ однако, не менѣе тѣхъ епископовъ, которые выражаютъ православныя убѣжденія, принадлежитъ къ Англиканской Церкви, *i.e.* 'Ussher is almost a complete Calvinist; but yet he, no less than those Bishops who give expression to Orthodox convictions, belongs to the Anglican Church. —[W. J. B.]

[quantity] changes the whole equation to an unknown quantity, even though every other datum be as clear and as positive as possible. Do not, I pray, nourish the hope of finding Christian truth without stepping out of the former Protestant circle. It is an illogical hope; it is a remnant of that pride which thought itself able and wished to judge and decide by itself without the Spiritual Communion of heavenly grace and Christian love. Were you to find all the truth, you would have found nothing; for we alone can give you that without which all would be vain—the assurance of truth.

Do not doubt the energies of Orthodoxy. Young as I am, I have seen the day when it was publicly either scoffed at or at least treated with manifest contempt by [too many in] our [high] society; when [I] myself, who was bred in a religious family and have never been ashamed of adhering strictly to the rites of the Church, was either supposed a sycophant or considered as a disguised Romanist; for nobody supposed the possibility of civilisation and Orthodoxy being united. I have seen the strength of the Eastern Church rise, notwithstanding temporary aggression, which seemed to be fatal, or temporary protection, which seemed to be debasing. And now it rises and grows stronger and stronger. Romanism, though seemingly active, has received the deadly blow from its own lawful child, Protestantism; and indeed I would defy anybody to show me the man with true theological and philosophical learning who is still at heart a *pure* Romanist. Protestantism has heard its knell rung by its most distintinguished teachers, by Neander, though unwillingly, in his letters to Mr. Dewar, and consciously by Schelling in his preface to the posthumous works of Steffens. The ark of Orthodoxy alone rides safe and unhurt through storms and billows. The world shall flock to it. Let us say with the beloved Apostle: 'Even so, come, Lord Jesus.'

Accept my thanks for your book. I consider it as a very valuable acquisition not only for your countrymen, but for all truly and seriously religious readers. The books contained in the parcel sent to me from Cronstadt I have forwarded to their respective addresses except the one for C. Potemkin, whose address I have not yet found out. Pray excuse the length of my letter and the frankness of some expressions which are perhaps too harsh, and believe me, most reverend Sir, your most obedient servant,

ALEXIS KHAMECOFF.

The 28th of November 1846.

CHAPTER VII

MR. KHOMIAKOFF'S VISIT TO ENGLAND

[1847]

Mr. Khomiakoff visits London and Oxford—His letter to the 'Moskvitjanin' about England—London and Moscow compared—An English Sunday.

I HAVE not succeeded in finding any answer from Mr. Palmer to this last letter. But as, shortly after it was written, Mr. Khomiakoff started on a journey to Western Europe, in the course of which he paid his only visit to England,[1] and spent some days at Oxford with Mr. Palmer, it is probable that the letter was never answered on paper, but that its contents were discussed *vivâ voce* on 'the green lawns' or under 'the deep shades' of Magdalen. Very few records remain of his impressions of England. He was not in the habit of keeping a diary, while of the letters which his wife wrote at regular intervals to his mother, giving an account of their journey, only those which were written from Germany have at present been found. In the first volume of his works, however, there is a reprint of an interesting letter which he wrote the following year for a Moscow periodical, entitled the *Moskvitjanin*, giving an enthusiastic account of his experiences in London and elsewhere. The greater part of this letter only touches indirectly upon ecclesiastical questions,[2] and would therefore be out of place

---

[1] This was in July 1847.
[2] Mr. Khomiakoff's views of English politics, and their connection with religious questions which are expressed in this letter, have been already explained in the Introduction.

in this correspondence, but the following passage from it, which is interesting as containing one of the very few favourable descriptions of the English Sunday which have been written by foreigners, and also as showing the friendly and sympathetic spirit with which he undertook the study of our customs and institutions, seems well worth translating.

'. . . It is not the first time that I have travelled in Western Europe, and I have seen not a few cities and capitals. But they are all nothing as compared to London, and this because each one of them appears to me to be nothing but a feeble imitation of London. If a man has once seen London, then, as far as living cities are concerned (for I leave *dead* cities out of the question), there remains nothing for him to see except Moscow. London of course is by far the larger, there is none more magnificent, or more thickly populated, while Moscow is more picturesque, and more varied, richer in atmospheric outlines, and more pleasing to the eye. In both cities their historical life and tradition is as yet healthy and vigorous. The native of Moscow may succumb to the enchantment of London, without compromising his own feelings of patriotism. London and Moscow alike have a great future before them.

'We wandered about London for two days on end: and everywhere we met with the same movement, the same swarming life in the streets. The third day after our arrival was Sunday, and accordingly we went in the morning to Mass at our Embassy chapel. The streets were almost empty, only here and there a few people were hurrying along the pavement, late for church. About two hours afterwards we returned. There was still no traffic in the streets: one met with nothing but people on foot, on whose faces there was an expression of thoughtfulness: they were on their way back from church. A similar silence continued all day. This is the way Sunday is kept in London. The emptiness of the streets, and the silence of the day in the midst of the huge noisy city with its constant movement, is indeed strange and striking, and it must be admitted that it is hardly possible to imagine anything grander than this extraordinary silence. For a short space the cares of commercial life had ceased, the allurements of luxury had disappeared. The shutters of those solid two-storied shop windows through which it seems as if all the treasures of the world are on view were closed; and so were the workshops in which unceasing labour is hardly able to provide its daily bread for itself; all the cares of life seemed to sleep: two millions of the most commercial, the most active people in the whole world had left their occupations, had made a break in their anxieties, and all this in obedience to one lofty idea. It was really delightful to me to see it. I could not help rejoicing over the high moral tone of national inclination, over this nobility of the human soul. It is extraordinary that there can be people in the world who neither understand nor appreciate the repose of an English Sunday: in this want of appreciation a certain pettiness of mind and scantiness of soul is displayed. It is of course true that not all, and indeed very far from all, Englishmen in reality keep Sunday holy anything like so far as they observe its external sanctity; it is true that while everywhere in the streets a respectable quiet may be observed, nevertheless, in many houses and sometimes in those of the best families things go on which are anything but satisfactory. But what of this ?—you will say that these people are Pharisees and hypocrites. Quite true, as far as they are concerned, but it is not true to say that the nation as a whole plays the Pharisee or the hypocrite. These failings and vices are those of individuals, but the nation itself acknowledges a higher moral law, obeys it, and lays its obligation upon its members. Let a German, and still more a Frenchman not understand this, their incapacity to appreciate it is excusable; but it is pitiable to hear Russians, or people who call themselves Russians, reiterating the language of Frenchmen or Germans. Do not we in Russia keep Easter-day itself just as strictly as Sunday is kept in England ? Do the people in the Russian villages dance or sing songs in Lent ? and is there any sort of entertainment in society even in the greater number of large towns in that season? Of course one comes across exceptions in the great towns, but these exceptions and their causes may be accounted for. The upper classes in Russia are so enlightened, and are inspired by such a highly spiritualised idea of religion, that they see no need of the external forms of national custom. England has not this good fortune, and accordingly is more strict in her observance of the common form. But perhaps you will say, If I am a Mohammedan I will keep Friday, if I am a Jew I will keep Saturday, but in either case what is the English Sunday to me? Quite true; but 'in a strange monastery one does not follow one's own rule,'[1] but on the other hand the English nation pre-supposes that when it is in England it is at home.'

---

[1] A Russian proverb, corresponding to our 'When at Rome do as Rome does.'—[W. J. B.]

CHAPTER VIII

MR. KHOMIAKOFF'S FOURTH LETTER TO MR. PALMER[1]

[1847-1848]

The unity of the Church—Self-contented Individualism of Protestant Germany—Contrast with England—Count Protásoff upon reunion—The Metropolitan Philaret's conditions.—Dr. Hampden's nomination as Bishop of Hereford—A call to join the Orthodox Eastern Church—The revolution in France and elsewhere.

September 18th, 1847.

DEAR SIR,—I am writing to you from the capital city of self-contented discord, from Berlin; and my first word shall be *Unity*.[2] Nowhere can I feel so deeply the necessity, the holiness, and the consoling power of that Divine principle. Unity? Not to be found in the vain and weak efforts of individual intellects (for every intellect makes itself its own centre, when indeed there is but one true centre: God); not to be hoped from the sympathetic power of nature (for that is nothing but the superstitious worship of an abstraction); but to be taken simply and humbly from the dispensation of God's mercy and grace. Unity! The substantial character of the Church, the visible sign of the Lord's constant dwelling on earth, the sweetest joy of the human heart.

An almost boundless Individualism is the characteristic feature of Germany, and particularly of Prussia. Here in Berlin it would be difficult to find one single point of faith, or even one feeling, which could be considered as a link of

---

[1] This letter was directed to Magdalen College, Oxford.—[W. J. B.]
[2] Khomiakoff wrote: 'and my word is—Unity.' The Russian version gives: 'I am beginning with the word Unity.'—[W. J. B.]

true spiritual communion in the Christian meaning of the word. Even the desire for harmony seems to be extinguished, and that predominance of Individualism, that spiritual solitude among the ever-busy crowd, send to the heart a feeling of dreariness and desolation. The hand of decay is on that country, notwithstanding its apparent progress in material improvements. I will not say : 'nothing is to be hoped for Germany.' The ways of the future are known to God alone, and a change may come quite unexpectedly ; but the present certainly gives but little reason for hope. Still the earnestness of the German mind in all intellectual researches is not quite so disheartening as the frivolous and self-conceited gaiety of homeless and thoughtless France. A mind given to reflection has time, and may perhaps feel a desire, to listen to the voice of Divine truth. Of all countries I have visited in my short journey, England is certainly the only one I have felt a deep regret to part with, the only one which I shall always think about with a deep feeling of sympathy. I know very well that England lacks, as much perhaps as Germany itself, the blessing of religious unity ;—the appearance of unity which exists there is more a show and a delusion than a truth ; but, delusive as it is, still its appearance is more consoling than its manifest absence. The numerous, and at times crowded, churches : the earnestness of prayer : the solemnity of ancient forms of worship not quite forgotten—even the rather Puritanical sabbathising of the Lord's Day—are full of deep and joyful impressions. They seem to indicate a community of spiritual life in the country. Even later, when the delusion is over,—when a closer observation has discovered the latent discord under the veil of outward and arbitrary unity,—there still remains a consolation in the evident longing for unity, which is felt by so many individuals, and which the multitude itself expresses by holding so strictly at least to its outward forms. Certainly a serious ignorance, searching for Divine truth, is much to be preferred to a proud or merry infidelity.

December, 1847.—I had begun but not finished this letter

in Berlin. Since that time some months have elapsed, but I leave the beginning as it was, because it expresses feelings which had been inspired by my travels through Germany. In Petersburg I have seen Count Protásoff[1] with whom till that time I had no personal acquaintance. He questioned me about England, and particularly about its religious movement. He listened to my answers with serious and, I hope, sincere interest. I think I may say he feels a true sympathy for religious questions, though he does not always understand their importance, and is somewhat inclined towards Latin views, *i.e.* formalism. The more agreeable was it to hear from him that he considered as of no importance at all some forms to which you have expressed your objections (as for example the use of the word Eastern in Ecclesiastical Rites), and that he could give me the assurance, which I think I gave you beforehand, that any form which could convey to the mind an idea of narrow locality would certainly be rejected as soon as it should be indicated or its rejection required. Indeed I expected no other answer. The undue exaltation of any locality whatever is exactly the antipodes of the very idea of a Christian Church which claims a living communion with the past and the future, with the visible and invisible world.

Some months have elapsed again since my visit to Count Protásoff. The health of my mother, the bad roads, and the cholera in Moscow have detained me in the government of Tula. I have but just now seen the Metropolitan of Moscow, Philaret. The conversation of that highly gifted

---

[1] The Chief Procurator of the Holy Synod. This post, which is analogous to that of the Imperial Commissioners in the Œcumenical Councils, is held by a layman appointed by the Emperor, whom he represents. He has a right to be present whenever the Holy Synod meets, and all matters which concern the temporalities of the Church, or its relations with the secular government, have to pass through him. He has, however, no vote, nor even a right to speak upon purely spiritual or dogmatic matters: and does not sit at the same table with the members of the Holy Synod, but at a separate table by himself.—[W. J. B.].

man has been more satisfactory still for me than my interview with Protásoff. I am even afraid that till now I have been unjust to our Metropolitan, though I should consider it as a gain if I had to confess an error in that case. His sympathy was unexpectedly warm and strong. He listened to many things with a joyful smile and with tears in his eyes. It was even a strange emotion to behold in a man of such concentrated feelings. He has raised my hopes. If you ask whether anything was positively promised, I answer: 'No'; no; but he said: 'Everything that can be done without offending the Christian conscience will be done'; and that was said earnestly. There was complete harmony between his face and his words. He said likewise that every plausible explanation in questions of seeming differences would readily be admitted; that every rite not implying a direct negation of a dogma would be allowed, 'Unity of rites being very desirable indeed, but unity of dogma being the only condition *sine qua non*.' Let us hope for the best.

I have had no direct news from England since my return. Newspapers inform us that the commercial crisis is at an end; that was expected, and yet I am glad to hear it. The words *commercial* crisis, and others of the same sort, are very short and unmeaning, but thousands of miseries are hidden under these short words. They are not much better than the likewise very short word *cholera*, which we know very well. Luckily, the latter is no more spoken of in Moscow, but this is not quite so in many parts of Russia. Victims have been very numerous in some governments, but the disease has not been quite so mortal as at the time of its first importation in 1830. I should be glad to think that all is going in England as well as possible; but I am afraid *another* crisis is unavoidable,—not a commercial but a religious one. Such at least are the consequences which in my opinion seem to follow naturally upon the nomination of the Bishop of Hereford. Dr. Pusey in a Church of which Dr. Hampden is a Bishop! Why, that is worse than affirmation and negation in the same sentence; and though the nomination is perhaps in itself nothing more than a bad trick of Lord John Russell, yet the manifestation of parties which have stood up and faced one another is most important. The hollowness of mere exterior Unity is growing evident. I am sorry for it, as I am sorry when anything happens that is a symptom of troubles and contention; and yet, it may be for the best. The divine logic of history is unavoidable. Every delusion must have an end, and noble spirits being freed from a delusive Unity, will seek and find the true one.

Let us seek it, dear sir! let us be earnest and bold in the task. Let us consider our actions as most important, not only for ourselves, but as either acting on or being symptoms of the times. A dozen ripe grains are not a ripe harvest, and yet the husbandman is happy to find two or three ripe grains in the field. They are a sign that the harvest is ripening fast.

If you are, as I suppose, in correspondence with Mr. G. Williams, pray be so kind as to give him my compliments. I hope he will not be offended if I say I have something of a brotherly feeling for him. There is so much in him that brings to my memory the dear friend I have lost lately. A friendly greeting to dear Oxford itself, with its twenty colleges, its green lawns and deep shades, and its stillness and quiet. I hope its salutary influence will outlive Whig ministers and German latitudinarianism.

My wife sends you her affectionate compliments, and even the two little ones hope that you have not quite forgotten them.—Your most devoted, ALEXIS KHAMECOFF.

March 14th, 1848.

A strange time! I was writing this letter when the great events of France and of all Europe came on so startlingly and unexpectedly. The highest questions are stirred up, and man hopes to solve them without the aid of religion. I am afraid humanity will pay dearly for the foolish pride of reason. May the impending storm be directed and moderated by the hand of Mercy! May England be spared! It is my heartiest wish.

CHAPTER IX

MR. PALMER'S ANSWER TO MR. KHOMIAKOFF'S
FOURTH LETTER

[1849]

Mr. Palmer's 'Appeal to the Scottish Bishops'—Compulsory auricular Confession—Preparations for a book upon the Patriarch Nicon—Plans for the future—Mr. Allies's book upon the Papal Supremacy.

Sunday of St. Thomas, 1849.

Христосъ Воскресе!¹

MY DEAR MR. KHOMIAKOFF,—It is nearly a year now since I received your most kind and interesting letter. If I have not yet acknowledged it, and thanked you for it, it is not that either it or you have been absent from my thoughts, but that I was desirous of being able to tell you something definite as to my own proceedings, and I had been confined to my room the whole of the preceding winter by a continued fit, or succession of fits, of the gout, so that I had made little or no progress, either in the work for publication, or in the prosecution of my Appeal in Scotland. Now, however, that an opportunity offers of sending a letter by one of the members of my own College at Oxford, Mr. Barmby, who is going out to take our chaplain, Dr. Law's, place at St. Petersburgh for the summer, I will delay writing no longer, and hope that this letter will reach you in time to bring you and Mme. Khomiakoff and the children my Easter salutations, at least before the halving of the Festival.² I shall ask Mr.

---

¹ 'Christ is risen,' the usual Easter greeting in the East.—[W. J. B.]

² This Festival (in Greek, ἡ Μεσοπεντηκοστή: in Slavonic, Преполовеніе Пятьдесятницы) is kept on the Wednesday in the fourth

APPEAL TO THE SCOTTISH BISHOPS

Barmby to put it into the post at St. Petersburgh, and tell him to call upon you personally, in case he should make a short visit to Moscow before returning to England.

After having recovered from the gout last summer (1848) I went to Scotland, and remained at Edinburgh all the winter, employed in printing in English a full account of the controversy between the late Scottish Bishop at Paris (and myself) and your country-woman, Princess G——. The whole makes a volume of 700 closely printed pages 8vo, which I hope to

---

week after Easter (after the 'Sunday of the Paralytic') and marks the middle of the fifty days between Easter and Whitsunday. The Eastern Church then commemorates the event in our Lord's life which is related in John vii. 14-30, which is the Gospel for the day. It must be admitted that this festival falls in admirably with the general scheme of the services provided in the Orthodox Church for these fifty days. While the first two Sundays after Easter—the Sundays of 'St. Thomas' (John xx. 19-31), and of 'the Myrrh-bearing Women' (Mark xv. 43—xvi. 8)—are devoted to events closely connected with the Resurrection, the three next Sundays of 'the Impotent man' (John v. 1-15), 'the Woman of Samaria' (John iv. 5-42), and 'the Blind Man' (John ix. 1-38) are devoted to events in our Lord's life before His Death and Resurrection, in which His divine power was manifested to men, in order that they might know Him as the Messiah, and believe in His Resurrection; while upon the last Sunday before Pentecost the 318 Fathers of Nicæa are commemorated, who (as the Synaxarion for the day puts it) taught that the Son of God was of one substance and of one honour with the Father, and who confessed that He was indeed the Son of God and perfect Man, and that He ascended into heaven and sitteth on the right hand of majesty (John xvii. 1-13).

The Gospel for the Feast of the Mesopentecost follows naturally upon that of the Impotent man, read on the previous Sunday. The words τῆς ἑορτῆς μεσούσης, with which it begins, and which primarily refer to the middle of the seven days during which the Feast of Tabernacles was kept by the Jews, are of course here applied to the great Week of weeks between Easter and Pentecost. There can be little doubt that the Gospel was originally continued so as to include our Lord's words spoken on the last day of the Feast; for in the service for the day there are constant allusions to the words: 'If any man thirst, let him come unto Me and drink.' As an example of this it will be quite sufficient to quote the Apolytikion of the day, a Troparion which in

send out to you before the end of this summer.[1] It is not to be published or sold by the booksellers, but is printed only for the information of the Bishops and clergy and lay communicants of the Church, in order to the prosecution of the Appeal as an Ecclesiastical document. I will not now enter into any details as to its contents, as I hope you will have it in your own hands before many months are over. Although I have not printed Princess G――'s name, it may, perhaps, be as well that I should not send copies of it to any persons holding official situations (such as the Count Protásoff, for instance); I therefore propose to send only two or three copies of the volume to Russia, and hope that, if by any chance the Count or others holding official stations should come to hear of it, or see it, they will attribute my reserve to the right cause, and not to any want of attention towards themselves. You will find in the volume some copious extracts from your own letters, or, rather, the letters themselves (only with some omissions), and hope that you will not disapprove of the use I have made of them. I wished to give

---

some respects liturgically answers to the collect for the day in the Western office books:—

'This being the midst of the Feast, do Thou, O Saviour, give unto my thirsty soul to drink of the waters of godliness: for Thou, O Saviour, didst cry unto all, saying, If any man thirst, let him come unto Me and drink. Glory be to Thee, O Christ our God, Who art the Fountain of Life.'

Liturgical students will not fail to mark the connection between the services of this festival and the other references contained in the Easter-tide services to the baptisms which took place at Easter and Pentecost. Its Gospel gives a key to the selection of the Gospels for the third, fourth, and fifth Sundays after Easter, the events mentioned in which took place at the Pool of Bethesda, Jacob's Well, and the Pool of Siloam respectively. A complement to the ideas contained in the 'Apolytikion' may be found in the Antiphon used by the Western Church during the same fifty days at the Asperges:—'Vidi aquam egredientem de templo, a latere dextro, alleluia: et omnes ad quos pervenit aqua ista salvi facti sunt, et dicent alleluia, alleluia.'— [W. J. B.]

[1] *An Appeal to the Scottish Bishops.* Edinburgh: 1849.—[W. J. B.]

something to represent such opinions and feelings as a member
of your Church might entertain on the subject of Unity, and I
was not likely to have found elsewhere anything so much to
the purpose, or anything so likely to be attractive in a good
sense to an Anglican reader as your letters, which seemed to
have been sent to me by Providence, and to deserve of themselves to find some wider sphere of usefulness than that of
merely being read by me, and then consigned to a portfolio.
I may add that already more than one person who has read
them has confessed to me that they have much modified the
prejudices he entertained before concerning the Eastern
Church. The volume has already been sent to the clergy of
that Scottish diocese (of St. Andrews), the Bishop of which
was the only one who received the matter favourably three
years ago in 1846, when it was brought only in the Latin
documents, without any detailed history of the case, or mis-
cellaneous illustrations such as now accompany it. The clergy
of the Diocese, having held a special Synod to deliberate on
the subject on the 27th of March (N.S.), have unanimously
concurred in decreeing the Appeal to be legitimate, and to
have been rightly referred to their Scottish Church, and have
recommended it to the other Synods of their Church, so that
it is now to be submitted to all the rest of the clergy of the
other Dioceses. This seems so far a favourable beginning;
but it will remain for time to show whether they will really
make any effort after an adequate reformation. And already,
even at this Synod, which has shown itself so favourable, a
strong attack was made upon the proposal which I had
brought forward,—as an ultimate issue to the Disciplinary
part of the Appeal,—namely, the institution of an *Examination*
for all applicants for the Holy Communion (at least at certain
times) on the three points of Ecclesiastical status, of Orthodoxy,
and freedom from excommunicable or mortal sins. This, it
is said, is simply to propose the restoration of the law of
'Compulsory Confession' (as they call it), which the Anglican
Church is thought distinctly to have abrogated and to have
blamed. And no doubt my proposal is indeed very much

what they assert it to be ; and though I do not think myself
that the Anglican Church has ever yet distinctly crowned
this heresy, that persons guilty of excommunicable sins may
re-admit themselves to the privilege of Communion whenever
they judge themselves to be sufficiently penitent, I yet must
confess that she has gone very near to doing so, by taking
away the law of Confession as a general pre-requisite to
Communion, without making any clear distinction at the
same time, and teaching the people that, though any person
who had kept himself free from excommunicable sins might
for the future communicate frequently (as in the early
Church) without coming every time to Confession, still, if at
any time he unhappily fell into any greater or excommunicable sin, he could not then be himself the judge of the
sufficiency of his own repentance, nor re-admit himself to the
right and place of those who had not fallen ; but must
confess and obtain the Absolution of the Church. I anticipate,
therefore, that there will be much opposition on this point ;
and indeed it may well be doubted whether the Anglican
Church, having gone so far as she has in the direction of
error on this subject, *can* now retrace her steps. And yet,
unless she does retrace them, I see not how she can prevent
every variety of heresy or of sin intruding itself upon her
Communion. I do not send you the book at once, because
some other Synods will have met before the end of the
summer, and I wish you to receive it with the addition of
whatever they may have done. If this disciplinary part of
the Appeal should ever be favourably decided, there would
still remain the Doctrinal part :—*i.e.* the consideration of
those propositions which were objected to me as the heresies
of the Anglican Church in the name of the Synod in Russia
in 1843, and to which I then said anathema ;—and if these
also were synodically rejected, the Scottish Church might
be in a condition to open conferences with the Eastern Church,
with some prospect of bringing them to a favourable issue.
In the meantime, there are individuals of considerable
reputation among our clergy, who have been consulted by

one, at least, of the Scottish Bishops, and who have recommended that the Scottish Church, instead of dealing with the Appeal as sent to Scotland from the Bishop at Paris, irrespectively of any indirect bearing which it may have on the question of Unity with the Eastern Church, should make it at once an occasion for expressing a willingness to open Conferences for unity on the basis of the Seven Œcumenical Councils. This advice is no doubt well intended, and shows good dispositions in the individuals who offer it: but I confess that I do not wish to see it followed, for reasons which you will see stated in the printed volume. If anything of the kind is ever to be done there must be a great practical reformation on our side; and it would be much better to begin by making the effort for its own sake, rather than offer to treat with others, who at present have too much reason to consider the Anglican Church simply as a Sect, and who would probably have little hope of any good result, and something perhaps of a formal, repulsive, and overbearing tone in their *manner* of conferring, if they were willing to confer at all.

As for my other work for publication, which is designed indirectly to subserve the cause of the Appeal, it has made (as I have mentioned above) but little progress during the last year—owing first to illness, and then to the necessary interruption caused by the other matter. However, I am now working at it again, and hope to do something in the course of this summer and the approaching winter—and if I keep free from illness may, perhaps, be ready to print it in the year 1850. I am just now translating part of the life of the Patriarch Nicon by Shusherin, and am curious to obtain some information on the points on which, perhaps, you may be able to inform me or to procure me information. First, I wish to learn in what year was born an illegitimate son of the Tzar Alexis Michaelovich—who was sent away from Court (then young, I suppose) with his mother soon after the Tzar's second marriage. I remember some connection between the name Mousin Poushkin and this incident. Also any other details, (as, for instance, concerning the time at which that illegitimate connection first commenced) would be acceptable to me. Secondly, I should like to have stated clearly to me those points in which Nicon might really have seemed to the Tzar to be unreasonable, or at least to be insisting upon privileges which were inconsistent with a good general administration of the temporal government. For example, I may suppose that the *imperium in imperio* resulting from the privilege of separate jurisdiction in civil or criminal causes accorded to the hierarchy, over all persons belonging to their own lands, may have been really an inconvenience, especially as the law administered by the ecclesiastics was not in all points identical with the law administered for all other subjects of the Empire by the civil authorities. And the introduction of a new Code, establishing one general system for all alike (at least in purely civil and criminal causes) might seem a measure of sound and enlightened policy, for the sake of which the State might require the hierarchy to give up some of their merely secular privileges. As for myself, I have, as I think you know, a pretty strong opinion in favour of Nicon, and attribute all the mischief that has ensued since his deposition to that one unrepented sin; but still, I should like to hear what is said by any learned and reasonable advocate of the other side. Thirdly, I should like to have a small ground-plan of the principal buildings of the Kremlin with the points of the compass marked, and the names to each, to refresh my memory. I do not care how roughly it is done— what you might scratch on one side of a sheet of letter-paper would abundantly answer my purpose. But at present I have forgotten the relative position and shapes of some of the Ecclesiastical or Imperial buildings within the Kremlin. If it is not making myself too troublesome, may I ask of you this favour?

If the Appeal in Scotland should seem likely to proceed unfavourably, I should look forward, after publishing the other work, to go to the East for some time, and seek from the four Patriarchs an affirmation of the same terms of reconciliation as were proposed to me in Russia, so as to make the case formally and not only virtually to be a precedent for the whole Eastern Church in dealing for the reconciliation of an Anglican. Having done this, I would return once more to the Scottish Bishops before finally giving the matter up.

However, it is not impossible that I may be occupied, if I live and am well, next winter by a very different duty, namely, that of accompanying one of my younger brothers, whose chest is delicate, to some warmer climate; which our physicians seem to look forward to for him, unless he should be unexpectedly better in the meantime. But at this present time I have one brother travelling (not, I thank God, for weak health) in Palestine, and in the last letters we received from him he spoke of having made acquaintance there with a Russian friend of mine, the Archimandrite Porphyrius, with whom and with some Russian ecclesiastics he was then about to make an expedition to Petra.

A friend of mine and a member of the University of Oxford, Mr. Allies, published some time back a book on the subject of the Papal Supremacy, which, if you have not already seen it, would, I think, interest you. He is disposed to send two or three copies of it as presents to Russia—in particular one to the Metropolitan of Moscow, for whom he has conceived a great veneration, and from whom he would much like to receive a blessing, if the contents of his volume seemed worthy of approbation. There are some eloquently written pages in it on the subject of the Eastern Church. If he sends his books through me, I will suggest to him to send that one which is the Metropolitan's to you in the first instance, that you may be able to read it. And if the Metropolitan does not read English enough to care to read it, he may, if he pleases, send it to the Library of the Spiritual Academy.

Pray make my most humble duty to him, as well as my best remembrances to Mme. de Khomiakoff and your children, if it is possible that they remember that they have been at Oxford; also to any acquaintances or friends of mine whom you may chance to meet, as Mme. de Dolgorouky, *née* Davidoff, or Professor Redkin; and believe me to be always, my dear Sir,—Yours most sincerely,

W. PALMER (Deacon)

CHAPTER X

MR. KHOMIAKOFF'S FIFTH LETTER TO MR. PALMER

[1850]

Letter of Pius IX. to the Oriental Christians — Reply of the Orthodox Patriarchs — The Church consists of the totality of the ecclesiastical body, not merely of the hierarchy — Orthodox theory of the Church vindicated — Hopes for the future both in Russia and in England — Ecclesiastical news from Oxford.

MOST REVEREND AND DEAR SIR,—More than a year has elapsed since I have received your kind letter, and I should confess myself guilty of a great tardiness in answering it if I had not a sufficient justification in a violent inflammation of the eyes which has confined me for weeks to a dark room, and made me for months unable to take a pen, or even a book, in hand. For a long while medical aid was not only of no use, but seemed rather to augment the intensity of the malady, till at length homœopathy was recurred to and achieved the cure in a very short time and only left a slight weakness in the eyes which does not hinder me in my habitual occupations.

The condition I was in during these ten months of involuntary and almost complete idleness was very disagreeable. Among many privations I consider as one of the most painful the impossibility of answering your letter, and of calling your attention to a very important event in the history of the Church. So many political events of high, or seemingly high, importance have troubled the last two years and engrossed the thoughts of all Europe that the one I mean has probably either passed quite unobserved or has been noticed by only a very few persons, and that rather accidentally than otherwise. No opinion is more common than that the abstract questions of religion are less interesting and less important than the practical questions of diplomacy and politics. I think that opinion very natural, and yet I believe there is none more erroneous and false, not only from the philosophical point of view (as religious questions refer to eternal truths, and to the only true welfare of man), but even from the historical point of view. For example, no man that is not altogether blind to the light of historical science can doubt for an instant that the Arian doctrine and its rejection at Nicaea have for centuries given a peculiar course to the destinies of European nations by having united the interests of Catholicism with some of the German tribes and having put them in opposition to other German tribes which were broken down in the conflict; or that the separation of East and West by a religious question has been of the most vital importance to the whole history of Europe by causing the western nations to sacrifice the Eastern Empire, and by reducing the East to an isolated, tardy, and insufficient development of its energy. The common answer to such examples is that they are exceptions; but in reality, instead of being exceptions, they are only manifest illustrations of the common rule. Even in our time the greatest part of the European commotions, though seemingly produced by material interests, sometimes of the lowest character, is indeed nothing but a veil to the deep religious questions which, without his being conscious of the fact, direct the actions of man. I am sure this opinion will find your approbation, and I hope that you will likewise admit that I was right in considering the following fact as a very important and remarkable event.

You have probably heard of the inroad the Pope attempted in the East when as yet he had not so much ado with Italy and his own rebellious subjects. This inroad was made in the form of an address directed to the Roman Catholic subjects of the Sultan, but was indeed an evident, though perhaps not quite fair, attack on Eastern Orthodoxy. The Patriarchs and Bishops of the East considered themselves called upon for an answer, and they gave an answer signed by thirty-one

Bishops. This fact is important in itself as being the only instance for more than a hundred years of a declaration of Faith coming so near to an œcumenical act, and as giving a splendid example of Unity; but some expressions contained in the answer are still more worthy of notice. I cannot quite approve of its general form and style. The phrases have a strong tendency to Byzantine rhetoric; but then it should be considered that, however strange to us, such a style is natural to men nurtured under the influence of a tasteless school. The polemical part, though not quite without merit, might certainly have been more powerful; but again that seems to be of only secondary importance. The expressions of the Synod, when speaking about their Roman adversaries, might have been milder; but this last circumstance, if not quite excusable, should not be judged too severely. In the last ten years or more the expressions of Roman writers when attacking the Eastern Church have been peculiarly harsh; it has even been very common with them to compare her with Arianism. No great mildness could have been expected in the reply. But a still more weighty excuse is to be found in the danger which seemed to threaten Orthodoxy in the East. Never had the missionaries of Rome been so active and, in some instances, so successful. The Pope had acquired a great personal celebrity; he seemed to be on the best terms with the Divan, and the energy of his mind and character were supposed to be bent towards attaining a political as well as a spiritual ascendency. There was much of fear in the harshness of the Grecian bishops. Still I do think that a milder tone would have been more dignified. But polemics belong to individuals, and never can have an ecclesiastical or œcumenical character. The only truly important part of the Patriarchal Encyclical is to be sought in the expressions which the Bishops use in speaking of their own Creed and Dogmas. These are of an immense importance, and have been a cause of joy to many of us, and indeed, I think, for all those who take a serious interest in religious matters. I daresay you have felt long since, as have most of us, that the difference between the Eastern Church and all the Western communities, whether Roman, or sprung out of Rome in the form of Protestations, lies not so much in the difference of separate dogmas or portions of creed as in something else which has not been as yet clearly defined or expressed. This difference consists in the different manner of considering the Church itself. I have tried in some straggling essays, and still more in some as yet unpublished historical disquisitions, to state that difference clearly and explicitly; still all explanations given by a solitary individual and by a layman had no authority whatever, and could not be considered as serious expressions of the Church's own self-notions. Doubts and direct negations were natural, and the more so as I must confess that my explanations were in evident opposition to many definitions of the Church and its essence given by some of our divines educated, I fear, under the influence of Western tendencies and science, which are rather predominant in Russian schools. The expressions used by a Synod of three Patriarchs and twenty-eight Bishops have a very high authority, and may be considered, now that they have been reprinted in Russia with the assent of our Church authorities, as something very near an œcumenical decision of the Eastern Church. These expressions, as worded in § 17, are of the following import: 'The Pope is greatly mistaken in supposing that we consider the Ecclesiastical Hierarchy to be the guardian of the dogma [of the Church]. The case is quite different. The unvarying constancy and the unerring truth of Christian dogma does not depend upon any Hierarchical Order: it is guarded by the totality, by the whole *people* of the Church, which is the Body of Christ.' Examples follow. The same idea is still more clearly illustrated, I think, in § 11 (I have not the Encyclical with me, and can only quote from memory); the meaning of the passage is as follows: 'No Hierarchical Order nor Supremacy is to be considered as a guarantee of truth. The knowledge of truth is given to mutual love.' It would be difficult to ask for explanations more positive and more clear. The gift of truth is strictly separated from the hierarchical functions (viz., from Sacramental and Disciplinarian power), and the essential distinction from the Roman notion is thus established; the gift of unvarying knowledge (which is nothing but faith) is attributed, not to individuals, but to the totality of the ecclesiastical body, and is considered as a corollary of the moral principle of mutual love. This position is in direct contradiction to the individualism and rationalism which lies at the bottom of every Protestant doctrine. I am happy to say that I consider one of the most important bases of our Catechism to be duly and solidly established for ever; and this fact I am inclined to deem almost miraculous when I reflect upon the deep ignorance, and perhaps moral debasement, of the Grecian clergy, and upon the tendency to spiritual despotism which I cannot but suspect in our more learned and enlightened churchmen. The strength of the vital and latent principle, when called upon, bears down before it all the obstacles which to our eyes and reason would seem unconquerable. I hope you will not blame me for my rather triumphant style; the joy we have felt in reading the Encyclical was the more intense inasmuch as it was quite unexpected. I am sure you will sympathise with us in this as you would sympathise in the many and many heavy feelings[1] which we experience daily.

The general aspect of things, at least in matters of religion, is very favourable in our country, and would be still more so if we had not too much of political religion, and if the State was more convinced that Christian truth has no need of constant protection, and is rather weakened than strengthened by an excessive solicitude. A greater share of intellectual liberty would go far to break down the innumerable heresies of the worst description which are constantly either springing

---

[1] In the original MS. this word is spelt 'fealings.' I had at first some doubt whether to correct it into 'feelings' or 'failings,' but I finally decided upon the former in deference to the Russian translation, which renders the passage thus: 'Just as you would sympathise in the painful (тяжелым, *lit.* heavy) impressions which we daily experience.'—[W. J. B.]

up or spreading their deleterious influence in the ranks of the common people. But then all this is nothing but a temporary error of rather timid politicians, and will pass; let the principles themselves be more clearly expressed and better understood, and all will go well. I hope such is the case with us. How does it stand with you, or rather with your country? The hopes that had so unexpectedly rewarded your constant exertions, are they likely to be fulfilled, at least in part? If they were, and if I could hear of such a fortunate event, I should consider that day as one of the happiest in my life. Believe me, these are not mere words. The spiritual welfare of England is one of the objects which are nearest to my heart. I do not say that I *sympathise* with your indefatigable exertions; that expression would be too weak. I can say that they are the theme of constant and anxious thoughts. I suppose that you were scarcely more rejoiced in seeing symptoms of a possible return or approximation to Catholicism during your journey to Scotland than I was in hearing of them. The country to which the world is so much indebted, I will not say for liberal institutions or for progress of sciences, but for the noble efforts of many of her children who have borne far and wide the name of Christ and the blessing of adoring Him, this country seems to me worthy of a clearer insight into the wonders of Christ's Church than any other. Such are likewise the feelings of our Metropolitan.[1] He was strongly moved by the perusal of your letter and highly approved all that you had done and proposed. The last news from Oxford is far from being satisfactory. It seems that some defections have taken place to ultra-Protestantism or to flat Rationalism, which is quite on the verge of infidelity, if, indeed, it is not a total rejection of religion. I think it could not be otherwise. The equivocal position of Anglicanism between Popery and ultra-Protestantism must manifest itself in its consequences. The noble genius of Newman has not avoided one of these

---

[1] The Metropolitan Philaret, of Moscow.—[W. J. B.]

deviations; others of less note, but perhaps of sincere tendencies to truth, fall in the opposite extreme. I hope these defections have not had any influence on your nearest friends or on your own energy. I feel it would be not only strange, but completely absurd, if I entertained an idea of giving you any advice, or of forewarning you against despondency. You know better than anybody the obstacles that lie in your way, and a struggle of many years has proved your energy and perseverance; but I could not avoid expressing my opinion on the fact I have heard of (perhaps a false rumour), and some slight anxiety lest this fact should have damped the hopes of your friends. No man is above a momentary weakness, and perhaps it will not be quite useless to you to know that in a country far distant from your own there are hearts which feel all the immense importance of the task you have undertaken, and are alarmed at hearing of things which may render it still more arduous, and pray God as fervently as they can for your ultimate success.

A friend of mine has promised to be the bearer of this letter to England, an excellent and very remarkable young man. His family name is Kossovitch; his line of occupation the ancient languages. Without any fortune, without any pecuniary means, without teachers, he has acquired a tolerable knowledge of the Semitic idioms, and has become very proficient in Sanscrit. The object of his journey to England is to acquire a greater perfection in this last branch of his studies, though it is joined to another object of a quite different sort, which is a rather strange idea of mine to take a patent for a new steam-engine of my invention. Very probably he will visit Oxford; a studious man cannot deprive himself of such a pleasure. If he does visit Oxford, he will most certainly call upon you, and I confide in your friendship for a welcome of which he is indeed worthy. But shall I be so happy as to meet you once more under the sweet and thoughtful shades of Oxford ? That is one of my hopes and of my *pia desideria*. Next year, perhaps—but I won't think of the future.

Accept, most reverend and dear sir, the assurance of the sincere respect and devotion.—Your most obedient servant

ALEXIS KHAMECOFF.

Oct. the 8th, 1850.

P.S.—I hope the book which I join to this letter will afford you some interest.[1]

---

[1] This letter, as will appear from a future letter, was not answered by Mr. Palmer until after Khomiakoff's sixth letter had been written. —[W. J. B.]

CHAPTER XI

MR. KHOMIAKOFF'S SIXTH LETTER TO MR. PALMER

[1851]

The Gorham judgment — The Papal aggression — Their real significance — Anglican position defined—Only one solution.

MOST REVEREND SIR,—England, in my opinion, has never been more worthy of admiration than this year. The Babylonian enterprise of the Exhibition and its Crystal Palace, which shows London to be the true and recognised capital of Universal Industry, would have been sufficient to engross the attention and intellectual powers of any other country; but England stands evidently above its own commercial wonders. Deeper interests agitate her, higher thoughts direct her mental energy. Europe, in its material tendencies and follies, does not understand the spiritual life, or at least the ardent longing for a spiritual life, which expresses itself in the agitation produced by the Gorham and Papal questions. The first has been laughed at almost everywhere as something childish and unworthy of an enlightened nation. The second is considered as something equally childish, and as a symptom of the morbid pride of England, and particularly of the English Church. I have lately heard a Frenchman and a countryman of mine concur in the following profound opinion:—'The self-love of all nations may console itself; England, the country of wonders, is foolish enough to speak whole months about the dogmatic frenzy of a parish priest and the unmeaning titles of a dozen bishops.'

Certainly such opinions only prove the mental degradation of those who utter them; yet it is impossible not to admit that the form which the religious agitation has taken in England has done much to conceal the importance of the debated questions. I am almost inclined to suppose that this form deceives even the greater part of your countrymen, and that perhaps they are glad of the deception which permits them to avoid the necessity of facing the true question in all its significance and importance. But it cannot be avoided.

In the Gorham case this form was a dispute about jurisdiction ; in the Papal question it is a dispute about titles ; in both the form is nothing but a pretext. The Gorham question was in itself no more than a disagreement between a Presbyter and a Bishop about a doubtful opinion in Theology, a revival of the old absurdity of *opus operans* and *opus operatum*. The true basis of the theological opinion, the only thing that could give it some importance, was the question whether unbaptized children are to be damned according to the mildly-looking hardness[1] of Augustine, or to be saved according to the spirit of genuine mildness which speaks in the Gospel. The question is one of pure curiosity, one about which nothing decisive is to be found in Revelation, nothing in Tradition, and which has been completely darkened by the subtleties of scholastic learning, or, rather, of scholastic ignorance. The decision of the civil authority is, in my opinion, a very reasonable one ; but the same decision admits, as a point of law, that questions of Ecclesiastical discipline are to be judged by the civil magistrate, and, what is more, that dogmatic doubts in the Church may be put aside by civil authority without having been decided by the Church. This is nothing but Prussian Protestantism. If the Church accepts the decision, it confesses itself to be completely Protestant, completely un-Catholic, and glides by an unavoidable necessity down into German Rationalism.

---

[1] I have left this passage as Khomiakoff wrote it. The Russian translation renders 'mildly-looking hardness' by words equivalent to 'the teaching of St. Augustine, which, while pretending to be mild (мнимо-кроткимъ) is in reality so cruel' (жестокимъ).—[W. J. B.]

The Papal Aggression is in itself still less serious than the dispute about Baptism. The Pope has an undoubted right to ordain bishops for Ireland; he has had for years *de facto* a right to direct the ecclesiastical affairs of Roman Catholics in England. Now he chooses to give his deputies in England *a local habitation and a name.* Where is the danger? Where is the serious offence? Geographical titles are important for a geographical, a *Roman* Church; but what is the importance of that whimsical pretension for England as a realm, or for Englishmen as Christians? If the Jacobite Patriarch was to send twelve bishops with twelve most pompous titles to England, would they be met by cries of anger? Peals of laughter would certainly be their only reception. Where is then the difference? Yet the effect has been quite different; and the reason of the difference is obvious. The Church of England, or rather a considerable part of it, though having broken the ties which made it dependent on Rome, felt itself menaced by ultra-Protestantism, and adhered strongly to a shadow of Catholicity, with a latent hope that some compromise might still be entered which would give Anglicans a right to say that they had always held tradition, and had never been quite estranged from one of the Churches of Apostolical foundation. Now Rome has decidedly rejected them, and has shown that she denies, or, rather, willingly ignores their existence as a Church. They are forced into Protestantism, which they feel to be the death of Religion, or reduced to confess that Anglicanism is no Church, but simply an Establishment. This seems to be the only key to the religious agitation of the last months. England has felt that Anglicanism, such as it is, cannot be upheld; and that England has felt it so deeply, so painfully (though indeed without confessing it), is a circumstance which reflects much honour on the earnestness and strength of her religious tendencies.

The Government of England and the Government of Rome have done all they could to put the question in the strongest light; and they have been understood. Numerous defections to Rome have happened in a short time, and have been much spoken of. The defections to ultra-Protestantism, though unnoticed, are more numerous still. Those who long for Catholicity feel that tatters of Tradition, arbitrarily chosen, without continuity and authority, and constantly exposed to doubt, cannot constitute a Catholic Church. Those who wish for the freedom of Protestantism feel that a liberty which is hemmed in by relics of Tradition and Authority is no true Protestantism. Every man takes to his own ways, and nobody is to blame. The position of Anglicanism is completely defined. It is a narrow ledge of dubious *terra firma*, beaten by the waves of Romanism and Protestantism, and crumbling on both sides into the mighty waters. The position cannot be maintained, but where is the egress ?

Romanism is an unnatural tyranny: Protestantism is an unprincipled revolt. Neither of them can be accepted. But where is unity without tyranny ? where is freedom without revolt to be found ? They are both to be found in the ancient, continuous, unadulterated Tradition of the Church. There a unity is to be found more authoritative than the despotism of the Vatican, *for it is based on the strength of mutual love*. There a liberty is to be found more free than the licence of Protestantism, for it is *regulated by the humility of mutual love*. There is the Rock and the Refuge.

Rome in the ninth century broke the blessed bond of Love, and fell into that Dogmatic Error[1] which you yourself, most reverend sir, have so candidly confessed and so powerfully confuted. The wound of the Christian world must be healed. Why should not England begin that blessed cure ? The more impending the crisis of the Anglican Church, the more powerfully are her members called upon to begin the work of renovation. Certainly nothing at first is to be expected from the totality or even the majority of Anglicans. In England, as everywhere else, incredulity, worldly cares, ignorance, prejudice, custom, and apathy hold the great number in

---

[1] The *Filioque*.—[W. J. B.]

their slavery; but God is not in numbers. Let a few speak and act boldly, and, though as few as the first Apostles, they may begin a rapid course of spiritual conquest, as did the ancient teachers of Christianity. I consider the present moment as eminently favourable, because it is eminently dangerous, and because the danger is manifest.

I hope you will not blame me for the frankness of my language. I cannot speak about the Church of England without an earnest emotion. I grieve for its present position, but I find a great source of hope in the zeal which is manifested by its members all over the world in the preaching of the name of Christ. May they find at home for themselves the peace of mind and spiritual joy they labour to spread over distant nations!

Accept, most reverend sir, the assurance of the sincere respect and devotion of a man who calls himself truly yours,

ALEXIS KHAMECOFF.

June $\frac{6}{18}$, Moscow.

CHAPTER XII

MR. PALMER'S REPLY TO MR. KHOMIAKOFF'S FIFTH LETTER

[1851]

Mr. Palmer's literary schemes—Outline of 'Dissertations upon the Orthodox Communion'—Journey to the East—In the South of Russia—Mr. Palmer applies for admission into the Greek Church—Question of Rebaptism—Question as to how far the laity have a voice in the teaching of the Church.

CONSTANTINOPLE,
Sept. 22 (*Oct.* 4), 1851.

MY DEAR M. KHOMIAKOFF,—I have been so long in your debt that I am ashamed to make any apologies, though you know, I daresay, as well as I could tell you how any intention which is long delayed is in danger of being delayed indefinitely. I cannot, however, now, after having been for some weeks in Russia, return to Athens without sending you a few lines to tell you how I had been calculating upon the possibility of seeing you personally, and how this hope or idea came to be disappointed. I think you know how I spent the winter of 1849-50 at Athens in company with my younger brother, for the sake of his health, and how afterwards, in the spring of 1850, we were with the Admiral Poutiatine in Palestine and at Constantinople, how, after the Admiral left us, I and my brother spent three weeks on Mount Athos, and then returned to England to spend the winter of 1850-51 with our family. During my stay in Athens with my brother, I procured a translation to be made into modern Greek of the chief documents relating to my previous controversies, and their ultimate termination in Scotland by the refusal of the Synod to give any decision either in favour of the more orthodox or in favour of the

more Calvinistic or Protestant party and tendency within the
Anglican Communion, or upon the merits of the particular
controversy brought before them by my appeal. These
documents so translated I printed as an explanation of the
motives which made me now to be ready to seek admission
to the Communion of the Eastern Church, in case no further
obstacle presented itself. I also agreed with my translator
to translate for me a number of Dissertations relating to the
Anglican Church (which you have seen in the thick volume
of my Appeal which I sent to you in English): and the thin
volume entitled *A Harmony of Anglican and Eastern Doctrine*
(which you also have in English). To these I proposed to
add some short Dissertations on the following subjects
connected with the Eastern Church :—(1) On the present
apparent separation and conflict of two attributes of the
true Church, namely 'Orthodoxy' and 'Catholicism'; (2) On
the present state and position and probable future prospects
of the Eastern Church; (3) On the apparent destinies or
mission of the Slavonic race and Empire, and of the Churches
connected with it: at the same time of the mission and probation of the first solemnly crowned Russian Tzar, *i.e.* John IV.
the Terrible, his failure of accomplishing it, and the extinction of his house; (4) Of the accusation commonly made in
the West against the Greek and especially against the
Russian Church, as having fallen too much under the Civil
Power, and of the grounds really existing for this opinion;
(5) Of the struggle between the Russian nobility and the
better part of the Hierarchy in the middle of the seventeenth
century, and of the consequences to Russia of the Deposition
of the Patriarch Nicon; (6) Of the method in which controversy should be managed; (7) Review of the present
state of particular controversies between the Latin and
Greek Churches; (8) Of Formalism or undue attachment
to the externals of religion; (9) Of superstition or credulity
in religious matters, and its tendency to produce the contrary
fault of scepticism and infidelity; (10) Of the need and duty
of instituting express prayers for the reconcilement of the

present divisions of Christendom ; (11) Of the improvements which the Eastern Church might make, if she pleased, so as to increase her influence upon others and strengthen her own position ; (12) Of the necessity of reconciling the discrepancy now existing between the Greek and Russian Churches on the subject of the reception of Proselytes, who have been baptized without the due observance of all the requisites of the Orthodox ritual, as by affusion instead of immersion, and by one immersion or affusion instead of three ; and lastly (13), of the lessons addressed to the Church in general, and especially to the Church and to Christians in the latter ages of the world, in the seven Apocalyptic Epistles addressed to the seven Churches of Asia. All this, it was agreed, my translator should translate during the winter ; and in the spring of 1851 I was to come out again to Athens, and revise with him and print there what he should have translated, so as to form of the whole a good-sized octavo volume. My idea then was, that this might be finished by July, and that then I might return to England through Russia by way of Constantinople, Odessa, Kieff, Moscow, and St. Petersburg : and I reckoned upon the possibility (*not* the certainty, as I knew people often are absent in the summer) of getting a sight of you by the way. This plan I had communicated by letter last spring to some of my friends at St. Petersburg, and they had even written to Odessa and Nicolaieff to bespeak the good offices of such persons as could be useful to me there when I should arrive. Thus things stood, when, just before leaving England on March 6th, N.S., M. Kossovich made his appearance at Oxford, and brought me your letter, dated some months before, October 8th, O.S., 1850. He also brought me a very handsomely printed thin volume, containing coloured representations and a description in letterpress of an ancient Church at Vladimir.[1] This present was

---

[1] This, there can be no doubt, must have been Count Sergius Stroganoff's beautiful monograph : The Cathedral of St. Demetrius at Vladimir on the Kliazma. Moscow, 1849.—[W. J. B.]

most interesting to me and to others to whom I showed it, as being a sign that the study of ecclesiastical architecture and decoration is beginning to have its votaries in Russia also. How I wish that this taste may spread and that before long, instead of the miserable bare whitewash and plaster inside and out (with green roof perhaps) which is now the general rule, your churches may again be painted, in the inside at least, after the old fashion, as are still all the churches (except one or two Russian) in the Monasteries of Mount Athos! We may hope too to see churches built upon true architectural principles, instead of the most barbarous structures in no style whatever which are now built, sometimes at considerable expense, when new Churches are wanted. I may instance the new Cathedral now building at Odessa. I was much interested in M. Kossovich's conversation, and sorry that his first visit to Oxford was so short. I shall be interested, too, to learn the fortunes of your new steam-engine.[1] This was something quite new for me to hear of you, that you were also an inventor of steam-engines.

But to return to my account of myself: I left England on the 20th of March, N.S., for Athens, and remained there printing till the 19th of July, N.S., when my translator absented himself, to pass six weeks of the hottest weather (being his vacation) in the islands. I then found that, instead of having finished my book as I had expected, I had only printed half of it, and that therefore I could not execute my project of returning to England through Russia, or of returning for the present at all. Still, having the time of my translator's absence free and at my disposal (as I could not continue printing without him), I determined to make a short excursion into the south of Russia, to see the Holy Places of Kieff, the ancient cathedral and catacombs at Chernigoff, and the recently restored monastery of Sviatija Gory between Izioum and Slaviansk in the Government of Kharkoff, when

---

[1] Shown in the International Exhibition that year in London.— [W. J. B.]

I was invited to visit M. de Potemkin. This I have now done, and have had the advantage at the same time of seeing two old friends whom I had not expected to see (viz., Mr. Mouravieff, who came to meet me at Sviatija Gory, and Philaret, Bishop of Kharkoff[1]), and of making acquaintance with several other persons of piety and learning, whom before I knew only by name. Among these the chief are Innocent, Archbishop of Kherson, M. Al. Stourdza, and Philaret, the venerable Metropolitan of Kieff,[2] who received me as if he had been my father. I owe also to an accident which caused me to be too late for the steamer of the 30th August, O.S., from Odessa to Constantinople, and so to have ten days to spare, a very pleasant addition to my tour, viz., that of seeing the Crimea, with the ruins of the two Khersons, near Sebastopol, then of several rock monasteries and churches, the Tatar capital and Bagtchi Serai, and the beautiful south coast, where I was most hospitably received (though before unknown to him) by Prince Voronzoff at Alupka. The accident to which I owed this was the overturning of my carriage at the first stage from the modern Kherson, when I was thrown out upon my head, and obliged to stay several days at Nicolaieff to be bled and to recover the sight of my eyes

[1] Better known as Philaret, Bishop of Chernigoff. His family name was Gumileffski. He was educated at the Moscow Ecclesiastical Academy, where he received his Master's degree in 1830, and that of Doctor of Divinity in 1860. He took the monastic habit in 1830, was made Rector of the Academy in 1835, was consecrated Bishop of Riga in 1841, and was translated to Kharkoff in 1848, was promoted to the rank of Archbishop in 1857, and was translated to Chernigoff in 1859, where he died on August 9, 1866, of cholera. Among his writings, which are of a very high order, and are deservedly popular in Russia, are *The Fathers of the Church*, *A History of the Russian Church*, *Dogmatic Theology*, and *Hymnographers of the Orthodox Eastern Church.*— [W. J. B.]

[2] Philaret, Metropolitan of Kieff, not to be confused with the more famous Philaret of Moscow. His family name was Amphiteatroff, and he occupied the Metropolitical See of Kieff (the second See of the Russian Church, St Petersburgh being the first, and Moscow the third) from 1837 to 1857.—[W. J. B.]

and the clearness of my head, which was at first confused. I am now on the point of returning to Athens, when I hope in about four months more, *i.e.* by Christmas, to finish my book, and will try to find some opportunity of sending you a copy (at least if you read Romaic), though I fear the fourth part, of which I have given you the heads, will scarcely be allowed by the Censors to enter Russia in the ordinary way. The extinction of the Family of Alexis, however delicately hinted at, and though for the purpose of showing that the present family has not inherited his sin, nor necessarily its punishment, but is now upon a separate probation or trial of its own, is too delicate a matter for any other Censor than the Emperor himself to be at all likely to estimate justly what may be written upon it.

I have been addressing in modern Greek a question to the Patriarch of Constantinople, of which I will send you a copy, whenever I have one myself.[1] It is on the subject of Rebaptism, the Russian Church now admitting as valid, though irregularly administered, Western Baptisms, and the Greek Church rejecting them as nullities and rebaptizing all proselytes who have been so baptized. Thus I am myself unable to be received to Communion, if I desire it, without either professing myself to be as yet unbaptized, contrary to my own belief and the declarations of the Russian Church, or being received by a part only instead of the whole of the Eastern Church, the Russian, while another part, the Greek, tell me that I am as yet unbaptized, and have been improperly received as baptized by the Russians. I am to receive an answer to this question to-morrow, and, from conversations I have already heard, know pretty well that it will leave the difficulty unremoved. My question was this: whether the Greeks, considering the contrary doctrine and practice of the Russian Church, could not rebaptize me conditionally instead of

---

[1] Ταπεινὴ ἀναφορὰ τοῖς πατριάρχαις. 'Αθηναῖς. 1850. A translation of this document, together with the reply, is to be found in Mr. Palmer's *Dissertations upon the Orthodox Communion*, 1853.— [W. J. B.].

absolutely; thus: 'The Servant of God N., if he is not already baptized, is baptized, etc., etc.,' or at least permit me to receive and understand their act of rebaptizing me as being virtually, even if not explicitly, *conditional*? But it seems they will not allow that the doctrine and practice of the Russian Church (being as they think wrong) could introduce any doubtfulness at all into the matter, or render the sense of the Eastern Church as a whole doubtful or indeterminate on the subject.[1]

I was very sorry to hear from M. Mouravieff, that besides inflammation of your eyes, mentioned in your letter of October last, your health in other respects has been indifferent for some time past. At least so he had heard, for I do not think he spoke as if he had seen you lately himself. I sincerely hope it may have been quite re-established long before you receive this letter. With regard to the proposition which you point out as being so important, I enter into what you say; and the proposition is both true and important. Nevertheless it is one which must not be pressed too far. Whatever share the common faith and charity of the Laity may have in the preservation of the true tradition of Doctrine, the mission to teach all nations, and the promise to be with them in teaching even to the end of the world, a promise which confers doctrinal infallibility so far as it may be necessary, is given to the united College of the Apostles and their successors: and to their public and Synodical decrees we must therefore at all times principally look. But I must conclude this letter. The conversions in England to Roman Catholicism still occur from time to time, and of very excellent and eminent persons; three or four most valued friends of my own have become Roman Catholics within the last year. How my own case stands at present, you will see from my question to the Patriarch of Constantinople when

---

[1] Both the Patriarchate of Constantinople and the Church of the modern kingdom of Greece have now conformed to the practice of the Russian Church, and now no longer rebaptize Westerns, whether Roman Catholic, Anglican, or Protestant.—[W. J. B.]

you receive it. I hope to write again to you after a shorter interval than the last; and in the meantime beg you to present my remembrances and my duty to your Metropolitan whenever you see him,—and to remember me very kindly to any other of my friends or acquaintances you may meet, especially to the Count Alex. Tolstoi, to Princess Dolgorouki, *née* Davidoff, or to M. de Levasheff, if you see any of them ; and believe me that a letter from you is always received by me with the greatest pleasure, and that I am always, my dear M. Khomiakoff, with best wishes and prayers for your health and happiness in all things, and that of all yours or connected with you,—yours most sincerely, W. PALMER.

CHAPTER XIII

MR. KHOMIAKOFF'S SEVENTH LETTER TO MR. PALMER

[1852]

The Archbishop of Kazan on Mr. Palmer's case—Death of Mme. Khomiakoff.

MOST REVEREND AND DEAR SIR,—After your kind letter which I received at the beginning of November, I was for a long while in a most painful position. I felt deeply and intensely your anxiety and your grief: I felt that my duty was to seek some means of giving you some aid or at least some consolation; but what could I do? I had no friendly acquaintance with the Spiritual Directors of the Russian Church. I had no means of being of any use to you, and yet my heart was torn with grief for you and your friends. At last I decided upon a line of action. I got acquainted with one of our young Bishops, a man of piety and feeling. He promised to do what he could, but after some fruitless correspondence with more influential persons he confessed that he could do nothing for you, or at least that he could give no hopes at present. I next took a rather bold step. I wrote a letter to one of the most eminent of our Divines and Archbishops, Gregory, Archbishop of Kazan, member of the Holy Synod,[1] whom I had never seen and who probably had

---

[1] Gregory Postnikoff received his education in the Ecclesiastical Academy at St. Petersburgh, where he took the degree of Master in 1814, and took the monastic habit the same year; in 1817 he was made Doctor of Divinity, and in 1819 succeeded Philaret as Rector of the Academy; in 1822 he was consecrated Bishop, as one of the Vicar-Bishops of St. Petersburgh; in 1826 he was translated to Kaluga, in

never heard about me. The day before yesterday I was rejoiced by a rather unexpected answer, and that answer contains most consoling assurances which I make haste to communicate to you.

If the Archbishop is well informed, there is a project of a petition from some of your friends in England to our Synod, and they are only waiting for your return to England to sign and send it. The project meets, it seems, with the most undisputed approbation from our Divines. Gregory promises (and his words are of no light character) that if the petition is signed and duly furthered to the Synod, every difficulty shall disappear, and every just request shall be met with the joy of Christian brothers and of men who consider the welfare of the Church as their dearest interest and its promotion as their only duty on earth. Do not be tardy, dearest sir, in the service of God's Kingdom! Hasten your return! Hasten to take the last and decisive step. The door of the Church is open. Brothers are ready to meet you with brotherly love. Your zeal, your humble constancy, have cleared away all doubts, all misrepresentations of which you were not even aware.

The Archbishop of Kazan excuses the Patriarch [of Constantinople] by the enmity in which all the Communions of Western Europe seem to vie with one another against the Eastern Church all over Greece, Syria, and Asia Minor. This certainly is a painful truth, and goes far to excuse temporary measures of self-defence. I have given you only the leading features of his letter. I cannot express the feeling of deep sympathy with your sufferings which forms its character, his high esteem for you, his Christian hopes and even the impatient expectation with which he looks forward to a decisive step from your friends. I am sure (I pledge myself to that) that

---

1829 he became Archbishop of Riazan, in 1831 of Tver, and in 1848 of Kazan, where he remained until 1856, when, shortly after the coronation of Alexander II., he was made Metropolitan of Novgorod and St. Petersburgh, which is the first See of the Russian Church. He died in 1860.—[W. J. B.].

in every just request you will find in him the warmest, and, I may add, the most powerful advocate.

The Lord has visited me with a heavy trial. On the 26th of January (O.S.) my wife died, and with her every possibility of earthly happiness for me. God's will be done! I try to be thankful. Fifteen years and a half of almost unmixed bliss is more than one man in a million has been allowed to enjoy, and a million times more than I can ever have deserved. Our mutual love was as boundless as an earthly feeling can be. It is not dead. We interchange prayers for one another, just as we interchanged words of affection during her lifetime. She was a pure, loving, and deeply religious soul. How often in our conversation about England have I heard her say: 'When shall we be so happy as to praise God in the same Church with MM. Palmer and Williams?' Her death has been childlike: no fear, no affliction, but a full reliance on God's mercy. We may be sure that she has met in Heaven a greater love than any love she could have found on earth. God's will be done!

Accept, dearest sir, the assurance of the sincere respect and affection of your most devoted, ALEXIS KHAMECOFF.

The 10 *of March,*
1852. Moscow.

As I am not sure of the address, I write to Constantinople, Athens, and Oxford. *N.B.*—A word in the letter of the Archbishop of Kazan is particularly important: 'What is Mr. Palmer doing in Athens when he is expected and called for elsewhere?'

[The direction on the outside of this letter is à Monsieur, Monsieur Palmer. à Athènes. Recommandée aux soins de la légation de Sa Majesté Britannique.]

CHAPTER XIV

MR. PALMER'S REPLY TO MR. KHOMIAKOFF'S
SEVENTH LETTER

Account of Mr. Palmer's 'Dissertations'—His present ecclesiastical position —Difficulty of joining either the Greek or the Russian Church—Claims of Rome.

St. Mary Magdalene College, Oxford,
July 5th, 1852.

My dear Mr. Khomiakoff,—All your letters sent in triplicate to Athens, Constantinople, and Oxford reached me at different times—and I really do not know how to express my sense of the friendly and charitable earnestness which you have shown towards me—and not only towards me, but also and rather towards the interests of truth and unity. Before I received any of your three letters I had already heard of your loss from a friend, Mr. Titoff, at Constantinople, and can feel for you the more from noticing that it was just at the same time that I lost my own sister. But we both have the same consolation, and a blessed one it is; of feeling that the departure of those whom we have loved was a happy one for them, and such as may be useful to us, and strengthen us in our efforts to live so that we may be found together with them at the last; the more sad losses we have experienced, the more deeply we can unite daily in those prayers which are made in the Liturgy for the living and the departed. I am now waiting here for the death of my father, who has been sinking rapidly for some months past, and is not likely to recover. Whenever that occurs, if I should myself have life and health, having done all that I could do towards the Greek and Russian branches of the Eastern Church, I may probably go and study at Rome, considering the obstacles which I have met with to prevent my being admitted to the communion of the Eastern Church, together with the impossibility of defending the Anglican Church, as signs that I ought to study more closely the Roman Communion, which, besides other superiorities, seems thus to be left, by a kind of exhaustive process, the only claimant on my allegiance.

But I am anticipating a little. I have not yet told you how I stand at present with regard to the Greek and Russian Churches, or what I see still remaining for me to do before I go to Rome. First, for the Greeks. After receiving at Constantinople, as you know, a refusal of the permission I desired, to accept their re-baptism in a conditional sense, I returned to Athens, and (after first printing a volume of 600 pages concerning the Anglican Church) printed in modern Greek some short dissertations on subjects connected with the Eastern and Latin Churches. There were fifteen of them, and they make in all a thin volume of 250 pages, on the following subjects:

I. Of the distinctive titles, present state, and probable future prospects of the so-called 'Orthodox' Communion.

II. Of the present apparent conflict between so-called 'Orthodoxy' and so-called 'Catholicism.'

III. Destinies of the Slavonian Empire. Probation and failure of John IV., the first solemnly crowned Tsar of Muscovy.

IV. Destinies of the Slavonian Empire. Of the conflict which took place in the seventeenth century between the civil power and the nobility in Russia and the Patriarch Nicon.

V. Of the right method of religious controversy.

VI. A brief review of the present state of particular controversies between the Eastern and the Latin Churches.

VII. On the bearing of the theory of doctrinal development on the question between the Eastern and Latin Churches.
VIII. A more particular exposition on the question of the Procession of the Holy Spirit.
IX. A series of Propositions, now commonly maintained in the Greek portion of the Eastern Church, respecting Baptism administered by heretics or schismatics; by lay persons, or in any other manner than by trine Immersion.
X. Three documents against and for the Re-baptizing of Westerns.
XI. Of the imputation of Formalism commonly urged in the West against the Eastern Church.
XII. Of credulity and superstition.
XIII. A list of things which seem wanting or desirable for the Eastern Church.
XIV. Of the duty of making more special and concerted Prayers for the restoration of unity between the Eastern and the Latin Churches, and of a future Œcumenical Council.
XV. Of the admonitions addressed to the Seven Churches of Asia, and, through them, to the Universal Church, in the Apocalypse.

Having printed this volume, and sent it to different parts of the Levant, I have done all I could towards the Greek part of the Eastern Church; and have now only to wait some sufficient time to see whether either those chapters of my book which relate to Baptism, or the communication from Russia of verified copies of those certain *Greek* (no less than Russian) decisions *against* Re-baptizing which *have disappeared* at Constantinople since 1756, produce any effect, or lead to any change in the practice of the Greeks in the Levant.

(2ndly) As regards Russia, the difficulty which with me seems insurmountable, is this :—that the present relations of the Spiritual and Civil Powers within the Russian Empire are such as to be inconsistent with the due exercise of the Apostolical Office. In Russia itself the administration of the Government and the Censorship keep all things quiet as they are, so that individuals neither perceive the true nature of many questions, nor the inevitable developments and consequences of principles which have once been admitted; and so they might be inclined to think that one were less scrupulous and would consent to be blind as they are blind, or silent as they are silent, and to acquiesce in and become a party to that which they find no difficulty in acquiescing in and being parties to. But to a Western seeking to join the communion of the Russian Church the case is very different. If I join the Russian Church, I must be able to defend myself to my own conscience, and to reasonable men (whether Protestants or Roman Catholics) in the West, for acting in a manner so contrary to their idea of reason. I cannot deny or dissemble the undue supremacy now held by the State in Russia; and if I were to make light of it, as if such usurpation had no essential bearing upon the Catholic faith and discipline of Christ, and as if one might allowably accept it and submit to it, I should be merely exhibiting myself in the eyes of all in the West as a fool or a madman, without in any way strengthening the position of the Eastern Church by my adhesion to her, or having the least chance of setting an example to be followed by others. If then this mountain of the undue State Supremacy crosses my way, I must either find some means of removing the mountain, which is not very probable, or I must turn aside myself and take some other road. Having these ideas, and considering the responsibility to lie with the Highest Personage in the Empire alone, if anything is wrong in Russia, I have determined not to address myself to any Bishop, or to the Synod, so long as things are in their present state, but I will send copies of those Dissertations which I have printed in the Levant to the Censorship of the Press in Russia, and request to be informed if a Russian translation of the same, either unchanged, or with only such changes or omissions as would not affect the theological completeness of the work, would be allowed to be printed and circulated in Russia. If it would be allowed (which I do not at all expect), I think that I *might then* seek admission to the Communion of the Russian Church. But if (as I make sure will be the case) it should be considered impossible to permit the publication of my Essays, I must then answer my friends who suggest to me to come again to Russia, that I could not satisfactorily defend myself, either to my own conscience or to my countrymen, if I sought admission to the communion of a particular Church in which I am not free to discuss freely and publicly (though in a spirit of sincere loyalty to all worldly authorities) matters which are of essential importance to religion. If the Russian Government and Censorship cannot accept or allow my mode of defending the Eastern Church and the interests of the Russian Empire and the Imperial Family, I have done all that I can (though certainly not for public, but merely for personal motives), and, having satisfied my own conscience, must step aside, and leave them to defend their Church and their Empire in their own way. After I have then done all I can towards the Russian as well as the Greek Church, I should probably, as I have said, go and study at Rome, with the hope of learning something there to enable me to change my mind and submit to her claims, since I can no longer defend the Anglican, nor find a satisfactory entrance to the Eastern, Church. If, after all, I should not be able to get rid of my present doctrinal agreement with the Eastern Church, then (as I could not profess to believe what I do not believe) I should have nothing open to me but to wait for any possible change which time might produce either in the Levant or in Russia, and, in that case, I might probably live a good deal in the Levant, perhaps at Mount Athos. I hope that—whatever the Providence of God may have in store for me, or by whatever way it may lead me—I shall never part with my present feelings of interest and regard for all the good that I have seen or known in the Russian Church and people. The *Greek* character (though they have some admirable natural gifts) is by no means attractive in a religious point of view. But there is very much about the Russian which ought, I think, to engage the sympathies of every Christian soul. And the unjust and bitter prejudices of so many in the West against those very things which are most admirable in the Russian Church and State is a strong additional reason for any one who has had opportunities of judging to feel all the more warmly in favour of what is unduly depreciated or calumniated. I am heartily sorry that these things are not in *all* respects as I could wish—that the Russian Church and Hierarchy is not in that position of just liberty which it held before the deposition of Nicon, that sovereigns and inferior organs of Government and the Censorship of the press are not likely to be able, or willing, to distinguish between a licentiousness or contumacy which springs from evil motives, and such a freedom of discussion as is healthy and conducive to the true interests both of religion and the throne. But I cannot make things to be other than they are. I must take them as I find them; and if what I think evil will not give place before my efforts or remonstrances, I must at least be excused if I decline for myself to submit myself to it, or to defend it as if it were good. I may be asked, indeed, how I can *wish* to change my mind on a number of points on which I now agree with the Eastern Church, rather than on one or two points on which I agree with the Roman Catholic Church. Why not, one may ask, try to see the present relations of the Imperial and Apostolical Powers in Russia with Russian eyes, rather than try to see the Procession, the Papal Supremacy, and four or five other questions, with Roman eyes? For this reason, I answer,—that the points of weakness or difficulty in the Russian Church are such as affect the definition of the Catholic Church itself, but the points on which I now differ from Rome are points of *detail*, capable of being ruled by the definition of the Church. My Roman Catholic friends put the matter to me thus: 'If you believe in a *visible* Church, the first and only necessary question is, what is that Church now on earth which is identical in essence (*e.g.* in the spirit and idea of universality, in zeal and charity for particular souls, and in its attitude of independence and, if need be, opposition to the powers of this world in spiritual things) with the Church of the first ages ? You will scarcely dare to say that the Eastern or Greek Church is this Church rather than the Roman Catholic. If, then, your conscience tells you that either the Roman Catholic Church is *the* Church, or else there is now no visible Church on earth which is the true perpetuation of that founded by the Apostles, you ought to have the sense to see that it is for the Church to teach you, and not for you to teach yourself or the Church ; and that therefore it is quite superfluous for you to discuss what may seem to you, or to any other smaller Community (which is not *the* Church), to be more orthodox or agreeable to antiquity concerning the Procession, the Papal Supremacy, Purgatory, Indulgences, or other particular points of doctrine.' This is what they now urge on me. What are my own sentiments you will see, I hope, before long from my Dissertations, which I hope to send you printed in English before the end of the summer, together, perhaps, with a more legible or more intelligible letter.

Accept once more my warmest thanks for all your kindness and friendship towards me ; and if you chance to see any persons, whether ecclesiastics or others, with whom I have any acquaintance, or who take any interest in my pursuit and wishes, pray offer them my most humble respects and desire for me a place in their prayers. I ought to name more especially the Metropolitan of Moscow and the Archbishop of Kazan, for whose truly Christian assurance to your letter I feel deeply grateful ;—and believe me to be always, yours most sincerely and affectionately,

W. PALMER.

CHAPTER XV

MR. KHOMIAKOFF'S EIGHTH LETTER TO MR. PALMER

[1852]

Sympathy with Mr. Palmer—Difficulty concerning Re-baptism, not without precedent in the early Church — Criticism of Mr. Palmer's attitude towards Rome and the East—Defence of the Greek Church, and of the Russian Church, against Mr. Palmer's strictures—Scheme for reconciling Anglicans to the Orthodox Church—A request—Communion with the departed—Proofs of the authenticity of the Gospels.

MOST REVEREND AND DEAR SIR,—I have just received your letter of the 5th of July and hasten to answer it. First I must say that I was the more rejoiced at receiving it, as, considering some circumstances, I was rather afraid that my letters or your answer were lost in some Post Office, which case is not very rare. Secondly, I am in many respects happy to know that you have for some time been back from the East, of which I suppose you are most heartily tired.

On the other side, I am very grieved to see how many difficulties and afflictions beset every step you take to find the true and direct way in the all-important question of Religion; but you will permit me to consider your position (though with the deepest sympathy, you will believe it), yet with a greater calm than, probably, you can have yourself.

Why is your position difficult?

If you were acting as an individual, seeking truth for yourself alone, there would, it seems, be no difficulty at all. I am very far from excusing the Patriarchs or approving their obstinacy; but still you must admit that the rite of Re-baptizing, having been at different times prescribed or rejected with regard to the same schisms or heresies in the early Church, the obstinacy of the Greek Bishops, though perhaps blameable, would not yet give occasion to any very important accusation. The discipline of a whole local Church cannot be expected to be altered for one individual, even were the change for the better. The case is different if you are acting as the representative of an opinion common to a certain number of your countrymen (which I take to be granted). Under these circumstances the stubbornness of the Grecian Church becomes offensive, and seems to indicate a certain want of charity and of desire to extend the realm of the true Faith. If you concede this point, and if you admit that you are acting, not as a mere individual, but as a representative of many others, you must likewise feel the extreme importance either of your failure or of your success; and then you will find it most natural that you should meet with the greatest and even the most unexpected difficulties. Such has been, and will probably ever be, the case when the spiritual futurity of a whole Society is to be decided. Mighty Powers will arise against truth, and will raise mighty obstacles by the permission of God, who wills that patience should be tried as well as faith.

Permit me to express the view I take of your position towards Rome and the Eastern Church, and to appreciate your objections to both. Certainly I may be biassed by my own convictions, and may be wanting in impartiality; no man can answer for himself. But one thing I may answer for, that I will express my opinion as candidly as if I were speaking to my own conscience before the visible Majesty of God.

First for Rome. You do not approve of many tenets of her Doctrine. I won't say you are right—this being my own particular opinion has nothing at all to do with your case—but I think you cannot join a Doctrine [of which] you do not approve. Your only answer to yourself, the only one given by your Roman friends, is: 'There must be a *visible* Church, and that Church must be a *free* one.' This I admit completely; but I must add, free in its *principles*, though not always free in its *actions or manifestations*, which depend much upon accidental circumstances. But I leave this aside. 'The Church of Rome is the only free one; *ergo* the only true one; and all other doubts must disappear.' This seems to me a false deduction. You doubt your individual judgment with respect to particular tenets. Well, I suppose you are right. But why do you not doubt of the boasted freedom of the Roman Church? It seems to me a matter of equal, I will say, of greater doubt still. I will admit the freedom of the Pope or of the hierarchical power; but is that the meaning of ecclesiastical freedom? The contrary would perhaps be nearer to truth than the affirmative. And shall such a doubtful test, for which we have no authority in the earlier time of Christianity, overrule convictions founded on a mature consideration of the teaching of the Church[1] as it is expressed by all ancient Fathers? That the Roman Church is independent I will concede; but that it has anything like ecclesiastical freedom, the liberty of the Spirit, I totally deny. To get rid of the difficulties of your present position you may lull your convictions to sleep, you may silence them, even conquer them; you will not uproot them. You will enter the Roman Communion, as it were, double-minded, with nothing even like a hope of finding the blessed peace of Christ in an undoubted Faith. Pardon me if I speak thus boldly; but the examples of Mr. Newman and Mr. Allies are, in my opinion, conclusive. They were certainly better Christians formerly than they are now; their open-heartedness is gone for ever; they have crippled themselves instead of expanding. For my part I will say that, happy as I should be if even a small number of Englishmen were to join

---

[1] I have substituted the words 'the teaching of the Church' here for 'the Ecclesiastical doctrine.' The Russian translator renders it: церковное учение, and these were evidently the words which Khomiakoff had in his mind, and which he intended to reproduce in English. [W. J. B.]

the communion of the Church, I could not rejoice if all England were to become Orthodox, with a mind divided by conflicting convictions. Pray tell me, dear sir, does any Symbol begin by the words: 'I *will* believe,' or, '*I will not doubt*'? Do not all of them begin by the words, 'I *do* believe'?

Now let us return to Greece and Russia.

Here you have no need to say: 'I *will* believe,' but you say with all your heart, 'I *do* believe' that the tenets of their doctrine are in every respect concordant with the ancient and traditionary Faith of the Church Universal. I think this is all in all. But you have objections against the two halves[1] of the Orthodox Church, against the one for its want of charity, against the other for its want of liberty. For the first, I believe their fault in your case is more a fault of ignorance than of cold-heartedness. That such is the true construction is, in my opinion, clearly proved by the extreme obstinacy of the Patriarchs. You may not have heard (I think you had left the East before that time) that the Constantinopolitan Synod has almost excommunicated the Russian Church for admitting Protestants and Romans without Rebaptism. The thing had gone very far, though I think it is now taking a more conciliatory turn. This event has been a scandal and a subject of grief to many of my countrymen; but, grieved as I was myself at the beginning, I soon felt my mind at ease. There was energy, though in a wrong direction, in such a step being taken by a poor enslaved community against the powerful Empire whose aid it wants continually. I respect the feeling. The error will soon be dispelled, and proves nothing against us; local Churches are often inclined to temporary errors, from which they are rescued by their belonging to a Catholic Union. I am even glad that you have given occasion to that misunderstanding. The question must and shall be brought to an issue either by the Greeks adopting our discipline through conviction, and

---

[1] *i.e.* the Greek and the Russian Church.—[W. J. B.]

then all is won; or by a declaration that a difference in Rite and Ecclesiastical discipline does not in any way affect the Unity of the Church. Much would be gained, even in that case, particularly for the future; but your difficulty would still remain unsolved. The error at any rate was, or is still, an error of ignorance, and proves nothing against charity. But I will confess that I am somehow suspicious of the Greeks. They have no lack of zeal or freedom (the two great reproaches brought against them by the Roman party); but they cannot get rid of a dangerous inheritance from Antiquity. They are Christians, but they are perhaps unconsciously too proud of their having been useful to the Church; Christianity belongs too much to their national history, and their hearts are not completely free from a certain un-Christian aristocratical feeling which makes them look down on other Christian nations, though Orthodox, as their inferiors. This feeling is akin to the one that has given rise to the Roman usurpation. Though being checked by a deeper understanding of the true doctrine, it cannot go the whole lengths it has gone in the West, yet it is not completely conquered; and it gives the Greeks that unbending stubbornness and that unamiable disposition which you have noticed and experienced. But as long as it does not break out in the assumption of undue pre-eminence and power, it cannot be considered as affecting in the least degree the ecclesiastical character of Greece.

Now for Russia. That the Church is not quite independent of the State, I allow; but let us consider candidly and impartially how far that dependence affects, and whether it does indeed affect, the character of the Church. The question is so important, that it has been debated during this very year by serious men in Russia, and has been brought, I hope, to a satisfactory solution. A society may be dependent in fact and free in principle, or *vice versa*. The first case is a mere historical accident; the second is the destruction of freedom, and has no other issue but rebellion and anarchy. The first is the weakness of man; the second the depravity of law. The first is certainly the case in Russia, but the principles are by no means deteriorated. Whether freedom of opinion in civil and political questions is, or is not, too much restrained, is no business of ours as members of the Church (though I, for my part, know that I am almost reduced to complete silence); but the State *never* interferes directly in the censorship of works written about religious questions. In this respect I will confess again that the Censorship is, in my opinion, most oppressive; but that does not depend upon the State, and is simply the fault of the over-cautious and timid prudence of the higher clergy. I am very far from approving of it, and I know that very useful thoughts and books are lost to the world, or at least to the present generation. But this error, which my reason condemns, has nothing to do with ecclesiastical liberty; and though very good tracts and *explanations of the Word of God* are oftentimes suppressed on the false supposition of their perusal being dangerous to unenlightened minds, I think that those who suppress the *Word of God itself* should be the last to condemn the excessive prudence of our ecclesiastical censors. Such a condemnation coming from the Romans would be absurdity itself. But is the action of the Church quite free in Russia? Certainly not; but this depends wholly upon the weakness of her higher representatives, and upon their desire to get the protection of the State, not for themselves, generally speaking, but for the Church. There is certainly a moral error in that want of reliance upon God Himself; but it is an accidental error of *persons*, and not of *the Church*, and has nothing to do with our religious convictions. It would be a different case, if there was the smallest instance of a dogmatical error, or something near to it, admitted or suffered without protestation out of weakness; but I defy anybody to find anything like that. It were a strange thing to see the Church judged and condemned for such a weakness of her members (let them be ever so high in the hierarchical scale) of which she can have no legitimate notion.[1] Every other Communion is to be judged on its principles; Orthodoxy alone is to be judged on the mere fact of historical accident! Where is the justice of such a test? Is there anything more scandalous than to see that the Headship of the Pseudo-Catholic Church has belonged for many centuries to men of Italian blood as a privilege? But this is accident and no principle; Romanism does not, and indeed ought not, to have to answer for it. Again, many Popes have been true slaves to the power of contemporary kings; Romanism does not and must not answer for it. Again, there have been Popes who have bought the tiara and have governed by constant simony; Romanism is not and cannot be made answerable for it. And yet if our Synod fails in courage and firmness—the Church must answer for it! Indeed, most reverend sir, I do not understand your objections. If Greece lacks science, and Russia freedom; well! Russia is enlightened for Greece, and Greece free for Russia! Both will reap the fruits of the particular merits of each of them. Do not, if you please, consider them apart from one another. You are not called to a *local*, but to a *Catholic*, Church. Let an Orthodox Community arise in the West (a thing which will happen most undoubtedly), its knowledge and liberty will again be the property of the whole ecclesiastical body. Do not give way (permit me to speak this freely) to momentary despondency, or impatience, or irritation. I understand, I feel, how very natural, how very lawful, they are to one in your position (speaking in a human, but not quite a Christian sense), and how guilty are those who, either by their ignorant obstinacy, or by their mean and cowardly cold-heartedness,

---

[1] I have left this passage just as Khomiakoff wrote it. In the Russian translation it reads as follows: 'It would be strange to judge and condemn the Church for such a weakness in her members, however high in the grades of the hierarchy they may stand, when the Church herself has not even a legitimate way of making inquiry about this.' (не имѣетъ даже законнаго пути къ дознанію этого.) —[W. J. B.]

have given occasion to such feelings; but you must, and I am sure you will, overcome them.

The little Essay [1] I subjoin to my letter will show you that the question which you have to decide for yourself and, I hope, for many others, has not yet, in my opinion, been quite satisfactorily stated, and that it is even much more important than it is generally thought to be.

I must request your indulgence. I know I have no right to give advice or to criticise your proceedings; but the interests at stake are too high to admit of any other language but that of a complete sincerity. You are not satisfied with the reception you have met from the Orthodox Communion, and you have an undoubted right to complain; but, in justice to yourself and to the Church Orthodox, you must consider whether the line you have followed has been such as to afford her a fair trial. As soon as you found that your convictions were in concordance with the doctrines of the Eastern Communion, you could have joined it by two different ways. Either you might have acted as an individual, or as being part of a society whose opinions harmonised with your own. In the first case every Russian priest had a right to receive you into our Communion without any difficulty; a congregation being formed, it would have organised itself naturally first into a Parochial, and later into an Episcopal flock. Such is the way in which the greater number of local Churches began; such is the way even with the Romanists in countries where there are no resident bishops. This was the simplest, though I will not say the best way, the more difficult one being often the best in God's Providence. It lies open even now, though perhaps it is no longer so easy as it would have been in the beginning. In the second case you could act as a member of a society with the consent and co-operation of its other members. The authority to which you would have had to address yourself in that case would no longer have been a priest, but either an independent bishop or a local

---

[1] For this Essay see p. 133 and the note on p. 134.—[W. J. B.]

Church. Your first steps were directed towards Russia. But what was the Society which asked for admission? And to what authority, to what representative of the Church, did it address itself? Has there even been an address? None; nothing but a project of address. Was it at least officially directed to the Synod? No, for some of the most important members of the Synod have only heard of it as a vague project without any serious import or object. This I can say with perfect confidence. What could be the answer? I know very well that an answer could have been given, if you had addressed the project to a member of the Synod zealous enough to have undertaken the whole business by himself, and to have been your advocate and your guide. You have not had that good luck. I neither know, nor want to know who was the man chosen to be your plenipotentiary, as I have no wish to blame or judge anybody harshly when I am not called upon to do so. God will judge the cold-hearted, or the ambitious, or the evil-minded, or the cowards who have not done their duty towards you and the Church. One thing I know, that Gregory of Kazan, one of the most zealous, active, enlightened and influential members knew nothing about the whole business, and thanked me for having given him information of it; and one thing more, that some persons [and M——ff is of the number] have been, and still are, very angry with me for having tried to bring the whole proceeding into notoriety and life. I do not want to accuse anybody, nor to awake suspicions that may be more or less unjust; but this much I must say for the vindication of the Church, and even of the Synod (though I have nothing to do with the reputation of the latter), that neither Church nor Synod can be accused of anything in your case. All has been going in a secret and stealthy manner, quite unworthy not only of the Church, but of those earnest and pious men who wanted to join her Communion. That neither you nor your friends are to blame, I am sure; but you trod on ground with which you were not acquainted, and you have met with dead formalities, known as such to all of us, where you thought to find life and action. But the Church is not to be blamed. She knows of nothing, has heard of nothing, has not been called to act or decide. Permit me to state my opinion upon the course you had, and I hope I may say, with God's blessing, you have to follow. I can add that this opinion is corroborated by a good and even a high authority.

If you believe earnestly, as I do not doubt you do, in the purity of the Orthodox Doctrine, and if you do not act as individuals (which would alter the case and bring you simply to call on the first Russian priest you meet with), but as a Society, that Society must act openly and boldly before God and man. It must choose a certain number (let us say, two or three) deputies and address them directly to the Synod with credentials. It must : (1) Make a direct Profession of Faith, shortly and distinctly worded, admitting that the Orthodox Church is in every dogmatical respect true to the ancient Tradition and to the seven Œcumenical Councils, and that every addition or change introduced by the Western Communities has been arbitrary and false. Nothing more is required on that point. (2) Ask for unconditional admission; —that is, without any concession on our side. (3) for priests, married or not, and for a short Liturgy to be completed at a later period, and (4) for a Bishop when the congregation has attained such or such a number, and for an independent Synod of Bishops when their number, if God blesses the good work, thus begun, amounts, let us say, to seven or five or even less. To avoid offending against the laws without necessity, the Bishops can be said to be residing in Great Britain, without any title of See or Province, and even without assuming the title of Bishops towards anybody but their flock; which is according to strict truth, for a man can be Bishop only in the eyes of God and of his own community—he is nothing to others. But this may be as you like. The deputies must be directed to the Russian Synod and have nothing to do with anybody but the assembly of Bishops. To prevent delays, or (as is likewise possible, as we may have more enemies than we know of) the hostile intervention of any evil-disposed influence or power, which might try to stifle or suppress the whole proceeding, *the deputation and its instructions ought to be made known and public by way of print as much as possible.* Letters should be directed, either in the name of the deputies, or of the Society, to all the Bishops of the Russian Church, and sent to them, requesting their good offices, and a letter circular must be addressed to the whole Church (*i.e.* Clergy and Laity) to the same purpose—*both made as public as possible.* I had forgotten one point. As you have addressed yourself to the Greeks (supposing they do not change their mind) you must say that you address yourself to the Russian Church because of her more indulgent discipline, although you do not question the right of the Greeks to maintain their own discipline. In case of any doubts, you must add a request that the Synod *should send a Bishop to England,* not only for the sake of obtaining information, but with a commission to admit converts, ordain priests, and introduce a Liturgy. Pardon me, dear Sir, for taking the liberty to give you these recommendations; but my excuse is, my earnest love, not only for you, but for your country and countrymen, which have been dear to me from my earliest childhood; and my desire to see the Church free from accusations, which are indeed groundless, however well grounded they may seem to be.[1] I may add that I am partly commissioned to make these communications. Supposing you cannot, or you do not, choose to follow this course, the only way left is the one I have spoken of in the beginning, viz., to act as individuals and rely for the future upon God, who can develop an atom to the size of the world. I am afraid every course will only give occasion to mistakes, misunderstandings, and unjust accusations. You have called into life a question between Russia and Greece which, though

---

[1] 'However well-grounded they may seem to be.' I have substituted these words for 'though perhaps seemingly well-grounded' in the original MS.—[W. J. B.]

productive of a temporary disturbance, will certainly be followed in time by favourable results. Let me hope you will yet, by God's Providence, be made instrumental in bringing to light the latent energy of our local Church, which is stifled, not by oppression (always easily resisted) but by a delusive (though unconsciously delusive) protection.

After having taken such liberties in giving advice, I will be more indiscreet still in addressing you a request. I have felt it a duty to answer some accusations which are often directed against us by the Romans, and to show, that the whole of religious conviction in Europe stands on such a false basis, that its triumph over infidelity is quite impossible. I hope I have shown that clearly. Perhaps I have too high an opinion of my own performances, but it seems to me that neither Protestants nor Romans will find it an easy task to answer the very simple explanation I have given of the difference which exists between the principles and character of the Eastern Church and the Western communities respectively. By putting the religious question in a new light, I hope I may be useful to many of those who are thirsting for truth but cannot find their way through the intricate web of theological Rationalism. This little tract I have written in the French language, inasmuch as it is the most generally known throughout all Europe. As I have said, I consider it a duty to take up the defence of the Church; I consider it an act of justice to make the voice of Orthodoxy to be heard to our long-estranged brethren in the West; but I have no possibility to give publicity to my Essay. I cannot do it in Russia, where it would be prohibited, either as useless, and giving rise only to unnecessary doubts, or as being simply contrary to the rules of the ecclesiastical Censorship. Both assertions would certainly be false; but I am tolerably well acquainted with the timidity of our ecclesiastical judges, and know that such would be the case. I cannot absent myself from Russia to have it printed anywhere else, and have no acquaintances out of Russia to undertake the task. At the moment I received your letter, being uncertain whether you had received mine, and whether you were in England or in the East, I had begun a letter to Mr. George Williams in Cambridge to ask him for that favour. In case you would have the goodness either to arrange for the printing of the MS. in England, or to send it over to Paris or Brussels to be printed (this would perhaps be the best plan) I subjoin a cheque for the sum which I suppose would be sufficient for its publication. If it is not enough, I will send more. I know that my request is a very bold one; but hope you will consider me as acting under a sense of justice and duty and that you will not refuse me that friendly service, if it does not give you too much trouble. I do not wish to have my name affixed to the publication, lest personal considerations should interfere with the impartiality of the readers; but if it were said by critics that the boldness of its opinions or expressions is owing to the Author's anonym, I would not only authorise you, but even beg of you to make my name public; for I am sure that I have said nothing but what is agreeable to the undoubted doctrine of the Church, and that nobody in Russia will ever dare to quarrel with me for having done so, though I hope that my expressions are quite strong enough, and even believe that they may perhaps not sound quite agreeable to ears little accustomed to the voice of truth.[1]

My firm conviction, most reverend sir, is, that Romanism is nothing but Separatism, and that humanity has only one choice:—Catholic Orthodoxy or Infidelity. All middle terms are nothing but preparatory steps towards the latter.

My life, dear sir, is quite changed. Its sunshine and holiday are over; nothing is left but the tug and the labour. Life itself would be worth nothing, but for duty. Certainly, I do not repine; although, if misery is to be measured by the

---

[1] This Essay, which was published as 'Quelques mots par un Chrétien Orthodoxe sur les Communions Occidentales,' under the pseudonym 'Ignotus,' is the first contained in the volume 'L'Eglise Latine et le Protestantisme, par Khomiakoff. Lausanne et Vevey, M. Benda, 1872.—[W. J. B.]

happiness lost, I might almost think that nobody has ever had more cause for grief than I have. Perhaps many others have had the same feeling, for every man is apt to consider his load as the heaviest; but, be it as it may, I do not and cannot repine. I had fore-warnings, but did not know or did not choose to understand them, or to make use of them. Everything is better as it is. It is better for her to be happier, as she certainly is; it is better for me to be no longer as happy as I was. Where goodness is lost, rigour is goodness.[1] My present state brings me to the following reflections. As I am now, with a good health, independence, and good little children playing and laughing around me, cannot I be happy? How many millions would consider such a situation a great blessing? Yet for me there is nothing in all this which is not an occasion of pain and affliction. Evidently happiness is only relative, and what I called happiness, what seemed to me the highest degree of possible happiness (for so both of us thought and thanked God for it), was only the shadow of possible happiness, probably because the earthly love which is the only source of happiness on earth is only the shadow of true love.

Will there still after death exist something of the relations that were so dear to us upon earth, or not? I am glad we know nothing about that; this is a merciful dispensation of God. Otherwise we should probably have a desire for something beyond the grave other than God's presence; and this ought not to be. This has nothing to do with the Communion of Souls, about which I have no doubt whatever. You will not, I hope, think these reflections out of season, as you have been yourself so lately visited by affliction.

Accept, most reverend sir, the assurance of the deep

---

[1] The Russian translation renders this passage: 'Where loving-kindness has proved ineffectual, rigour is likewise loving-kindness.' The Russian word, *милосердие*, corresponds exactly to the Latin *misericordia*.—[W. J. B.]

respect and sincere affection with which I have the honour to be, your most humble and obedient servant,

A. KHAMECOFF.

Sept. 4th.

P.S.—If you meet or correspond with Mr. Williams, pray be so good as to recall me to his friendly remembrance.

I have lately chanced to read in the *Christian Remembrancer* a critical article about Alford's edition of the New Testament, where I have found some reflections about the proofs for and against the genuineness of the Gospels. I think that the proofs [given] of their being the work of the Apostles are generally insufficient, or rather, not well chosen. The most important proofs have always been left aside. I mean the proofs which are felt to be so by the artist and the man more than by the learned book-worm. In St. John, considering the spiritual and mystical character of the whole, a most important fact is the omission of the Eucharistical Narrative. It evidently proves that the work had no pretensions to stand by itself, and was intended only as a supplement to written narratives known to the members of the Christian community. The absence of parables and the scanty mention of miracles[1] will be found to lead to the same conclusion; but the most evident proof is certainly in the last chapter. An impartial reader cannot doubt that this chapter is an addition to the first edition which was terminated by *the last verse* of the foregoing one. Scepticism itself cannot dispute that. Now, let anybody explain how this chapter can have been added to a complete edition by anybody, or in any other time, or for any other reason, excepting by St. John himself or by his first disciples, either to dispel a false opinion current in the community, or to explain the unexpected death of the author of the preceding narrative. Is there any other possible explanation? But a disciple would not have added

---

[1] After having related so few (though the most striking) miracles, the Apostle evidently has in mind the great number of miracles related by others in the last verse of his Gospel.

the last verse, and even that supposition (though improbable) would still prove that the first twenty chapters were the work of St. John, or at least *thought to be so in his time*. I will add (but this is a digression) that this last chapter has an immense prophetical significance. At any rate the stamp of contemporaneity is as evident as if we had the first authenticated copy of the book. Again, in the last chapter of St. Luke's Gospel we find proof of authenticity which will be perfectly clear to a mind [1] open to the feelings of what I would call artistic or human truth. 'Did not our hearts burn within us?' There is not a word like that in the whole Gospel, which never speaks of the feelings of the Apostles but in the most vague expressions. But here we do not read, as might have been expected, 'Were not his words Divine?' or something to the same purport, but,—'*Did not our hearts burn within us?*' The eye-witness is evident. A common forger could not have invented such a master-stroke, while a man of genius would not have contented himself with only one. In St. Mark the end of the last chapter is again an author's signature, though perhaps less evident. He had not seen our Lord; he was not one of His personal disciples. He is the only one who speaks at any length of the signs by which later disciples were to be known. Is not that a most conclusive feature of what I might call *personal interest* natural to man, even to the inspired instrument of the Word of God? I find that there is a great want of simplicity in the criticism of Scripture,[2] and this is greatly

---

[1] The beginning of this sentence, which I have re-written from the Russian translation, in Khomiakoff's MS. is as follows : 'In St. Luke's (in the last chapter) proof is again clear to a mind.'—[W. J. B.]

[2] I leave this passage as it stands. The Russian translation gives: 'To speak generally, it seems to me, that all the critical literature concerning the Scripture sins by reason of a complete absence of simplicity in its aims and views.' The Russian word, простота, corresponds exactly to the Greek word ἁπλότης, and is used for it in every case in the Slavonic version of St. Paul's Epistles, Rom. xii. 8; 2 Cor. i. 12; viii. 2; ix. 11, 13; xi. 3; Eph. vi. 5, and Col. iii. 22, whereas in our authorised version it is rendered by *simplicity, liber-*

due to the book-worm character of the great critics of our time, the Germans (though I have the greatest admiration for them), and to the rhetorical tendency of the earlier critics, the Greeks.

---

ality, or *singleness*. I translate it *simplicity* so as to keep as closely as possible to Khomiakoff's text, but it perhaps would be better rendered by 'singleness'—*cp.* Eph. vi. 5, Col. iii. 22.—[W. J. B.]"

CHAPTER XVI

MR. KHOMIAKOFF'S NINTH LETTER TO MR. PALMER [1]

[1852]

Mr. Khomiakoff's commission to Mr. Palmer—Further proofs of the authenticity of the Gospels.

MOST REV. AND DEAR SIR.—Some months elapsed, after I had received your friendly letter of the fifth of July, before I could give you an answer. My answer was written in the month of September; but as it was with a parcel rather too heavy for the post, I sent it over to Petersburg to one of my friends, as an opportunity was more likely to be found there than anywhere else. I am informed that the parcel has been forwarded to England; but I am as yet quite uncertain whether you have received it or not. I should be very sorry if it was lost, as some parts of the letter (such as the P.S. about proofs of the authenticity of the Gospels) must have been worthy of your attention, and others, such as the commission which I was bold enough to thrust on your friendship (with a little cheque enclosed in the letter) were of great interest to me. In this uncertainty I have made inquiries in order to ascertain whether the parcel may not have been lost. It has passed, it seems, through many

---

[1] This letter and the tenth are not included in the Russian edition of Khomiakoff's works, but were first published in their original English, accompanied by a Russian translation, in 1892 in the January number of the *Russki Archiv*, a well-known Moscow periodical, edited by M. P. Bartenieff. They are neither of them dated, but the first was evidently written before Mr. Khomiakoff had received Mr. Palmer's reply to his last letter.—[W. J. B.]

hands, but at last it must have found its way to the Foreign Office in London, where it is not improbable it may yet be found in a state of quiet uselessness. As this may be the reason for your silence (though there may certainly be many others) I thought I was bound to give you this information, and I hope you will not accuse me of obtruding on your attention without necessity. Excuse me if I do so.

I can say but little about myself. My life is going on rather wearily, though not perhaps uselessly. I am now seeking after a remedy against the Cholera as I have done for other less apparent ills; success or failure in that, as in everything, comes from God. Our duty and perhaps our only true happiness is to seek incessantly after every useful truth. Accept, dear sir, etc.

In the P.S. of my letter I spoke of the proofs of authenticity of the Gospels of St. John, St. Luke, and St. Mark. In the first of these the proofs seem to me to be unanswerable, clear in the second, though not so evident in the third. I had not spoken of St. Matthew. Its anteriority seems to be out of question for any impartial reader. Still, I will add for more sceptical critics that, though the person of the author may be disputed, no reasonable doubt can arise as to the time when this Gospel was written. Any critic endowed with something like common sense can see that it was written in Palestine, and not only before the fall of Jerusalem, but even before the successful preaching of St. Paul in Greece. The one is proved by the great importance given to prophecies about little towns in Palestine; the other by the ardent attacks on Pharisaism all over the book and more particularly in the 25th chapter. This indicates a violent struggle not against an almost abstract or fallen system, as Pharisaism must have been after the conquest of Jerusalem, nor against a local difficulty which must have lost much of its importance when Christian preaching had invaded Greece and Rome, but a deadly struggle against a dangerous enemy and a living power in the centre of its action. I think that those who do not feel the truth of this remark, will be found rather deficient in the rules of enlightened Criticism. This seems to me as plain a truth as the one that St. Mark's Gospel has been written out of Palestine. The explanation of the Jewish customs at their meals (which is not to be found in St. Matthew) cannot be otherwise accounted for.

CHAPTER XVII

MR. PALMER'S ANSWER TO KHOMIAKOFF'S EIGHTH[1] LETTER

[1853]

Mr. Khomiakoff's commission—Mr. Palmer's plans—His literary work—Ecclesiastical movement in England—Mr. Palmer's own position—The question of Re-baptism—Reasons for turning towards Rome—Criticisms of an Essay by Mr. Khomiakoff—Communion with the departed.

FINMERE, NEAR BUCKINGHAM,
April 5 (N.S.), 1853.

MY DEAR MR. KHOMIAKOFF,—Your letter, dated Sept. 4, 1852, together with the essay in French and an order on Messrs. Schroeder & Co. in London for £39, 1s. 3d. to pay for the expenses of printing it, reached me at Oxford on the 1st of January 1853, N.S. I was then confined to my room by a very tedious, but not painful, attack of gout, which had come on in November and continued until about three weeks ago. Now I am well again, and not disinclined to do anything in my power towards executing your wishes respecting the publication of your essay—but since you have sent me the commission at a venture you must be content to wait my convenience, and perhaps longer than either of us wish, for its execution. To print a French essay in England would be simply throwing away your money. It must be done, if at all, at Paris or Brussels, at neither of which places have I any acquaintance with publishers, nor any other acquaintances such as I could request to execute the commission.

---

[1] This letter was evidently written before the receipt of the last letter, but did not reach Mr. Khomiakoff before it had been sent.—[W. J. B.]

MR. PALMER'S PLANS

If you do not send me instructions to hand the essay and money-order over to some other person better qualified than myself to execute your wishes, and to execute them more speedily, I shall look forward to taking the first opportunity when I am at liberty to going myself to Paris or Brussels for a few days and intrusting your MS. to some publisher. I will do the best I can for you—but you must take your chance—and it is very possible that I may not do the best that could be done for obtaining for your essay the circulation you would desire, as I am ignorant (as I have said) of all that relates to the publishing and circulating of pamphlets and books in France, or to the choice of a publisher. I am always inclined to do (so far as I properly can) what is asked of me; but I hope that you will not again send me such a commission, especially in such a way as makes me feel less free to decline or delay executing it. I should have liked, at any rate, to know your wishes first, and have been able to write you word whether I saw any prospect of being able to execute them, and was besides willing to undertake the commission before you sent me the money to pay the printer.

Now I will tell you how this commission has found me, and what prospect I have before me. I have already said that till March I was confined to my room at Oxford by the gout. Since then I have been staying here with my father, waiting for his decease, which is now seemingly very near; and whenever that takes place (which will probably be before many days are over) I shall be wanted by my mother and sisters to assist them in settling their family matters for some time—so that I really do not know how many months it may be before I am at liberty to leave them. But probably I shall be at liberty in the course of the coming summer. My own plans are, to put an end to my connection with the University of Oxford, and with the College of which I am a member there, shortly after my father's decease. So long as he lived, I was unwilling to do anything which my conscience did not absolutely require, and that might give him pain, as showing increasing and settled dissatisfaction with the Anglican Church, from which he knew that I was willing to separate, but hoped that I might change my mind on finding obstacles to my reception to the Communion of the Eastern Church. Having done this, I shall probably go abroad again, and live for some time at Rome, with the wish to study and, if possible, find some way to overcome those difficulties which hitherto have made me incline rather to the Eastern side, though I see great difficulties there also. While I was at Athens I published in Greek some Dissertations about the Eastern Church,[1] of which I sent you a copy last autumn, and I hope that you have before now received it, though you had not done so when you wrote your letter to me or the French Essay accompanying it. Since then I have published the same Dissertations in English,[2] with considerable additions, and the English volume also I hope you will receive soon after you receive this letter. One of the Dissertations added in it is on a subject which, I think, will interest you, namely, on 'Civil Government, Authority, and Liberty, in their relations to Orthodox Christianity.' One or two of my Russian friends, who have as yet seen only the Greek edition, have been blaming me for touching upon certain politico-ecclesiastical questions of Russian history, and think that if I had avoided them my book might have been allowed by the Censors of the Press in Russia. But I do not myself think that this would have been the case; and I could not possibly avoid or dissemble those questions on which the deepest prejudices and objections of Western Christians, Protestant and Roman Catholic alike, against the Russian Church chiefly turn. When you see the Dissertations you will be able to judge for yourself. During my confinement with the gout, I have been occupying myself chiefly with researches concerning the history of the Holy Places at Jerusalem, having the intention to write something on that subject.

[1] Διατριβαὶ περὶ τῆς 'Ανατολικῆς 'Εκκλησίας. 'Αθηναῖς, 1852.—[W. J. B.]

[2] Dissertations concerning the Orthodox Communion. London, 1853.—[W. J. B.]

I have been disappointed to find that only one part of the
MS. of Arsenius Souchanoff has as yet been published, while
two other parts (those on ritual matters, and his description
of the Holy Places) are still in MS. I wish that some friend
to Ecclesiastical and Russian literature would exert himself
to get these two remaining parts published. Also, I am
curious to know whether any account of a Greek MS. of the
Archbishop Paisius of Gaza, who conducted the proceedings
against Nicon in the seventeenth century, has recently been
published in Russia; as such an account was, I know, written
and sent to Russia by the Archimandrite Porphyrius, and
I should much like to have it. The Bishop of Kharkoff
(Philaret), when I was in the south of Russia in 1851, promised to get me a transcription made of the Воапатепia[1] of
the Patriarch Nicon against or upon the 'questions' sent by
the Boyars to the Patriarchs of the East, and upon the
answers to the same questions returned by the Patriarchs.
But I have not received anything from him since, and I fear
he must have forgotten me. I should be most willing to pay
all necessary expenses for causing such transcription to be
made, as I told him; and if it were sent either to the English
Chaplain, Dr. Law, at the Church of the English Factory at
St. Petersburgh, or to Mr. A. S. Noroff, it would be sure to
reach me. Now, I have told you all I have to say about my
own circumstances and plans, and it is time that I advert
to the contents of your letter and essay.

I feel much the warmth of your Christian kindness and
zeal in all that you have written and suggested, but perceive
that at present you have only an indistinct and somewhat
inaccurate idea of the religious position, both of myself and
of many others in England. You write as if there was some-
where an organised party or school, with distinct views of
union with the Eastern Church. That is not the case.
Within the Anglican Church there is an increasing spirit, or
tendency, in many individuals unfavourable to Protestantism,

---

[1] Replies.—[W. J. B..]

and even to Anglicanism such as it has hitherto existed, and favourable, more or less, in some perhaps to Eastern Orthodoxy, but in many more to Roman Catholicism. The disposition to think and speak favourably of the Eastern Church, and to dream of some union with it, rather than with Rome, exists only in those who are as yet tenacious adherents of the Anglican Church, but invariably diminishes and disappears in proportion as they come to doubt the Anglican Church, and to contemplate the necessity of abandoning her for some other 'Communion'—or rather, I should say, of submitting to the Roman—for the thought of abandoning the Anglican Church and submitting to Easternism as being the true Catholicism or Universality never so much as crosses their mind. For myself, I am acting certainly, and have been all along, merely as an individual, and do not much trouble myself with the question whether the Greek Patriarchs are, or are not, unreasonable in what they do or say about Baptism. But for me, as an individual, Baptism, past or future, is, or must be, the beginning of my Christianity; and the first practical question for me in seeking any communion is this: Have I already been baptized, or must I now seek to be baptized? If the communion to which I address myself either tells me what I cannot believe on the subject, or tells me two contrary propositions at once, which is equivalent to telling me nothing and making no answer, I must consider this fact to be an obstacle to my continuing to seek their communion. I must say to them, that they must be able to tell me distinctly whether I am baptized or unbaptized, before they can deal with me, or I with them, on any ulterior matter. I did indeed suggest an expedient by which this question might be got over, viz., by a conditional rebaptism, or by allowing a conditional sense to be put upon the rebaptism by the party baptized. But they would not allow this. So I have now done all I could. I cannot for a moment listen either to the Russians saying: 'Never mind the Greek Patriarchs; *we* tell you that you are baptized, and are ready to receive you; and we are the

DIFFICULTY ABOUT BAPTISM

Eastern or Orthodox Church'; or to the Greeks saying: 'Never mind the Russians: we tell you that you are unbaptized, and we are the Orthodox or Catholic Church, which you must listen to, and not to your own private judgment.' I see plainly that neither the Greeks alone nor the Russians alone are that Society, or Church, in the name of which alone they can baptize or teach with authority. The discrepancy may, or may not, be of secondary importance, as a question of virtue and of fact, in itself; but to *me*, to the *individual*, it is absolutely necessary (physically necessary) that I should be able to assume this or that position. I cannot think that you regard a person come to years of discretion as a mere subject upon which any ritual is to be performed without his taking any part in it. He who comes to be baptized is either most sacrilegiously trifling, or he must be able sincerely to seek from God the grace of Baptism, which he cannot seek if he believe that he has received it already. But neither can he well be received by the Russian Church, as to the communion of the whole Eastern Church, when the Patriarchs tell him to his face that the Russians are doing wrong, and that he is all the same unbaptized. If, indeed, the particular Russian Church said to me: 'Since your belief on the point agrees with our practice, be received by us, as to the communion of the local or particular Russian Church, and leave us to settle the question afterwards with the Greeks'; and the Russian Church at the same time imposed upon me no merely national or local peculiarities which would be a hindrance and prejudice to Catholic Christianity among my own countrymen, I might be inclined to seek such admission. But the Russian Church would not do this. She would act in the name of the whole *Eastern* Church, and would seek to impose on me Eastern (and not only Russian) peculiarities, while all the time she was acting in direct contravention of the Eastern or Greek customs, and the Greek Patriarchs entirely disallow the act which she does in their name, as well as in her own. Besides this, there is in the present state of the Russian Church a peculiar reason for one to entertain great unwillingness to seek her communion otherwise than as a mere part of the Eastern or Orthodox whole—that is, the undue supremacy of the Civil Power. On this account, if I were inclined to repeat the attempt to obtain admission to the Eastern Church, or to any part of it, the Russian is the very last part which I should think of. Absurd as such a step would appear to all Englishmen and to all Westerns, it would appear only as an innocent, though unintelligible, extravagance or monomania, so long as the proselyte was not mixed up with the politico-ecclesiastical system of Russia. Only imagine a learned and enlightened Roman ecclesiastic, or a Greek or Russian, submitting himself, on grounds of religious conviction, to Queen Victoria's supremacy, and to that of the Acts of the English Parliament! The very idea is absurd. But it is conceivable, that a Roman or a Greek should adopt the opinion of the Quakers, the Scotch Calvinists, or the Scottish or American Episcopalians on grounds, however mistaken, of religious conviction. And if he were inclined to do so, it would be manifestly disadvantageous to his character and chance of influencing others, if he betook himself to the Anglican Episcopal Church, which to the eyes of all at a distance is so much under the influence of the state, that its religion seems rather to depend on the Civil Government, than Civil Government on its religion. For the same reason, if any one were inclined to seek union with the Eastern Church, it would be impolitic and undesirable for him to address himself to the Russian part of it, until things were in a very different state from that in which they now are.

I think that you must have seen or heard of some exaggerated and misrepresented account of my proceedings at Constantinople and their consequences, when you wrote that 'the Constantinopolitan Synod had almost excommunicated the Russian Church for admitting Protestants and Romans without re-baptism.' This, I expect, is merely an echo of the lively article or articles of a Jesuit friend of mine (a Russian by origin) which he inserted in the *Univers* before I left Athens, and the materials for which his strong and imaginative zeal had found in a letter which I had written to him myself. I scolded him for his inaccuracy on my way through Paris and told him that there was no sign of any such zeal or warmth in the matter, on which he exclaimed to my amusement, 'Oh! that is the case, is it? So much the worse for them. That shows them in so much the worse light. I will make another article in the *Univers* in that sense!' And in fact this is the worst sign about the Greeks, that they are careless and hypocritical, rather than over-warm in the matter. For instance, these very Patriarchs and Bishops not only receive themselves, by a hypocritical dissimulation or economy, all those *unbaptized* persons, who have just been received by the Russians, but *occasionally* have permitted themselves to allow, even in the Levant, the same practice as is used in Russia. The second wife of the present Russian Consul at Athens (who is a Greek) was so received after the Archbishop of Patras had twice declared it to be utterly impossible. The lady was a Roman Catholic of French extraction, and her friends objected to her being re-baptized, and eventually the husband obtained from the Patriarch of Constantinople (not the present) a special licence, with which the Archbishop of Patras was satisfied, and received her by Chrism only. About this thing itself I am inclined to agree with your anticipations, and those of M. Mouravieff, that the present abusive custom will fall almost of itself in the Levant, so soon as the question comes to be more attended to, and the more authoritative and earlier documents known, and the influence of the Russian Church to be properly exerted to bring it to a settlement.[1] But in the meantime that is nothing to me, and the personal difficulty, *until* the matter is settled, remains insurmountable. I do not agree with you in thinking that a declaration that the existing difference does not affect the unity of the Church would be a possible solution; because this would amount to a

---

[1] This is just what has happened during the last twenty-five years both in the Patriarchate of Constantinople and in the Church of the Kingdom of Greece. See note on page 63.—[W. J. B.]

decision that is unnecessary for proselytes to know whether they are baptized or not, and that they may take the matter easily, and say equally, if it so happen, 'O God, I seek from Thee the grace of regeneration which I have not yet received' or 'O God, I thank Thee for that grace of regeneration which I have already received, and pray Thee now for such other graces as are offered by Thy mercy to believers.' This, I must repeat, would be the most profane trifling with holy things. When we speak to God, it is not a matter of indifference whether we say one thing or the contrary, and it is to me a rather disagreeable fact that no single member of the Eastern Church, who has talked with me in the Levant or in Russia on the subject, has seemed to feel or understand, that the person to be baptized has any part to perform in the ceremony, beyond that which might be equally sustained by a new-born infant or a block. There is something wrong in this. I admit your distinction between an undue subservience to such influences in *fact* only, or also in *principle*: and I am far from imputing to the Russian Church the latter. The excesses or thunderings of censors, or other subordinate agents of governments, are matters of secondary importance. What I find fault with is, not the undue timidity or subserviency of a Metropolitan or Patriarch or a Synod, but the permanent existence of irregular institutions calculated and introduced by the Civil Power expressly to transfer to itself upon the whole, and by virtue of the system, a large portion of that power which belongs essentially to the Apostles. The idea of catching the Apostles or their chiefs, and shutting them up in a room or house, and indirectly governing Christianity by allowing its existence within certain limits, but taking care that the Apostles shall neither have food, nor money, nor servants, nor messengers, nor even send a letter except through the paid officers of Cæsar, appointed to be at once the servants of Cæsar and of the Apostles,—this is only an ingenious, though somewhat comical, variety and refinement of the tyrannies of more barbarous ages. The canons of the Universal Church require a *personal* Primate (he might indeed be *assisted* by a Synod) in every Province and Nation: and the four Patriarchs of the East had no more right nor power to legitimatise the Synod, or Kollegium, of Peter I., than Peter himself had to initiate it. Again, the Bishops have a natural right to the same freedom of action in their own spiritual spheres which every landlord and free subject has in his worldly sphere; and if the Civil Government administers their property, appoints, salaries, and displaces their servants, and prevents them from doing anything except through such channels, and the Bishops submit to this; this is somewhat more than a casual and temporary subserviency in fact. The admission of such machinery into the permanent institutions of the Church is the indirect admission of a principle subversive of the Apostolic mission and authority. When you say: 'Russia is enlightened for Greece, and Greece for Russia. Do not, if you please, consider them apart from one another. You are not called to a local [Russian][1] but to a Catholic [or at least to an Eastern][1] Church': I admit your thought and have shown myself prepared to act upon it, till I found the two parts of the Eastern Church split asunder on the first preliminary question and step. And after this, whatever they may be in themselves, or abstractedly, *to me* they must be regarded as separate and divided, till they speak to me with a single, and not with a double voice. There may indeed be underneath the double and discordant voice only one being, or Church, which ventriloquises, and thinks it of no great consequence so to mock and perplex individuals with a double voice. But I feel no sort of divine call upon my conscience to become a party to such trifling.

I am not conscious of any despondency, impatience, or irritation whether against the Scottish or Anglican Hierarchy, with whom I have now worked out and finished my ecclesiastical problem, nor against the Greek Patriarchs, or the Russian Civil Government, against which I am now still

---

[1] These parentheses are both contained in Mr. Palmer's manuscript. —[W. J. B.]

occupied in an intellectual process similar perhaps to that of Don Quixote against the wind-mills. What I do, I do for the sake of my own conscience and personal responsibility only; not with the smallest expectation that ecclesiastical or secular mountains can be moved by my efforts, but because I think it is my duty to act in the first instance towards them as if they could. When I discover, or think that I discover, an obstacle in the Russian or in the Greek Church to my seeking in the way proposed to me its communion, I think it is a duty which I owe to them to state fully my objections, before I recede from my attitude towards them, or take the obstacles I meet with as signs intended to divert my mind to some other quarter. But I know too well the nature of things and institutions to think it strange that when an individual like myself knocks his head against a wall or a mountain, the wall or the mountain stands firm as before, and his head only is driven back. Insects which are blind, and some too which have eyes, feel their way by their heads, or antennæ, coming in contact with the objects around them, the contact or collision serving not to remove the obstacles (to which the force of the insect is quite unequal), but to show it in which direction its path does not lie, or cannot lie; so, being driven back, it turns back or turns aside, and finds at last some direction to which there is no obstacle. Or if, by some unusual chance, the obstacle which meets the antennæ gives way (though this is contrary to the common order of things), it may hold on its course, having ascertained by the collision that the obstacle was not insurmountable. I grant that in the case of the Anglican Church, to which I was originally and naturally attached by so many ties, it was not without pain and reluctance that I gradually admitted unfavourable doubts and convictions. But having made this sacrifice, I have no feeling of pain or despondency at finding difficulties to lie in the way of my joining the Eastern, rather than the Roman Catholic, Church, for I have no sort of reason to wish to find the lesser section of Christendom right rather than the greater, the Eastern than the Western, or Constantinople than Rome. Of course, so long as my personal opinions and belief agree on points of detail rather with the Easterns than with the Westerns, I am forced by the duty which I owe to truth and sincerity to avow this; and I cannot, to please Rome or to obtain her communion, say that I believe, or will believe, what I do not believe.[1] But I can say this, and do, that I would wish to agree with Rome rather than with Constantinople, and that, seeing great and increasing reason to doubt the conclusions of my own understanding when they agree with inferior authorities against superior, I will listen attentively to all that the superior authority can say to me, and will do my best to find out that it is right, and that my individual mind and the inferior authority, with which at present I rather agree, is mistaken. I will not say much in reply to the remarks you make on my conduct hitherto towards the Eastern, and especially towards the Russian, Church, because they proceed from the not unnatural mistake which I have noticed at the beginning of this letter, that I have been acting upon some general plan, and for some public object, and in concert with others, instead of being merely an individual blockhead or monomaniac, who was led on from one thing to another, in the attempt to do his own personal duty in a certain particular case. When I was first in Russia in 1840-41, I was far from feeling it my duty to seek admission to the Russian communion as a proselyte; because at that time I still firmly believed the Anglican Church to be essentially Orthodox and defensible; and, having no sort of public mission, I could do no more towards unity than profess my own personal desire of inter-communion, which was countenanced by my immediate ecclesiastical superiors at Oxford. At that time, too, though I thought the Greek and the Latin Churches must *mean* the same thing on the subject of the Procession, I had no doubt that the Latin phraseology was the fuller and more Orthodox confession of the faith.

---

[1] This refers to Mr. Khomiakoff's remark on page 125.—[W. J. B.]

If I had then held the contrary opinion (as I do now), not knowing of the existence of any discrepancy between the Russian and the Greek Eastern Church as to the validity of my baptism, but supposing it to be exactly the same thing whether I was received at St. Petersburgh or at Constantinople, I should no doubt have sought for admission from any Russian priest, within whose district I happened to be. But afterwards, when I had at length come to change my mind about the Procession, and had entirely and finally failed in my attempt to procure attention either to that, or to other questions which I had raised, from the Scottish and British Bishops, I also discovered the existence of an obstacle to my joining the Eastern communion which I had not before suspected. With that project of an address to the Russian Synod two years ago, which you mention, I had nothing to do, though the two individuals who were most concerned in it and who have since both become Roman Catholics, wrote to me on the subject before I left England for Athens. I had no expectation that it could lead to any result, even if there had been a much greater number of persons wishing to be parties to it, because none of those *persons* would think of the *Eastern Church* as possessing the attribute and claims of the universal Church, and the Russian Synod, on the other hand, if it dealt with them at all, would deal with them on that, and on no other hypothesis. The gentlemen who would have sent that memorial to the Russian Synod are now zealous in their friendly wishes to open my eyes to the unreasonableness of those admissions, which I am still obliged to make, in favour of the Eastern Church. The course of action which you point out as fit to be pursued, if there were only a conviction, and a sufficient number of individuals united in that conviction to pursue it, is quite such as I should myself have recommended, except only that the difference about Baptism could not be alluded to as a thing indifferent.

I will now add only a word or two concerning your Essay.[1]

---

[1] See note on page 134.—[W. J. B.]

I find very much in it which I think true and valuable—and it is all (as any you wrote is sure to be) interesting and suggestive; but there are in it reflections which seem to me to be put too generally and absolutely, so as to lessen their effectiveness, and to give an advantage to opponents. If, for instance, I say that the *Church* of Rome is a *state*, and unites by political treaties discordant dogmas, this is an exaggeration, and unjust, and easily answered: just as if I said, on the other hand, that the Russian Church has admitted in principle the supremacy of the Civil Power in ecclesiastical matters. Such propositions must be put forward only with limitations. So again, if I say that the Roman Church puts the Pope into the place of Christ, it is a mere calumny; but if I say only that she does so in a manner, in tendency, and in a certain undue proportion, the accusation may be true or plausible. So your idea of the Christian people being the guardians of the faith of the Church is in a sense and degree very true, but, if carried too far and put absolutely, a very mischievous error; for the Hierarchy are sent to teach all nations, with the promise of Christ's presence in doing so, even to the end, and the nations are thereby required to submit to the teaching of the united Apostolate.

You must understand the grumbling, with which I began this letter, to arise, not from unwillingness to take a little trouble and serve your views in printing your Essay, but simply from fear that I may not be able to do it so soon or so satisfactorily as I could have wished.

I sympathise much with what you say of your own feelings. But the time that we are to be here is short. The departure of those whom we have loved before us, when they have departed in faith and hope, gives us so many more strong links and cables, fixed already to the shore of the other world, by which we may draw our own vessels to the same moorings. Where our treasure is, there our heart will be also. For myself, I attach no great importance to natural emotions of feeling in themselves; they are given us merely as means to an end, to help and quicken our efforts after increase of grace and good habits. But I see, as life advances, more and more danger of the very variety and frequency of Divine warnings and admonitions inducing callousness of feeling. Two things are good remedies against this: one, the study of the Gospels, and the other, the practice of acts of charity and mercy towards our fellow-men. I tremble to think of the luxurious abundance of food and clothing and other earthly goods, which I have enjoyed all my life, and the little service I have ever done to others, and the coldness I have felt in such things. In speaking of the study of the Gospels, I am tempted to ask whether a work in four volumes, Greswell's *Harmony and Dissertations on the Gospels*, is known in Russia. If it is not, it is well worth procuring. You write: 'Will then after death there still exist something of the relations that were so dear to us?' Who can doubt this? The notion that natural recognition and memory are to cease in the next world is only a varied form of Sadduceeism and infidelity, utterly absurd, and contrary to every word of Holy Scripture, and as far from my thoughts as it is from yours.

Accept my thanks for all your charity and zeal; they are due to you from my personal feelings, although you have also higher motives than personal friendship and interests; and believe me to be always, with best wishes for the approaching festival of Easter, and at all times, yours most sincerely,

W. PALMER.

If you see any Russian acquaintances of mine, I would beg of you to make my best remembrances to them, and especially, with my dutiful respects, to the Metropolitan of Moscow.

P.S.—My address is still for the present to Magdalen College, Oxford.

CHAPTER XVIII

MR. KHOMIAKOFF'S TENTH LETTER TO MR. PALMER

[1853]

Mr. Palmer's objections inapplicable to the whole Orthodox Eastern Church— They refer to mere local and temporary defects—No books yet received from Mr. Palmer

MOST REV. AND DEAR SIR,—Accept my thanks for your kind, though (as you call it) grumbling letter, and pray excuse the extreme indiscretion of the commission I had burthened you with. My excuse is in my total ignorance of foreign life and the supposition that intercourse between England and France or Belgium was more frequent and easy than I now find it to be. But I have at last found means to put you out of any difficulty or inconvenience on that account. Only be so good as to send the letter here enclosed, with the essay and cheque, to the subjoined address without even a word of your writing, and all I want will be done. I will add a request that you should bear me no ill-will for my indiscretion, considering the extreme difficulty of my position, which you can only partially guess from some words of my preceding letter.

I was wrong perhaps in supposing that your mind was labouring under some irritation or fatigue, and yet pardon me if I still continue to suppose that something of that feeling is indeed working in you, though you are not perhaps aware of it, and is driving you in a direction which I cannot consider otherwise than erroneous. Your letter has shown me more clearly than ever all the difficulties against which you have been and are still struggling, and the intricacy of the questions which have been for a long time agitating your conscience; but I cannot consider them as being insoluble in a straightforward way. Do not suppose that, when I have been speaking rather lightly about the ritual difference existing between Greece and Russia in the admission of Romans and Protestants, I was paying no attention to the feelings and conscientious doubts of the convert. You seem to indicate as much by saying that a Sacrament is operated 'on a man, and not on a block. A man must know whether he is to ask for a grace, or to thank God for the grace received and pray for strength to continue in it.' I must say that there is an evident misunderstanding in the question. The Russian Church as well as the Eastern one ([*i.e.*] the whole Catholic Church) does not admit that the full grace of Baptism can have been conferred by schismatic Baptism. The only difference is, that the Russian considers the rite as fulfilled, the Grecian finds the rite uncanonical, and considers its more canonical repetition as commendable. Both suppose in the convert the conviction that he has not yet received the *Grace of Baptism* and that he is to pray for the [full] grace of the Sacrament which he receives either by the repetition of the Rite or by the prayers of reconciliation giving power to a rite otherwise powerless. In both cases the feelings and mental action are exactly the same, and the difficulty melts into nothing; and yet it seems to me that it is the only serious one which affects your particular case. The fact which you advance against the Russian Church (or I should rather say against the Russian Diocese[1] of the Catholic Church) is unfortunately a true one; but you admit it to be a fact and not a principle, and therefore not binding upon any

---

[1] Khomiakoff uses the word 'Diocese' here, and throughout this letter, as an equivalent to the Russian word enapxin, which is used, as is ἐπαρχία in ecclesiastical Greek, either for 'diocese' or for an 'eparchy,' or Province forming a national Church. It is, of course, in the latter sense that it is used here; but I have retained the word 'diocese' because of its use further on with regard to the Roman See.—[W. J. B.]

conscience, and by the same reason quite out of the domain of Faith. If the fact has been working even for a hundred years or more, well—this cannot have changed its nature—it is still nothing but a fact. The Roman See has been for more than two hundred years the monopoly of Italian blood.[1] This is certainly an anti-ecclesiastical fact; but it is no principle, and cannot be adduced against Romanism; and yet it is far more important than the tyrannical policy of the Russian State, as you, not without some appearance of reason, call it. The one affects the whole Church, the other affects only a Diocese. Whether the Russian hierarchy has been, or has not been, deceived into an undue subjection by the semblance of protection, is an historical and not an ecclesiastical fact, and has nothing in common with the principles of Anglican submission to the State, so long as the Russian Church does not arrogate to itself an independent position in the Catholic Church. Your moral sense is revolted, and well it may be, by the visible action, or rather inaction, of the different Dioceses of the Catholic Church. The feeling is just and reasonable; but it must not bear away your impartial reason. A Christian, dear sir, belongs to his Diocese only in his outward life (Discipline, Rite, and so forth). In his inward life he belongs to the universality of the Catholic Church and is in no way affected by the vices of the Diocesan hierarchy, which he counteracts in a mild and peaceful way, as long as the Diocese itself has not run into separatism, as the Roman See, or rather, the whole of the western communions have done. The ways of God are inscrutable, and perhaps it may not be sinful to suppose that the Russian hierarchy has been allowed to fall into a dependent situation until the time when the other Dioceses, having regained their full dignity and action, can stand forth as her equals in every respect, lest she should have fallen into the temptation of undue pride and anti-ecclesiastical ambition. This supposition

---

[1] As a matter of fact, the last non-Italian Pope was Adrian VI., A.D. 1523-1534.—[W. J. B.]

(a false one perhaps, for where is the man who is able to judge of the unrevealed designs of God?) does not seem to me quite unreasonable. Do not, dear sir, ascribe an undue importance to secondary facts; and do not shut your eyes to the evident *separatism of the Roman west, which is the only true plague of humanity*, as I hope to have shown in my Essay.

I am sorry I can say nothing about your tracts, either in the Greek or the English edition. The very simple reason of my silence is that I have not as yet received them. It is, as you may see, no easy thing to send books over to Russia if their contents are not agreeable to our ecclesiastical or political rules. The thing becomes still more difficult if the books bear my address. Such is the reason why I must beg of you most instantly in no case to return my Essay to Russia, but to send it as soon as possible with the enclosed letter to Paris by the subjoined direction, without even giving me any written answer about the whole concern (at least by post).—Accept, dear Sir, etc.[1]

---

[1] This letter I have reprinted as it stands, from the *Russki Archiv* of January 1892.—[W. J. B.]

CHAPTER XIX

MR. KHOMIAKOFF'S ELEVENTH LETTER TO MR. PALMER [1]

[1853]

Mr. Khomiakoff's commission—Mr. Palmer's book upon 'The Holy Places'—
A Russian opinion upon Mr. Palmer's 'Dissertations.'

DEAR AND MOST REVEREND SIR,—I feel myself quite unable to express my gratitude for the pains you have taken about the little MS. which I sent you. Indeed, I should never have had the boldness to ask for even a little part of the kindness you have bestowed on me, and of the trouble you have undergone. I need not add that without your friendly aid the MS. would undoubtedly have been lost, as well as the money directed to a very wrong address; but do not accuse me of having been imprudent. I could not act otherwise than I did. In Moscow we are so far from London and Paris, or any other European city, that there is no possibility of getting any correct information, and I had some misgivings (though far from the reality) of the risk I was undergoing.

The idea you have suggested to our Chaplain of publishing

---

[1] I have not been able to find Mr. Palmer's reply to the last letter, neither have any traces of it been found amongst Mr. Khomiakoff's papers, although it is evident that there must have been one. In the Russian edition of Mr. Khomiakoff's works the translation of this present letter is erroneously put seventh in order, and at the end is inserted a date, December 26, 1852. But there is no trace of this date in the original MS. from which I myself copied the text here printed; while its contents show that it was written in answer to some letter written later than Mr. Palmer's letter dated April 5, 1853.
—[W. J. B.]

L

in England the newest polemical writings of our Church is an excellent one, and I should be happy and proud to appear in the company of such men as our Metropolitan, though always under the condition of my pamphlet remaining anonymous. I am quite content to do my duty as a soldier in a line of battle, and do not feel any ambition to appear alone in the lists, or to undertake a battle single-handed as a Knight-errant or a fabulous Hercules. If I have acted otherwise in the publication of the French MS., my excuse is that I could not act otherwise. At any rate, I must say that the MS. and the sum for its publication are quite at your disposal. You have given me an evident proof that you will arrange things better than I can suggest, and that your friendship is sure to choose the best way.

Accept my thanks, my dear Sir, for your vindication of our rights in the question of the Holy Places. I have received your little book from our Chaplain, and consider your proofs as quite undeniable; but I suspect that the question is one of those in which might makes right, and that the strongest hand will be thought to indicate the justest cause. A sorry thing it is that it should stand so; but I am afraid all peace-congresses are nothing but humbug as long as there is so little Christianity in the world at large, and as long as even in the members of the Peace-Congress there are those who are just as ready as any others to cry 'to arms' as soon as their own interests or prejudices are at stake. Still the words of justice and reason may not remain quite unnoticed. Public opinion may sometimes listen to them, and thanks are due to those who fear not to speak them even amidst the roar of ignorant passions.

I have been unlucky with your publications upon religious questions, and although they may certainly have been way-laid by accident, still I must say that this sort of accident is of such frequent occurrence with me that I cannot but suspect that accidents have their rules. In a fortnight or so I hope to see the Metropolitan, and will ascertain whether he has been luckier than I (which I suppose to be the case). When I get to Moscow I will do my utmost to execute your commission and get the books you want. But for two or three weeks there is no probability of my getting to town, and of being free from an immense quantity of domestic affairs which still detain me at our country place near Tula.

Accept, dear Sir, the expressions of my esteem, devotion, and gratitude.—Your most humble and obedient

AL. KHAMECOFF.

P.S.—This letter was not closed and sent to the post when I met by accident one of our learned Ecclesiastics who had read your publications. He did not admit your opinions as a whole, and accused you (whether rightly or wrongly I cannot say) of having given to the word *Catholic* too much of a geographical meaning; but I am happy to say that he spoke of the work itself with great approbation and esteem, and admired particularly the clear distinction which you establish between dogmatic and ritual questions. I rejoiced very much at hearing such a favourable and quite candid account given by an Ecclesiastic of a work which interests me so much.

CHAPTER XX

MR. KHOMIAKOFF'S TWELFTH LETTER TO MR. PALMER

[1854]

Mr. Khomiakoff upon the Eastern Question—His opinion of Mr. Palmer's 'Dissertations'—Distinction between the two higher Sacraments and the other five—Mr. Khomiakoff's letter upon the outbreak of the Crimean War.

DEAR AND MOST REVEREND SIR,—The strangest thing in the world, and the most unexpected for me, is to find myself writing about politics. But every political question has its social meaning and, if well understood, its religious tendency. This is particularly the case with the Eastern question, and I have been naturally impelled to show how this side of a great political event acts on the mind of the reflecting few, and the unreflecting but deep-feeling mass in Russia. I think the exposition of the public opinion as it stands in our country may be of some use even for the public opinion in England. I should be very glad if it was possible to have the lines which I send[1] printed either in a newspaper or as a flying pamphlet with an English translation. The first course would certainly be the better, supposing any newspaper would admit my little article. You yourself, dear Sir, and some few others, perhaps, will, at least in part, sympathise with us, but even you will find my expressions rather, perhaps even very, harsh; yet I am sure that the printing of such opinions and language cannot bring any disagreeable consequences to anybody, as it may be preceded by an

---

[1] See page 166.—[W. J. B.]

introduction disclaiming anything like a total concordance of feelings and views, but asking at the same time for Russian opinion a right of publicity which has been given even to Chinese opinions and manifestoes. My expressions are not official (this you know very well); and they are perhaps the more interesting as being the most free and the most unsophisticated representation of the feelings which pervade the whole country of which Petersburgh and the court are no very adequate representatives, though in the present case they are brought nearer to the country than in common occurrences. I will add a few words more which I have not said in the French article. The conditions exacted from the Sultan are quite ridiculous—another name for *harratsch*: and the right of standing witness before a Mohammedan judge, whose Codex is the Coran—very important indeed! That would have mightily saved the Armenian Jacobites when they were slaughtered by Beder Khan! It would be laughable, if it were not an abominable trick and a dirty pretext for getting an apparent right to fight against Christians.

I know too much of history to indulge in a feeling of indignation against any political tricksters such as Lord John Russell and Lord Palmerston. Machiavelism is no very new invention, and very worthless deeds have often been crowned by success; but I am sorry that England should become the instrument of a shabby intrigue, when it could have played such a noble part in the present events, without letting Russia usurp any exorbitant influence in the East. I should be glad, if I could be assured that Gladstone does not approve of this guilty and wicked war.

I have not yet had an occasion to inform you that I have at last received your Dissertations. Permit me to say that, though dissenting in some important points from your opinion, I cannot speak without admiration of the conscientiousness and earnestness of your researches and of the deep feeling of love for truth which pervades the whole work. After having read your magnificent chapter about the Seven Sacraments I have been struck by an idea which I do not remember having met anywhere. Would not the following division answer some difficulties ? viz., that the two higher Sacraments belong to the relation between man and the whole Church, and the five others to the relation of man to the earthly Church and its organism. This remark I submit to your impartial judgment. Of the work in general, I hope to write on the very next occasion.

I feel I am trespassing unpardonably upon your leisure and kindness, but I hope you will pardon me, considering the utter impossibility of us Russians to have any communications by print with other nations. I need not say that if the publication of my French letter is possible, it should go without the name of the writer.

Accept, dear Sir, the assurance of my sincere respect and gratification for your constant friendship, and believe me to be, your most humble and obedient,

ALEXIS KHAMECOFF.

March the 9th,
1854.

A LETTER TO A FOREIGN FRIEND BEFORE THE COMMENCEMENT OF THE WAR IN THE EAST [1854][1]

CHÈR ET RESPECTABLE AMI !—L'année qui vient de commencer laissera des traces profondes dans l'histoire. Les forces de toutes les nations s'avancent et se mesurent des yeux. Une lutte terrible va s'engager. L'opinion publique de l'Europe se manifeste dans des livres, des brochures, des journaux lus et connus de tout le monde. Il ne se peut pas que vous ne trouviez quelque intérêt à savoir ce qui se passe silencieusement dans l'opinion publique du pays, contre lequel s'arment tous les autres.

---

[1] This letter, the history of which we have already seen, is reprinted from vol. i. of Khomiakoff's Works, (Moscow, 1878) where the original French is given together with a Russian translation. The title I have translated from the Russian.—[W. J. B.]

Les évènements historiques, les rapports diplomatiques entre les gouvernements sont remplis de détails accessoires et surchargés de formes inutiles, qui échappent à l'opinion et surtout au sentiment des peuples. Je n'entrerai donc pas dans les détails, j'élaguerai les formes diplomatiques et j'aborderai le fond de la question considérée de notre point de vue. Vous ne condamnerez pas, je l'espère, l'acerbité de mon langage. Une franchise sérieuse doit être sans réserve. Tout en nous blâmant peut-être d'avoir les convictions que je vais exprimer, vous ne me blâmerez pas d'exprimer les convictions que nous avons.

Le peuple Russe est lié par la fraternité du sang aux peuples Slaves; il est lié aux Grecs par la fraternité de la foi; car leurs aïeuls ont été, comme le dit St. Paul, nos pères en Jésus Christ. Ce sont des liens que nous ne pouvons ni oublier ni méconnaître. Ignorans des finesses politiques, peu éclairés sur les idées de devoirs conventionnels, nous connaissons nos devoirs réels envers nos frères par le sang et l'esprit. L'histoire de nos rapports avec la Turquie en porte témoignage. L'Europe s'était contentée de repousser la force redoutable des Ottomans. La Russie, à peine sortie des fers de l'étranger et des convulsions intérieures, a fait renaître des peuples oubliés par le reste du monde. Témoins le Monténégro protégé et la Grèce rappelée à la vie, plus tard sauvée avec la coopération de l'Angleterre et de la France sur les eaux de Navarin, plus tard encore consolidée pour toujours par nos armes seules dans les champs de la Roumélie; témoins la Moldavie et la Valachie arrachées au joug de la Turquie et purgées de l'opprobre et de la tyrannie qui pesaient sur elles depuis des siècles; témoin la Servie sauvée de l'esclavage et élevée au rang des puissances presque indépendantes; témoins les églises relevées de leurs ruines dans toutes les parties de l'Empire Ottoman, le culte rétabli, l'intelligence réveillée. Témoins surtout les secours de charité, de sympathie, de consolation que nous offrons tous les jours et de tous les points de notre vaste patrie à nos frères souffrants encore sous la domination musulmane. Oui, nous avons rempli une partie de notre devoir; nous ne l'avons pas encore rempli tout entier.

La Turquie avait manqué à ses obligations envers nous; elle avait violé ses promesses au détriment des droits de nos frères. La Russie a demandé des garanties; elles ont été refusées; elle a demandé au moins des promesses plus solennelles; elles ont été refusées. L'opinion publique s'est émue, la Russie a senti que la justice devait être appuyée par la force devant une nation qui ne comprend ni la justice, ni la miséricorde, ni la sainteté des promesses. L'Angleterre et la France, sous prétexte de soutenir l'équilibre européen, qui n'était pas menacé, ont soutenu le refus de la Turquie. Sans rien offrir en place des garanties que nous demandions, excepté peut-être quelques vagues promesses dans l'avenir; sans respect pour nos sympathies, sans souci des devoirs les plus simples de l'humanité, elles ont relevé les espérances de la Turquie par leur alliance et leurs secours; elles ont réveillé le courage des Musulmans, elles ont fanatisé leurs passions. Grâce à l'Angleterre et à la France, et à elles seules (et cette page ne sera jamais rayée de leur histoire), l'oppression et l'ignominie, le pillage, le meurtre et le viol, toutes les souffrances, toutes les misères versées à grands flots sur nos frères en Bosnie, en Bulgarie, dans l'Anatolie et dans la Roumélie,—telle a été la réponse, que la Turquie a envoyée à nos justes réclamations. Notre devoir en est devenu plus difficile à remplir; il en est devenu plus impérieux, et il sera rempli.

La Russie s'arme. Je voudrais, cher et respectable ami, que vous fussiez au milieu de nous, pour voir le mouvement intérieur du pays en ce moment. Ce n'est point l'armement orgueilleux de l'Angleterre, ni l'ardeur belliqueuse de la France; non, c'est le mouvement calme et réfléchi de l'homme qui a consulté son cœur, écouté sa conscience, consulté son devoir et qui prend les armes, parce qu'il se croirait coupable s'il ne les prenait pas. Cet homme—c'est un peuple, et qu'il me soit permis de le dire, un grand peuple. Croyez-moi, il y a quelque chose d'imposant dans un pareil spectacle. Le peuple Russe ne pense point à des conquêtes : les conquêtes n'ont jamais rien eu qui le séduisît. Le peuple Russe ne pense point à la gloire ; c'est un sentiment qui n'émeut jamais son cœur. Il pense à son devoir, il pense à une guerre sacrée. Je ne la nommerai pas une croisade, je ne la déshonorerai pas de ce nom. Dieu ne nous donne pas à conquérir des pays éloignés, quelques précieux qu'ils puissent être à nos sentiments religieux, mais il nous donne à sauver des frères, qui sont le sang de notre sang et le cœur de notre cœur. La guerre, criminelle dans le premier cas, est sainte dans le second. C'est ainsi que la Russie comprend la lutte qui va s'engager, et c'est pourquoi elle s'arme avec joie, prête, s'il le fallait, à s'élever toute entière. Voyant la décision de l'opinion populaire et la modération prudente du gouvernement, il en est qui sont prêts à l'accuser de faiblesse, et à croire qu'il n'est pas à la hauteur de la nation. Ceux qui pensent ainsi sont dans l'erreur. Le gouvernement est et doit être retenu par beaucoup de considérations politiques, par les formes de la diplomatie européenne, par une certaine routine même, qui ne saurait être abandonnée à la légère, par toutes sortes d'entraves, qui n'ont pas d'influence sur l'opinion dont les décisions sont plus absolues, parce qu'elles n'emportent pas de responsabilité, et surtout par l'amour même qu'il porte à la nation, à laquelle il ne doit permettre d'autres sacrifices que ceux qui sont indispensables. Le gouvernement modère un mouvement qu'il partage.

Certes, le sentiment noble et désintéressé, qui anime notre peuple, avait droit aux sympathies des autres ; certes, une guerre commandée par les devoirs d'une fraternité de sang et d'esprit, une guerre dont le but était d'arracher des hommes et des Chrétiens à l'oppression la plus sauvage, à la mort et au déshonneur, devait nous donner des alliés dans toutes les nations civilisées. La politique pouvait prendre ses réserves et demander ses garanties ; mais le devoir de toutes les nations était de s'unir à nous pour imposer un frein à la férocité des Turcs et pour délivrer des Chrétiens du joug, dont les écrase la loi du Coran. La direction opposée était immorale et honteuse, et c'est pourtant celle qu'on a choisie. Je ne vous le cache point ; il y a à nos yeux quelque chose d'odieux et de déshonorant dans la conduite des peuples, qui, soit pour consolider leur propre prépondérance, soit pour diminuer l'influence d'un autre peuple, déclarent la guerre aux sentiments les plus vrais, les plus naturels, les plus saints du cœur humain, et prennent sous leur protection même temporaire la plus infâme tyrannie, exercée sur des victimes sans défense par des barbares, dont les lois sont atroces et les actions plus atroces encore. En un mot, il y a quelque chose d'indigne dans la conduite d'hommes se disant Chrétiens qui tirent le glaive pour priver des Chrétiens du droit de protéger leurs frères contre les caprices de la cruauté et de la luxure des Mahométans. C'est avec douleur qu'on voit l'Angleterre se précipiter la première dans cette carrière d'ignominie, qu'on voit cette tache indélébile s'attacher au front d'une nation, a laquelle l'intelligence humaine doit tant de dons précieux, le cœur humain tant de belles et nobles jouissances, l'âme humaine tant de hautes aspirations, et la société humaine toute entière tant d'améliorations et de perfectionnements. Cette douleur, ressentie par tout homme ami de la civilisation, de la justice, et de la liberté, je la ressens plus vivement encore, moi, qui, comme vous le savez, porte à l'Angleterre une affection tellement vive, que j'ai été bien des fois soupçonné de l'admettre dans mon cœur à une secrète rivalité avec ma propre patrie. Mais la vérité ne doit pas être déguisée. L'Angleterre en ce moment paraît viser à la primauté dans l'ignominie. Certes, il y a quelque chose de bien redoutable dans ses armements, de bien imposant dans l'échelle sur laquelle se déploient ses forces et son activité, de superbe dans le dédain, avec lequel elle porte un défi à tout ce que l'humanité a de plus respectable ; mais que l'Angleterre ne l'oublie pas ; la honte ne devient pas glorieuse pour avoir atteint des dimensions gigantesques. Moins grandiose dans ses préparatifs, moins décidée dans son attitude, mais poussée par une animosité peut-être plus vive encore, la France se précipite dans la carrière cherchant inutilement à devancer sa rivale, et à remplacer par un zèle plus chaud et par des rapports plus amicaux encore avec la Turquie, ce qui lui manque en grandeur et en energie réelles. 'Elle est,' dit-elle avec raison, 'une vieille amie des Ottomans, elle les a appuyés bien souvent dans le passé, elle les a bien des fois lancés sur les Chrétiens. C'est une liaison respectable et antique ; c'est une vieille et douce habitude, que les dynasties se liguent l'une à l'autre.' Rien de plus vrai, et nous devons le comprendre ; la honte du passé doit justifier l'infamie du présent. L'Autriche suit l'Angleterre et la France d'un pas plus indécis. Elle a bien quelque sympathie pour la Turquie, evec laquelle elle se sent une ressemblance intérieure ; elle a bien quelque animosité contre la Russie, mais elle est aussi tourmentée de mauvais pressentiments et préférerait à se tenir loin de la querelle. Elle ne le peut pas, il y a un mobile qui l'entraîne, une force irrésistible ; c'est son amour pour la putréfaction et sa haine contre toute nationalité vivante, haine plus ardente contre les nationalités qui l'ont sauvée, que contre celles qui l'ont menacée. Plus lente encore et plus indécise dans ses démarches, la Prusse suit l'Autriche. Elle n'a pas de sympathie pour le mal ; elle n'a pas de haine contre les nations, elle n'est enfin poussée que par un seul principe ; ce principe, c'est la crainte de paraître coupable aux yeux des grandes puissances, si elle persistait à rester innocente de leurs crimes. Au reste ce noble mouvement se propage au loin ; il embrasse presque toute l'Europe Occidentale. Il n'est pas jusqu'à l'Espagne, qui sortant de son atonie séculaire, n'envoie ses chevaleresques enfants porter quelque petit secours et quelques petites consolations aux Mahométans, menacés de ne pouvoir plus insulter, décimer ou écraser à leur gré les Chrétiens d'Orient. Il n'est pas jusqu'à Naples même, qui poltronnement brave ne demande à l'Angleterre et à la France, quelle sera la petite part d'ignominie, qu'on lui fera dans l'ignominie commune.

Mais au milieu de cette honte générale, il y en a une plus apparente que les autres, quoique passive, plus criante quoique silencieuse, c'est celle de Rome. Le soi-disant vicaire du Christ, le prétendu chef de la Chrétienté, qui dernièrement encore avait fait retentir sa trompette polémique pour une charge malheureuse contre les Églises d'Orient, ne trouve pas une voix, pas un accent de charité pour arrêter les peuples, ses enfants spirituels, ses chères ouailles, au moment où ils se lancent au combat contre la liberté des Chrétiens. Pas un mot d'intercession, pas une parole d'amour, pas une larme de compassion. Cet indigne silence, je n'en puis parler sans regret. Le vieux guerrier ottoman, le terrible conquérant, le farouche pirate retrouve avant sa fin quelque chose de son ancienne énergie. La providence historique donnera à cet homme du glaive, ce qu'elle lui doit, la mort par le glaive, et un lit ensanglanté. Rome défaillante ne devait-elle pas retrouver aussi avant sa chute quelques unes de ses nobles paroles, qu'elle a fait de temps en temps retentir en faveur de l'humanité aux temps de sa gloire ? Mais non : elle se tait. Hélas pour Rome ! Cependant, ce que nous disons à regret, peut-être devrions-nous en parler avec joie. Rome doit tomber, non devant le Protestantisme qui se meurt, non devant l'incrédulité, car Rome garde encore quelque chose des forces du Christianisme ; elle doit tomber devant la parole de Vérité, et le futur évêque de Rome, rentré dans le sein glorieux de l'Église, bénira les voies de la Providence, qui, par un lâche silence, erreur politique ou crime moral de Pie IX., aura hâté le triomphe de la fraternité chrétienne.

La guerre se déclare. A qui sera la victoire ? Les décrets de Dieu ne nous sont pas encore révélés et nul ne peut dire avec assurance, à qui Il réserve les succès ou les revers dans les combats ; mais nous n'avons pas besoin de deviner à qui sera le triomphe véritable. Il est déjà acquis à la Russie sans retour. C'est déjà un triomphe que d'avoir pris les armes pour une cause aussi sainte, pour l'humanité souffrante, pour les Chrétiens opprimés par le Coran, pour la pureté des vierges, pour la chasteté des femmes, pour la vie des hommes, pour la liberté du culte, pour le développement de l'intelligence. Cette gloire nous est assurée et ne saurait nous être enlevée. Les revers peuvent éprouver notre constance ou punir nos propres fautes, que nous n'osons ni déguiser, ni excuser devant Dieu, mais je le dis hardiment : la victoire même matérielle ne peut appartenir aux nations coalisées sous la direction de l'Angleterre et de la France que dans le cas où elles deviendraient les protecteurs des Chrétiens et les ennemis réels, quoique non avoués peut-être de leurs oppresseurs, c'est-a-dire, dans le cas où ils nous voleraient nos armes et notre drapeau. Soit. L'intelligence humaine ne s'y trompera pas : elle rendra le drapeau victorieux à celui qui l'a déployé et la gloire des armes à celui qui les a préparées et fait briller le premier. L'humanité fera justice d'un escamotage historique, quelque adroit qu'il puisse être.

Quoiqu'il arrive, la Providence a marqué notre temps pour faire époque dans les destinées du monde. Dorénavant deux grands principes sont à l'ascendant : le premier, le principe Russe ou plutôt Slave, celui de la fraternité réelle de sang et d'esprit. Le second bien plus haut encore, celui de l'Église—et ce n'est que sous ses ailes bienfaisantes que le premier a pu se conserver au milieu d'un monde de trouble et de discorde, et ce n'est que grâce à sa divine puissance qu'il pourra passer de l'état de tendance presque instinctive d'une seule race à la dignité de loi morale guidant les pas futurs de l'humanité.

La guerre va éclater, et le prétexte en est aussi frivole que la raison en est odieuse. Les puissances, qui avaient déclaré que l'occupation des provinces Danubiennes n'était pas un cas de guerre, se rejettent sur la destruction de la flotte Turque à Sinope, comme contraire, à ce qu'il paraît, aux lois de la guerre défensive que la Russie avait promis d'observer. Après la surprise d'un fort sur notre territoire, après l'infâme ravage d'une province, après des tentatives avouées de donner des secours et des armes à nos ennemis dans le Caucase—nous n'avions pas le droit d'intercepter une flotte destinée à porter des renforts et des munitions de guerre aux troupes ennemies, et, qui plus est, à des troupes qui avaient franchi notre frontière. L'attaque d'un convoi sur terre, en mer, ou dans une rade est défendue par les lois d'une guerre défensive,— l'attaque d'une force moindre par une force supérieure est un attentat et un guet-apens, contraire à toutes les lois de la guerre entre peuples civilisés. Une guerre agressive n'est pas l'occupation d'un territoire ennemi dans un but de conquête : non, c'est la destruction d'une flotte ennemie armée contre nous : c'est enfin (car les deux cas sont évidemment parallèles) la destruction à coups de canon d'une troupe ou d'un convoi de guerre, qui longerait la frontière du pays pour porter des secours ou des munitions à l'armée qui l'aurait déjà franchie ou se préparerait à la franchir. Cette absurdité est par trop palpable ! Vous faites une guerre défensive, eh bien ! Combattez le corps d'armée, mais ne vous avisez pas de canonner la réserve qui n'a pas encore donné : autrement vous manquez à vos engagements. Vous avez devant vous une force égale ou supérieure, vous pouvez attaquer ; mais vous rencontrez une force moindre, n'osez pas la toucher ; autrement vous êtes des barbares, des assassins et vous manquez aux lois de toutes les nations civilisées. Non : je ne ferai pas à l'intelligence la plus étroite l'affront de lui supposer de la bonne foi, si elle tenait ce langage, eût-elle même l'honneur de diriger les conseils de la reine d'Angleterre, ou de se faire entendre dans le cabinet de l'empereur des Français, se nommât-elle Russell ou Drouyn de Lhuys. La raison de la guerre est ignominieuse : son prétexte est un infâme mensonge.

Le canon de la grande lutte n'a pas encore retenti, et déjà la question se complique. Les Grecs et les Slaves de la Turquie ont levé l'étendard de la révolte. Ce ne sont plus les Russes à combattre, ce sont les Chrétiens protestant en armes contre leur joug séculaire. Que feront l'Angleterre et la France ? Enverront-elles leurs flottes et leurs soldats massacrer les populations Chrétiennes, pour en faire des sujets dociles du Sultan, et pour rétablir la plénitude des droits de vie et de meurtre ? Cet acte serait horrible, mais il y aurait au moins de la franchise dans le crime. Ou bien diront-elles au Sultan de placer leurs troupes aux endroits menacés par les Russes, pour qu'il ait plus de forces disponibles à lancer sur les Chrétiens révoltés ? Le crime du renégat se couvrirait ainsi des protestations d'un Christianisme menteur. C'est la marche la plus probable, ou plutôt ce ne serait que la continuation d'une marche adoptée dès le commencement et qui a déjà donné de beaux fruits : car les horreurs, commises par les Turcs depuis plus de six mois, ne viennent pas, comme l'ont prétendu des bouches menteuses, des menaces de la Russie devant lesquelles la Porte tremblait, mais des promesses données par l'Angleterre et la France, qui ont rendu aux Turcs le courage du crime en leur en assurant l'impunité. Une voie si noble ne doit pas être abandonnée, quoiqu'en disent les bigots. Lord Palmerston l'approuve. Vite, mylord : les Grecs vont être passés au fil de l'épée, et leurs femmes et leurs filles livrées aux Turcs par les Anglais. Vite, mylord : un bon dîner, des phrases élégantes et un toast en l'honneur des armes de l'Angleterre, de la France, et du Sultan.

Cette guerre nous est imposée par les devoirs de notre fraternité avec les Chrétiens d'Orient. Quelqu'en soit la marche, le triomphe du principe est indubitable. Et c'est dans le moment où nous levons les armes pour défendre la cause d'une fraternité réelle et sainte, fondée sur les liens du sang et de la foi, que nous voyons s'élancer contre nous et à l'avant-garde de nos ennemis les prédicateurs d'une fraternité conventionnelle et fausse, sans base morale et sans foi religieuse. Apostats ou amis des apostats, assassins des faibles ou alliés des assassins, grâces leur en soient rendues—ils ont séparé leur cause de la nôtre, ils nous justifient par leur inimitié, ils nous honorent par l'ardeur de leur haine.

Grâces soient aussi rendues aux puissances Occidentales. Elles hâtent sans le vouloir le moment où deux grands principes, jusqu'ici relégués dans l'ombre, vont se produire au grand jour et prendre l'ascendant dans le monde ; elles poussent sans le savoir la Russie elle-même dans une voie nouvelle, à laquelle elle était inutilement conviée depuis bien des années. Instruments aveugles des décrets de Dieu, elles acquirent des droits à notre reconnaissance, et non seulement à la nôtre, mais encore à celle de toutes les générations futures, qui marchent à la clarté d'une lumière plus pure que celle, qui a lui sur les générations passées.

Le sang humain est précieux, la guerre est horrible—mais les desseins de la Providence sont impénetrables, et un devoir doit être rempli, quelque rigoureux qu'il soit.

Flottez, pavillons! Sonnez, trompettes de la bataille! Nations, ruez-vous au combat! Dieu fait marcher l'humanité!

CHAPTER XXI

MR. PALMER JOINS THE ROMAN COMMUNION

[1855]

Mr. Palmer's Profession of Faith upon joining the Roman Church.

THE correspondence between Mr. Khomiakoff and Mr. Palmer was brought to an end, partly by the breaking out of the Crimean War, and partly by the secession of the latter from the Anglican to the Roman Communion. It seems to me that this volume cannot be better brought to an end than by three documents which show the exact state of mind in which each of them found himself at its conclusion. The first of these is a 'Profession of Faith' which Mr. Palmer wrote for circulation among his friends when he joined the Church of Rome. It was originally written in Latin, but was afterwards translated into several languages. I first came across it in Russia in a French translation obtained from the Archives of the Russian Holy Synod; but through the kindness of the late Lord Selborne I am able to give an English version which is no less valuable and authentic than the original Latin Text. It is a translation written in Mr. Palmer's own handwriting which Cardinal Newman returned to Lord Selborne, together with some other papers which had belonged to his brother.

PROFESSION OF FAITH BY W. PALMER
1855

Having been asked by friends to whom I owe deference write something in order to guard against any inaccuracy

M

rumours which may be circulated, I put into their hands the following :—

'The reader may imagine the case of a young Englishman, too self-confident, and not free from sins, undertaking the study of theology, with the belief (derived from the Creed and from Anglican tradition) that there is one holy Catholic and Apostolic Church, and this a visible, not an invisible society; nevertheless that this Catholic Church is at present torn asunder and divided into three parts, the English, the Roman, and the Greek, so that, while on all points on which these three parts teach alike, private judgment ought to submit itself absolutely, it is yet the duty of every man—of every Anglican at least—in respect of all other points on which there seems to be as yet a difference between conflicting authorities, to labour by assiduous prayer to God as well as by attention and diligent use of all reasonable means, to develop and fill up that truth which he already holds, and to discover and correct (for himself at least) any errors which may lurk beneath the tradition of his particular Church.

'Add next, that such an one, after passing seven years (1833-1840) in thus cultivating and filling up or correcting his inherited Anglican tradition, finds himself to agree with the Greek or Eastern Church on all points of doctrine except one, respecting the Procession of the Holy Ghost. Again, that after seven years more (1840-1847) he comes to agree with the Easterns on this point of the Procession also; and besides is forced by a gradually accumulating necessity to confess, though most unwillingly, that the Anglican Church in which he was baptized and bred up has fallen into grave errors. Lastly, that for eight years more, reaching down to the year 1855 now current he remains without further change, having his heart meantime more and more drawn towards the Roman Communion, but without any such conviction of its plenary and exclusive authority as would require or enable him to make an act of faith in its doctrine on one or two particular points contrary to the doctrine of the Eastern Church, and to his own private judgment assenting to the Greek rather than to the Latin Theology.

'We may add further that the person referred to has made during the last eight years both in Russia and in the Levant repeated attempts to obtain admission as a proselyte to the 'Orthodox' or Eastern Communion; and that these attempts have always failed, owing, chiefly, to a discrepancy existing at present between the Russians and the Greeks as to the validity of Western Baptisms. For a proselyte from the Westerns, received by the Russians after their manner by Chrism only, is told by the Greek Patriarchs that he is simply and absolutely unbaptized (πάντῃ πάντως ἀβάπτιστος) though by a certain dissimulation or connivance they would give him the Communion; while on the other hand if a man were to put himself into the hands of a Greek Bishop to be re-baptized, he would be acting not only against the synodical decrees of the Russian and of the Roman Church, and perhaps against his own conscience, but also against the canonical discipline of the Greeks themselves decreed by the Synod of A.D. 1484, and since abrogated in 1751 only by the personal authority of the Patriarchs.

'Under these circumstances his R. C. friends, of their zeal and charity, begin to urge him as they had done before, but especially after his arrival at this place, insisting: That he cannot rightly as an individual remain so long outside the true Fold; that for the last eight years by his own confession he has been only passively and unwillingly a member of the Anglican, and in no sense at all a member of the Greek, Church; that like other people he has need of the Sacraments, and, even supposing him to have been baptized, still he has need of a valid Absolution and Communion, and of these he is deprived, so long as he remains outside of the Church, passing his judgment upon all visible Churches, and having no certain ground on which to stand himself; that death is approaching to all men, and the time of death uncertain; it may come suddenly, and then to die without the Sacraments is most dangerous; that he himself confesses his opinion of the

Catholic Church being a visible society and yet divided into two conflicting Communions to be paradoxical and difficult to maintain; he confesses, too, that neither can the whole Catholic Church, nor any particular Church within it be *permanently* severed from the Roman Chair. And he cannot deny that even when he thought himself obliged to seek admission to the Communion of the Greek or Eastern Church he dreaded rather than wished for success, while on the contrary, even when he was most fighting against Rome, his heart wished for the Roman Communion. That under such circumstances he ought immediately to submit himself to the Roman Pontiff as to the chief doctor and ruler of the Apostolic Church, and be ready to make oath in such form or words as he prescribes, even though the form may contain some things inconsistent with his own private judgment not only on certain particular doctrines *but even respecting the Definition of the Church*, on which they depend.

'In answer to such exhortations as these it may be objected that though on all points of doctrine or practice which are ruled by the authority of the Catholic Church the private understanding has nothing else to do than to learn, and to follow with docility the Apostolic authority, still with respect to the definition of the Catholic Church and of that plenary authority which is to be followed as the rule of faith and practice in all details, the case is different. For as he who comes to God must first believe that God is, and that He is the rewarder of them that seek Him, so also he who comes to any particular Community (as to the Roman) as to the true Church with an unreserved submission and submits his private judgment and the judgment of other communities on particular points to its teaching, must first be fully persuaded that this same Community is really the whole Catholic Church exclusively of any other Communities whose judgment it requires him to disregard. And until he has this full persuasion, however closely a man may seem to approximate to the Roman Church, he is not yet ripe to be admitted as a proselyte to her Communion. All that can be done with such an one is to exhort him to give closer and more habitual attention to those points on which he still doubts, especially to the primary question of the definition of the Church, to search and examine more narrowly his own conscience, and more earnestly to implore help and mercy of God, Who alone can reveal to a man such sources of error as may be lurking in the heart or understanding, and lead him into all truth.

'Such an answer may seem to some just and reasonable. Still, in the case of a person who needed valid Absolution and remission of his sins, it seemed morally safest to submit himself to the undoubted Primate of the whole Apostolic College, so as to take from him upon trust, not only some definitions of doctrine, but even to a certain extent that definition of the Church itself which is the first principle and on which particular doctrines may depend, committing himself to the mercy of Almighty God, and trusting that the result will be such as his friends (who in past time blamed his hesitation, and urged him to the step) most confidently anticipated for him and promised.'

[There is no date upon the copy of the translation from which this is printed, and which, as has been already said, was in Mr. Palmer's own handwriting; but at the end of the French translation, which I obtained in Russia, I find: 'Ecrit à Rome le 7 Mars, 1855.']

CHAPTER XXII

MR. PALMER'S LETTER TO THE CHIEF PROCURATOR
OF THE RUSSIAN HOLY SYNOD

[1858]

Mr. Palmer in the Roman Communion—Journey in Egypt and the Holy Land—Visit to Constantinople and Asia Minor—Last attempt at Philadelphia to join the Eastern Church—Starts for Rome—Stops at Corfu on the way—Makes his terms of submission to Rome with Fr. Passaglia— His present feelings with regard to the Eastern Church—Symbolical pictures—St. John Chrysostom, St. Thomas of Canterbury, and the Patriarch Nicon.

THE following letter, written to Count Alexis Tolstoi, the Chief Procurator of the Holy Synod, throws considerable fresh light both upon the circumstances which led to Mr. Palmer joining the Roman Communion, and to the views which he continued to hold with regard to the Orthodox Eastern Church. It is here printed for the first time in its original form, which was given me by M. Peter Bartenieff, the Editor of the *Russki Archiv* at Moscow, in which a translation of it appeared last year, and created considerable interest and surprise in Russia. M. Bartenieff received it from the present Chief Procurator of the Holy Synod, M. Constantine Pobédonostzeff.[1]

ROME, 13 DIETRO LA TRIBUNA DI TOR DI SPECCHI,
20 *March* 1858.

MON CHER COMPTE,—I am availing myself of the opportunity afforded me through the kindness of Prince Cherkassky to send you a few lines. The Russian Chaplain in London, M. Popoff, has several times given me a friendly

---

[1] See *Russki Archiv*, May 1894.

word of greeting from you, and this winter in Rome, where I have for the most part been living during the three years that I have been a Roman Catholic, I had the still greater pleasure of making the acquaintance of your friends or relations Prince and Princess Obolensky. As for myself, I have neither in my thoughts nor in my prayers abandoned those whom I knew in past times before the war and before the personal change which I made in the matter of religion. For one of your relatives in particular, Mme. de Potemkin, I preserve, and always shall preserve, an affection as deep as if she was one of my own dearest relations; and if I have not written to her during these three years, this was because I well knew not only that proselytes are generally more or less suspected by others, but also because they very often deserve it: and that accordingly a proselyte ought to be an object of suspicion to himself, and this is why I wished to pass a little time alone by myself, without seeking to continue or renew the relations with others which I formerly had whether in England or in Russia. Besides, during the war, and even after it, I had not the same facilities as formerly for sending or receiving letters.

Now I will tell you in a few words what I have been doing during these last years. When I left Odessa in the autumn of 1852 I addressed a letter to the late Emperor [Nicolas] upon the subject of the relations of the Russian Church with the state, and I afterwards heard that this letter, although it was sufficiently frank, did not offend him. I think that I also heard that he had showed it to Mme. de Potemkin. In the autumn of 1853, after the death of my father, as I had for several years past suffered more and more from the gout, I went to Cairo in Egypt, partly to read there, and, if it were worth while, to translate a history in manuscript of the trial of the Patriarch Nicon, written in modern Greek by the unfortunate archbishop of Gaza, Paizios; for I had always intended (and still have not abandoned the idea) to complete my researches upon the life of this great and holy man, and even to publish his life in English or in Latin, if I should have succeeded in seeing the most necessary unpublished documents, so that my work should not be too incomplete.[1] But at Cairo I only found the first of the three books of Paizios, and even, in the case of the first, not the original text, but a copy made by the orders of the Greek Patriarch for M. Andrew Mouravieff. The Patriarch, on finding that the manuscript was difficult to decipher and that the copy already made of the first part was full of mistakes, had sent the original manuscript to Mouravieff in Russia, giving him permission to keep it as long as he required it, and requesting him to send it back to Cairo whenever an opportunity presented itself.

Afterwards, at Jerusalem, I obtained leave from the Archimandrite Porphyrius to copy some extracts which he had made from the second and third books; but if the war had not prevented me I had intended to return to Egypt by Georgia and Southern Russia and then up the Volga, in order that I might both see the manuscript in the hands of M. Mouravieff, and also perhaps obtain permission to examine other unpublished documents concerning the trial of Nicon which are still preserved in Russia. In Egypt I went up the Nile as far as the first cataracts, and finding that the proper names of the kings upon the monuments are extremely easy to make out, I became immensely interested in them, and I even venture to think that I was able by chance to make a few discoveries which will be useful both for science and for religion. Whether this is so or not scholars will perhaps later on have occasion to judge. But supposing that I am not mistaken, it will be to the interest and affection which I had for the Patriarch Nicon (and partly also to the gout) that they will be indebted for my discoveries.

From Cairo I went by Mount Sinai to Jerusalem, where,

---

[1] This work (six volumes, octavo) was published in 1871-1876 by Trübner.—[W. J. B.]

notwithstanding the war, I stayed for some time with the
Russian Archimandrite; and afterwards at Athens I suc-
ceeded in translating into modern Greek and printing my
Dissertations upon the Orthodox or Eastern Church, of which
I think I sent you a copy in English. After having been
for a last visit to Constantinople, where the Patriarch with
his Synod pretended to be ignorant of the custom of the
Russian Church (which indeed is the sole canonical custom,
for the Greeks no less than for the Russians) of receiving
Latins into the Orthodox Church without rebaptizing them,
I made a short journey into Asia Minor in order to see the
churches of Smyrna and Philadelphia (especially the latter);
the two Churches out of the seven of the Apocalypse which,
having alone received praises and promises from our Saviour
without any admixture of blame or warning, are also the
only ones which have been preserved down to the present
time amidst the ruins of the five others. At Philadelphia
I experienced for myself that the charity, the type of which
this Church is chosen to bear, is still preserved there and
shows itself in a very touching manner. As for the idea
which I had in my mind in going there—namely, there to
make a last attempt to be received into the Orthodox Church
as a proselyte without being rebaptized,—it gave occasion
to an interview of a most comical description with the Bishop.
It was from Philadelphia, externally the feeblest and poorest,
but mystically the most honourable of all the Churches, that
I turned myself towards Rome — the greatest and most
puissant of all the Churches. On my way thither I passed
through Corfu, and found that there they had more or less
changed their tone on the subject of the rebaptizing of Latins
since my last visit there in 1852. At that time they pretended to act by economy, by a spirit of abuse which it
was difficult to justify in the presence of the great Church
of Constantinople—in short, through fear of the English,
just as in former days, when they admitted proselytes without rebaptizing them, they pretended that it was because of
their fear of the Venetians. But in 1854 they had just

republished the text of the Council held in the fifteenth century upon the acts of which the Patriarch Macarius of Antioch and the Patriarch Nicon insisted when they were engaged in Russia in correcting the abusive custom of re-baptizing, which had been introduced under the Patriarch Philaret;[1] also in 1854 they took their stand at Corfu on this Council, and were rather proud of having preserved the ancient canonical custom which the Patriarchal decrees of the eighteenth century alone were unable to abrogate.

Having arrived at Rome, and having been persuaded by some very enthusiastic friends of mine to make a retreat, I came into connection with a very distinguished theologian, Father Passaglia, who informed me of an 'opinion' which I had never thought of, and which served to facilitate my conviction,—namely, that having, as I had, Greek rather than Latin convictions upon certain important points of controversy, I could all the same be received into the Roman Catholic communion by merely suspending my private judgment and by making up my mind to affirm nothing contrary to the known dogmas of the Roman Church, nor to entertain by preference any such thoughts. Accordingly I followed his advice, for it seemed to me neither right nor justifiable, with the sins of my past life on my soul, and persuaded as I was long since that it was impossible to defend the Anglican Church, to pass all my life in studying, and even to some extent *judging*, all Churches, without belonging in God's sight to any one of them. My Roman Catholic friends, themselves proselytes for the most part, predicted to me in a tone of absolute assurance that my singular partiality for the Russian and Eastern Church would cease all in a moment, when once I should become a Catholic, and that my understanding would be fully enlightened, so as to know and recognise the true orthodoxy upon all points. As a matter of fact, I am very glad to think that I never allowed myself

---

[1] Philaret Romanoff, third Patriarch of Moscow, A.D. 1621-1633, and father of the Tzar Michael, the father of Alexis and grandfather of Peter the Great. Nicon was Patriarch A.D. 1653-1667.—[W. J. B.]

to be carried away by their promises, and accordingly I have not been disappointed. I have obtained from the step which I resolved upon a real peace and a religious position which I am able to defend; but, as for my intellectual position, it has remained almost without change; only in respect to the Roman See and, in general, in respect to general arguments favourable to the pretensions of Catholicism, I find it much more agreeable to be on the side of the stronger, rather than on that of the less strong.[1] As to the great theological

---

[1] As this is the most important portion of the letter, I give the original French as Mr. Palmer wrote it :—

'Quant à l'idée que j'avais eu y allant, d'y faire une dernière tentative pour être reçu comme prosélyte sans être rebaptisé, elle a donné lieu à une conférence avec l'Évêque, qui était une des plus comique. C'est de Philadelphie, la plus faible et la plus pauvre extérieurement, mais mystiquement la plus honorable de toutes les églises, que je me suis tourné vers Rome—la plus grande et la plus puissante de toutes les églises : et en passant par Corfou j'ai trouvé qu'on avait changé plus ou moins de ton, etc. . . .

'Arrivé à Rome, et ayant été persuadé par quelques amis très zélés à faire une retraite, je suis venu en rapport avec un théologien fort distingué (le père Passaglia) qui m'a annoncé une opinion inattendue qui servait à faciliter ma conviction, c'est à dire, qu'ayant, comme je les avais, des convictions grecques plutôt que latines sur certains points de controverse importants, je pouvais néanmoins être reçu à la communion Catholique Romaine en faisant seulement suspens de mon jugement privé, en me déterminant de ne rien affirmer de contraire aux dogmes connus de l'église romaine, ni d'entretenir de préférence de pareilles pensées. Ainsi j'ai suivi son avis, ne le trouvant pas convenable, ni justifiable, avec les péchés de ma vie passée sur mon âme, et convaincu depuis longtemps que l'église Anglicane n'était pas à défendre, de passer toute ma vie à étudier et à *juger* même de quelque manière toutes les églises sans appartenir à aucune d'elles. Mes amis catholiques romains, prosélytes la plupart eux-mêmes, me prédirent avec un ton d'assurance absolue que ma partialité singulière et aveugle pour l'église Russe et Orientale cesserait tout d'un coup aussitôt que je serais catholique, et que mon entendement serait pleinement éclairé pour reconnaître en toute chose la vraie orthodoxie. Quant au fait, je suis très heureux de penser que je ne me suis jamais laissé entraîner à leurs promesses : ainsi je n'en ai pas été désappointé. J'ai obtenu de ma conviction ce que j'espérais, une paix solide, et une position religieuse que je puisse raisonnablement défendre ; mais pour

question which divides the Orientals from the Latins, if I thought myself free to dictate a private opinion of my own to others, I should support, as I did before, the theology—or better to say, the phraseology—of the Greeks, as being the most ancient, and in itself quite sufficient. But I am fully persuaded by general considerations, that there must be some way of reconciling and uniting the two formulas of the Greeks and Latins which seem to contradict each other: and although I dare not think that I have as yet discovered the solution of this question, I have nothing better to wish than to pass the rest of my life in studying it; and if it pleased God to allow me of His grace to serve as His instrument for advancing the cause of unity, however little, in this respect, I shall say my *Nunc Dimittis* with tears of joy and gratitude. For after all (although God has no need of us) it is both natural and part of our duty to desire to do something in His service, and not to eat and drink and live in abundance quite uselessly all one's life, while so many of the poor, who till the land with their hands, make hardly enough to live upon.

I send you traced upon thin paper a copy of a composition which I put together, last year, and which I have recently had painted in colour. With a little attention you will easily guess, at least so I think, all the applications of the texts drawn from the life of Nicon which I wish to make. I will only add that this composition follows upon a series of paintings chosen from among those of the catacombs at Rome,

---

l'entendement, il est demeuré presque sans changement ; seulement par rapport au siège Romain, et en général, par rapport aux arguments généraux favorables aux prétentions du catholicisme, je trouve qu'il est beaucoup plus agréable de se trouver du côté du plus fort que de celui du moins fort. Quant à la grande question théologique qui divise les Orientaux et les Russes des Latins, si je me croyais libre de dicter aux autres une opinion particulière, je soutiendrais comme auparavant la théologie, c. à. d. la phraséologie grecque comme étant la plus ancienne et en elle-même suffisante. Mais je suis pleinement convaincu par les considérations générales, qu'il doit exister quelque manière de concilier et unir les deux formules des Grecs et des Latins qui semblent se contredire : etc. . . .'

and grouped together with the idea of presenting in a compendious manner the Christian symbolism of the first three, and of the early part of the fourth, centuries. In the composition which I send you you will see the Ark of Noah (at the top); the rainbow, in which are represented the Patriarchal Churches; the stone throne on six steps, with the dove, the golden candlestick (without, however, the Greek inscriptions with the two lighted mouths), the representation of Daniel in the midst of the lions, with the hand of Habakkuk bringing him loaves of bread, the representation of Job seated on his dung-hill; those of symbolical animals and birds, of Susanna (that is to say the Church) falsely accused by the elders, of the bread which signifies the incorruption of the sacred bodies of the Disciples of Jesus Christ, of the Phœnix (signifying the resurrection and immortality), of the partridge (the soul in trouble under persecution like the soul of David pursued by Saul), of the sparrow and of the dove, are all taken from various frescoes discovered in the Roman catacombs. If you are sufficiently interested in my composition to wish to help me to complete it, I will ask you to procure for me and send me, either in a letter or on some other opportunity which may present itself, two or three sketches of objects or of places for which I have for the present been obliged to substitute either pure imagination or a description grounded upon my inexact recollections related to the artist, who moreover has added further inexactitudes of his own. The sketches which I should like to obtain are:

1. A view of the Church of the new Jerusalem at Voskresensk to put with Sion and Noah's Ark at the top of the principal picture. 2. A sketch of the tower or hermitage of Nicon, on the banks of the Istra, at the same place; 3. one of the Calvary [in the Church of the Monastery] with the tomb of Nicon, and the chains which he used to wear next his body: 4. one of the monastery of Therapontoff on the White Lake with the winter road crossing the ice, and the little island made in the lake by Nicon, where he planted a cross with an inscription; I don't know whether the monastery

still exists, but at any rate the island, the lake, and the town remain the same as they were. If you will provide me with these materials (the smaller the sketches are, the better they will be for the end I have in view, as you will see if you look at the vignettes in which they are to be put), I shall show you my gratitude by sending the whole composition, painted in colours, together with another one in which I have also introduced the name of Nicon. In this one there may be seen in the middle King Nebuchadnezzar arrogating to himself a part of the obedience due to God and to His Church; on one side an officer is showing the three Hebrews the image of the king and is commanding them to adore it. Opposite to these I have put some names, to the first the name of St. John Chrysostom, whose history was related by Nicon to the Czar Alexis as a reason for the translation of the relics of St. Philip the Metropolitan of Moscow;[1] to the second the name of St. Thomas à Becket, Archbishop of Canterbury; and to the third that of the Patriarch Nicon. On the other side of the king appear the same three confessors in the burning fiery furnace.

It is with respect to this picture that I have put amongst the extracts taken from the life of Nicon, the first of which relates his deliverance in his youth from the stove, with the name of Xenia (the stranger) who drew him out of the fire of persecution. As to the two pictures on the sides, on the one side may be seen King Herod pretending that he wishes to adore the child Jesus, and feigning, as he questions the three Magi, to be filled with reverence and admiration. This king is symbolical of a second kind of impiety by which the secular power pretends to honour religion and the Church,

---

[1] St. Philip was driven from Moscow, and afterwards strangled in prison by the orders of John the Terrible, whom he had rebuked for his cruelties. His remains were taken to Solovetzki Monastery in the White Sea, of which he had formerly been Abbot; but under the Tzar Alexis, they were, at the instigation of Nicon, solemnly translated to the Cathedral of the Assumption at Moscow, where they have ever since rested in a great silver shrine just outside the iconostasis at its south end.—[W. J. B.]

with the secret desire all the time to make use of them as instruments of human policy. On the other side opposite are the three Magi hastening with their gifts to adore the true King in the arms of the holy Virgin. In one of the crypts of the catacombs of St. Agnes there exists a very beautiful variation of this thought, in which the three Hebrews on one side of a tomb are depicted as refusing to worship the image of the king of the earth, while on the other side the same three, that is to say the Magi, who are in some manner identified with them, are hastening with their gifts to adore their true King, the King of Heaven and of the earth, and the Image of the only true God, in the arms of His Mother.

But I have already written more than enough to weary at least your eyes, and so I shall end by begging you to give my kindest remembrances to Mme. de Potemkin, and also, according to the degree of our friendship, to all of those whose acquaintance I made and who have not forgotten me, nor bear me a grudge on account of my change of religion. I will mention more especially M. Noroff, M. Wagner, and, amongst ecclesiastics, the Metropolitan Philaret of Moscow, and Archbishop Philaret of Kharkoff, whenever you happen to have occasion to see or write to them: always praying that you might be able to do something (something however small) to diminish and abate the scandal and the division which it has taken more than two centuries to ripen,[1] and which consequently we cannot hope to see disappear all at once and in one day.—I am always, my dear Count Tolstoi, with much friendship and affection, your most humble and obedient servant in Jesus Christ,

WILLIAM PALMER.

---

[1] For Mr. Palmer's views with regard to the events which took place in Russia in the seventeenth century, see his *Dissertations upon the Orthodox Communion* (Masters, 1853), No. v., headed 'Destinies of the Slavonic Empire,—Probation and failure of the Tzar Alexis Michaelovitch, with the Nobility and Hierarchy of Russia, in the seventeenth century.' The 'division' to which he here refers is the *Raskol*, or schism of the Old Believers, which, although it began before the fall of Nicon, would probably have disappeared had it not been for the changes after his disgrace, and under Peter the Great.—[W. J. B.]

CHAPTER XXIII

MR. KHOMIAKOFF'S ESSAY ON THE CHURCH

[*Circa* 1850]

Introduction—§ 1. The Church is one—§ 2. The Church on earth—§ 3. Her notes—§ 4. She is One, Holy, Catholic, and Apostolic—§ 5. Her Scripture, Tradition, and Works—§ 6. They are manifestations of the gifts of the Spirit; of faith, hope, and love—§ 7. The Church's Confession of Faith— The clause 'Filioque' not a part of it—§ 8. The Church—Her visible manifestation—Baptism—Other Sacraments—The Eucharist—Ordination —Confirmation—Marriage—Penance— Unction of the Sick—§ 9. Inward life of the Church—Gifts of the Holy Spirit—Faith—Justification by faith, and works—The Church, but no single individual within her, is necessarily infallible—Distinction between '*opus operans*' and '*opus operatum*' superfluous—The law of adoption of sons, and of love which is free—Communion of prayer—Invocation and worship of the Saints— Prayers for the living and the dead, and also for those as yet unborn—No presumption in praying even for the Saints—The worship of the Church an expression of her love—The use of images sanctioned by the Church— The Liturgy—§ 10. The Church's hope—The Resurrection of the body— The Last Judgment—Orthodox doctrine of grace—The distinction between 'sufficient' and 'effectual' grace superfluous—Faith, hope, and love are eternal, but love alone will preserve its name—§ 11. The Orthodox Eastern Church is the whole of the Catholic Church now living upon earth—The titles 'Orthodox' and 'Eastern' merely temporary— The whole world belongs to her.

HAVING seen the final development of Mr. Palmer's views, we must now endeavour to ascertain those of Mr. Khomiakoff. They are admirably set forth in the following Essay. It is not exactly known when it was written, but although it was not printed until the year 1863, three years after the death of the author, when it received the sanction of the Ecclesiastical Censureship and appeared in the Moscow 'Orthodox Review,' it is certain that it was written towards the end of the time of Mr. Khomiakoff's correspondence with Mr. Palmer, and was largely circulated in manuscript form amongst the author's friends. It is now to be found at the beginning of the second volume of his works, of which some account has already been given in the Introduction. An excellent translation of it was made by the Baroness von Rahden with the assistance of Mr. G. Samarin, and published at Berlin in the year 1870, under the title of 'Versuch einer katechetischen Darstellung der Lehre von der Kirche.' References both to it, and also to the correspondence between Samarin and Baroness von Rahden with regard to it, will be found in the foot-notes of the following translation.

ESSAY ON THE UNITY OF THE CHURCH.[1]

BY A. S. KHOMIAKOFF.

§ 1. THE Church is one. Her unity follows of necessity from the unity of God; for the Church is not a multitude of persons in their separate individuality, but a unity of the grace of God, living in a multitude of rational creatures, submitting themselves willingly to grace. Grace, indeed, is also given to those who resist it, and to those who do not make use of it (who hide their talent in the earth), but these are not in the Church. In fact, the unity of the Church is not imaginary or allegorical, but a true and substantial unity, such as is the unity of many members in a living body.

The Church is one, notwithstanding her division, as it appears to a man who is still alive on earth. It is only in relation to man that it is possible to recognise a division of the Church into visible and invisible; her unity is, in reality, true and absolute. Those who are alive on earth, those who have finished their earthly course, those who, like the angels, were not created for a life on earth, those in future generations who have not yet begun their earthly course, are all united

---

[1] The title written by Mr. Khomiakoff himself at the top of the manuscript from which this Essay was first printed is: Церковь одна, 'The Church is one.'—[W. J. B.]

together in one Church, in one and the same grace of God; for the creation of God which has not yet been manifested is manifest to Him; and God hears the prayers and knows the faith of those whom He has not yet called out of non-existence into existence. Indeed the Church, the Body of Christ, is manifesting forth and fulfilling herself in time, without changing her essential unity or inward life of grace. And therefore, when we speak of 'the Church visible and invisible,' we so speak only in relation to man.

§ 2. The Church visible, or upon earth, lives in complete communion and unity with the whole body of the Church, of which Christ is the Head. She has abiding within her Christ and the grace of the Holy Spirit in all their living fulness, but not in the fulness of their manifestation,[1] for she acts and knows not fully, but only so far as it pleases God.

Inasmuch as the earthly and visible Church is not the fulness and completeness of the whole Church which the Lord has appointed to appear at the final judgment of all creation, she acts and knows only within her own limits; and (according to the words of Paul the Apostle, to the Corinthians, 1 Cor. v. 12) does not judge the rest of mankind, and only looks upon those as excluded, that is to say, not belonging to her, who exclude themselves. The rest of mankind, whether alien from the Church, or united to her by ties which God has not willed to reveal to her, she leaves to the judgment of the great day. The Church on earth judges for herself only,[2] according to the grace of the Spirit, and

---

[1] Во всей ихъ жизненной полнотѣ, но не въ полнотѣ ихъ проявленій. On the true meaning of the last word Samarin wrote:—Je n'ai rien à redire à 'Selbstoffenbarung,' mais décidez vous-même si 'Erscheinung' ne serait pas plus exact dans le sens que donnait Kant au mot 'Erscheinung' en l'opposant à l'idée d'essence (das Ding an sich). Samarin, *Correspondence with von Rahden*, p. 108.—[W. J. B.]

[2] Церковь же земная судятъ только себѣ. I have translated this quite literally, rendering the dative case, себѣ by 'for herself.' Baroness von Rahden translates the passage, 'Die irdische Kirche richtet nur auf ihrem eigenen Gebiete.'—[W. J. B.]

the freedom granted her through Christ, inviting also the rest of mankind to the unity and adoption of God in Christ; but upon those who do not hear her appeal she pronounces no sentence, knowing the command of her Saviour and Head, 'not to judge another man's servant' (Rom. xiv. 4).

§ 3. From the creation of the world the earthly Church has continued uninterruptedly upon the earth, and will continue until the accomplishment of all the works of God, according to the promise given her by God Himself. And her notes are: inward holiness, which does not allow of any admixture of error, for the spirit of truth lives within her; and outward unchangeableness, for Christ, her Preserver and Head, does not change.

All the notes of the Church, whether inward or outward, are recognised only by herself, and by those whom grace calls to be members of her. To those, indeed, who are alien from her, and are not called to her, they are unintelligible; for to such as these, outward change of rite appears to be a change of the Spirit itself, which is glorified in the rite (as, for instance, in the transition from the Church of the Old Testament to that of the New, or in the change of ecclesiastical rites and ordinances since Apostolic times). The Church and her members know, by the inward knowledge of faith, the unity and unchangeableness of her spirit, which is the spirit of God. But those who are outside and not called to belong to her, behold and know the changes in the external rite by an external knowledge, which does not comprehend the inward [knowledge] just as also the unchangeableness of God appears to them to be changeable, in the changes of His creations. Wherefore the Church has not been, nor could she be, changed or obscured, nor could she have fallen away, for then she would have been deprived of the spirit of truth. It is impossible that there should have been a time when she could have received error into her bosom, or when the laity, presbyters, and bishops had submitted to instructions or teaching inconsistent with the teaching and spirit of Christ. The man who should say that such a weakening of the spirit of Christ could possibly come to pass within her knows nothing of the Church, and is altogether alien from her. Moreover, a partial revolt against false doctrines, together with the retention or acceptance of other false doctrines, neither is, nor could be, the work of the Church; for within her, according to her very essence, there must always have been preachers and teachers and martyrs confessing, not partial truth with an admixture of error, but the full and unadulterated truth. The Church knows nothing of partial truth and partial error, but only the whole truth without admixture of error. And the man who is living within the Church does not submit to false teaching or receive the Sacraments from a false teacher : he will not, knowing him to be false, follow his false rites [обрядъ = *ritus*]. And the Church herself does not err, for she is the truth, she is incapable of cunning[1] or cowardice, for she is holy. And of course, the Church, by her very unchangeableness, does not acknowledge that to be error, which she has at any previous time acknowledged as truth; and having proclaimed by a General Council and common consent, that it is possible for any private individual, or any bishop or patriarch,[2] to err in his teaching, she cannot acknowledge that such or such private individual, or bishop, or patriarch, or successor of theirs, is incapable of falling into error in teaching; or that they are preserved from going astray by any special grace. By what would the earth be sanctified, if the Church were to lose her sanctity ? And where would there be truth, if her judgments of to-day were contrary to those of yesterday ? Within the Church, that is to say, within her members, false doctrines may be engendered, but then the infected members fall away, constituting a heresy or schism, and no longer defile the sanctity of the Church.

---

[1] не хитратъ. Countess de Rahden, at the advice of Samarin, translated this, ' sucht sich nicht durch Kunstgriffe zu helfen.' In French the verb хитрять might be exactly reproduced by 'finasser.' Mr. Khomiakoff is evidently referring to a policy such as is described on p. 7, in his first letter to Mr. Palmer.—[W. J. B.]

[2] As for instance, Pope Honorius, whose teaching was condemned at the sixth General Council.—[Author's note.]

§ 4. The Church is called One, Holy, Catholic, and Apostolic; because she is one, and holy; because she belongs to the whole world, and not to any particular locality; because by her all mankind and all the earth, and not any particular nation or country, are sanctified; because her very essence consists in the agreement and unity of the spirit and life of all the members who acknowledge her, throughout the world; lastly, because in the writings and doctrine of the Apostles is contained all the fulness of her faith, her hope, and her love.

From this it follows that when any society is called the Church of Christ, with the addition of a local name, such as the Greek, Russian, or Syrian Church, this appellation signifies nothing more than the congregation of members of the Church living in that particular locality, that is, Greece, Russia, or Syria; and does not involve any such idea as that any single community of Christians is able to formulate the doctrine of the Church, or to give a dogmatic interpretation to the teaching of the Church without the concurrence therewith of the other communities; still less is it implied that any one particular community, or the pastor thereof, can prescribe its own interpretation to the others. The grace of faith is not to be separated from holiness of life, and neither any single community nor any single pastor can be acknowledged to be the custodian of the whole faith of the Church, any more than any single community or any single pastor can be looked upon as the representative of the whole of her sanctity. Nevertheless, every Christian community, without assuming to itself the right of dogmatic explanation or teaching, has a full right to change its forms and ceremonies, and to introduce new ones, so long as it does not cause offence to the other communities. Rather than do this, it ought to abandon its own opinion, and submit to that of the others, lest that which to one might seem harmless or even praiseworthy should seem blameable to another; or that brother should lead brother into the sin of doubt and discord. Every Christian ought to set a high value upon unity in the rites of the Church: for thereby is manifested, even for the unenlightened, unity of spirit and doctrine, while for the enlightened man it becomes a source of lively and Christian joy. Love is the crown and glory of the Church.

§ 5. The Spirit of God, who lives in the Church, ruling her and making her wise, manifests Himself within her in divers manners; in Scripture, in Tradition, and in Works; for the Church, which does the works of God, is the same Church which preserves tradition and which has written the Scriptures. Neither individuals, nor a multitude of individuals within the Church, preserve tradition or write the Scriptures; but the Spirit of God, which lives in the whole body of the Church. Therefore it is neither right nor possible to look for the grounds of tradition in the Scripture, nor for the proof of Scripture in tradition, nor for the warrant of Scripture or tradition in works. To a man living outside the Church neither her scripture nor her tradition nor her works are comprehensible. But to the man who lives within the Church and is united to the spirit of the Church,[1] their unity is manifest by the grace which lives within her.

Do not works precede Scripture and tradition? Does not tradition precede Scripture? Were not the works of Noah, Abraham, the forefathers and representatives of the Church of the Old Testament, pleasing to God? And did not tradition exist amongst the patriarchs, beginning with Adam, the forefather of all? Did not Christ give liberty to men and teaching by word of mouth, before the Apostles by their writings bore witness to the work of redemption and the law of liberty? Wherefore, between tradition, works, and scripture there is no contradiction, but, on the contrary, complete agreement. A man

---

[1] Внутри же Церкви пребывающему и пріобщенному къ духу Церкви. The two participles are difficult to translate at once clearly and fully. Countess de Rahden translates the whole passage thus :—' Demjenigen aber, der in der Kirche und in der Gemeinschaft des Geistes der Kirche bleibt, dem ist die Einheit ihrer Aeusserungen in Schrift, Tradition und Werken, durch die ihr innewohnende, lebendige Gnade offenbar.'—[W. J. B.].

understands the Scriptures, so far as he preserves tradition, and does works agreeable to the wisdom that lives within him. But the wisdom that lives within him is not given to him individually, but as a member of the Church, and it is given to him in part, without altogether annulling his individual error;[1] but to the Church it is given in the fulness of truth and without any admixture of error. Wherefore he must not judge the Church, but submit to her, that wisdom be not taken from him.

Every one that seeks for proofs of the truth of the Church, by that very act either shows his doubt, and excludes himself from the Church, or assumes the appearance of one who doubts and at the same time preserves a hope of proving the truth, and arriving at it by his own power of reason: but the powers of reason do not attain to the truth of God, and the weakness of man is made manifest by the weakness of his proofs. The man who takes Scripture only, and founds the Church on it alone, is in reality rejecting the Church, and is hoping to found her afresh by his own powers: the man who takes tradition and works only, and depreciates the importance of Scripture, is likewise in reality rejecting the Church, and constituting himself a judge of the Spirit of God, who spake by the Scripture. For Christian knowledge is a matter, not of intellectual investigation, but of a living faith, which is a gift of grace. Scripture is external, an outward thing, and tradition is external, and works are external: that which is inward in them is the one Spirit of God. From tradition taken alone, or from scripture or from works, a man can but derive an external and incomplete knowledge, which may indeed in itself contain truth, for it starts from truth, but at the same time must of necessity be erroneous, inasmuch as it is incomplete. A believer knows the Truth, but an unbeliever does not know it, or at least only knows it with an external and imperfect knowledge.[2] The Church

---

[1] Sie bleibt jedoch Stückwerk in dir, und hebt nicht vollkommen die dir innewohnende Lüge auf.—[Von Rahden's translation.]

[2] For this reason, even he who is not sanctified by the spirit of

does not prove herself either as Scripture or as tradition or as works, but bears witness to herself, just as the Spirit of God, dwelling in her, bears witness to Himself in the Scriptures. The Church does not ask: Which Scripture is true, which tradition is true, which Council is true, or what works are pleasing to God: for Christ knows His own inheritance, and the Church in which He lives knows by inward knowledge, and cannot help knowing, her own manifestations. The collection of Old and New Testament books, which the Church acknowledges as hers, are called by the name of Holy Scripture. But there are no limits to Scripture; for every writing which the Church acknowledges as hers is Holy Scripture. Such pre-eminently are the Creeds of the General Councils, and especially the Niceno-Constantinopolitan Creed. Wherefore, the writing of Holy Scripture has gone on up to our day, and, if God pleases, yet more will be written. But in the Church there has not been, nor ever will be, any contradictions, either in Scripture, or in tradition, or in works; for in all three is Christ, one and unchangeable.

§ 6. Every action of the Church, directed by the Holy Ghost, the Spirit of life and truth, sets forth the full completeness of all His gifts,—of faith, hope, and love: for in Scripture not faith only, but also the hope of the Church, is made manifest, and the love of God; and in works well pleasing to God there is made manifest not only love, but likewise faith and hope and grace; and in the living tradition of the Church which awaits from God her crown and consummation in Christ, not hope only, but also faith and love are manifested. The gifts of the Holy Spirit are inseparably united in one holy and living unity; but as works well

---

grace may know the truth even as we hope that we know it: but this knowledge is in itself nothing but an hypothesis, more or less sound as an opinion, logical conviction or external knowledge, which has nothing in common with inward and true knowledge, with faith which sees the invisible. And whether we have faith or no is known to God alone.—[Author's note.]

pleasing to God belong more especially to love, and prayer well pleasing to God belongs more especially to hope, so a Creed well pleasing to God belongs more especially to faith, and the Church's creed is rightly called the Confession or Symbol of the Faith.

Wherefore it must be understood that Creeds and prayers and works are nothing of themselves, but are only an external manifestation of the inward spirit. Whereupon it also follows that neither he who prays nor he who does works nor he who confesses the Creed of the Church is pleasing to God, but only he who acts, confesses, and prays according to the spirit of Christ living within him. All men have not the same faith or the same hope or the same love; for a man may love the flesh, fix his hope on the world, and confess his belief in a lie; he may also love and hope and believe not fully, but only in part; and the Church calls his faith, faith, and his hope, hope, and his love, love; for he calls them so, and she will not dispute with him concerning words; but what she herself calls faith, hope, and love are the gifts of the Holy Spirit, and she knows that they are true and perfect.

§ 7. Holy Church confesses her faith by her whole life; by her doctrine, which is inspired by the Holy Ghost; by her Sacraments in which the Holy Ghost works; and by her rites, which He directs. And the Niceno-Constantinopolitan Symbol is pre-eminently called her Confession of Faith.

In the Niceno-Constantinopolitan Symbol is comprised the confession of the Church's doctrine; but in order that it might be known that the hope of the Church is inseparable from her doctrine it likewise confesses her hope; for it is said: '*we look for*,' and not merely, 'we believe in,' that which is to come.

The Niceno-Constantinopolitan Symbol, the full and complete Confession of the Church, from which she allows nothing to be omitted and to which she permits nothing to be added, is as follows:—' We believe in one God the Father

Almighty, Maker of heaven and earth, and of all things visible and invisible. And in one Lord Jesus Christ, the Son of God, the only-begotten, who was begotten of His Father before all worlds, Light of Light, very God of very God, begotten, not made, of one substance with the Father, by whom all things were made; [Who] for us men and for our salvation came down from heaven, and was incarnate of the Holy Ghost and the Virgin Mary, and was made man; and was crucified also for us under Pontius Pilate, and suffered, and was buried, and rose again the the third day according to the Scriptures, and ascended into heaven, and sitteth at the right hand of the Father, and He shall come again with glory to judge the quick and the dead; Whose kingdom shall have no end. And in the Holy Ghost, the Lord, the Giver of life, who proceedeth from the Father, who with the Father and the Son is together worshipped and together glorified. [Who] spake by the Prophets. In one Holy Catholick and Apostolic Church. We acknowledge one Baptism for the remission of sins. We look for the Resurrection of the dead, and for the life of the world to come. Amen.'

This confession, just as also the whole life of the Spirit, is comprehensible only to one who believes and is a member of the Church. It contains within itself mysteries inaccessible to the inquiring intellect, and manifest only to God Himself, and to those to whom He makes them manifest for an inward and living, not a dead and outward, knowledge. It contains within itself the mystery of the existence of God not only in relation to His outward action upon creation, but also to His inward eternal being. Therefore the pride of reason and of illegal domination, which appropriated to itself, in opposition to the decree of the whole Church (pronounced at the Council of Ephesus), the right to add its private explanations and human hypotheses[1] to the Niceno-Constantinopolitan Symbol is in itself an infraction of the sanctity

---

[1] The Russian word, догадка, literally means a 'guess' or a 'conjecture.'—[W. J. B.].

and inviolability of the Church. Just as the very pride of the separate Churches, which dared to change the Symbol of the whole Church without the consent of their brethren, was inspired by a spirit not of love, and was a crime against God and the Church, so also their blind wisdom, which did not comprehend the mysteries of God, was a distortion of the faith; for faith is not preserved where love has grown weak. Wherefore the addition of the words *filioque* contains a sort of imaginary dogma, unknown to any one of the writers well pleasing to God, or of the Bishops or successors of the Apostles in the first ages of the Church, and not spoken by Christ our Saviour. As Christ spoke clearly, so did and does the Church clearly confess that the Holy Ghost proceedeth from the Father; for not only the outward, but also the inward, mysteries of God were revealed by Christ, and by the Spirit of Faith, to the holy Apostles and to the holy Church. When Theodoret called all who confessed the procession of the Holy Ghost from the Father and the Son blasphemers, the Church, while detecting his many errors, in this case approved his judgment by an eloquent silence.[1] The Church does not deny that the Holy Spirit is sent not only by the Father, but also by the Son; the Church does not deny that the Holy Ghost is communicated to all rational creatures not only from the Father but also through the Son; but what she does reject is that the Holy Ghost had the principle of His procession in the Godhead itself, not merely from the Father, but also from the Son. He who has renounced the spirit of love and divested himself of the gifts of grace cannot any longer possess inward knowledge—that is, faith—but limits himself to mere outward knowledge; wherefore he can only know what is external, and not the inner mysteries of God. Com-

---

[1] Silence on the part of the Church in not rejecting a writer is of great significance; but this silence becomes a decisive sentence when the Church does not reject a decision brought against a doctrine of any sort; for in not rejecting the decision she maintains it with all her authority.—[Author's note.]

munities of Christians which had broken away from the Holy
Church could no longer confess (inasmuch as they now could
not comprehend with the Spirit) the procession of the Holy
Ghost, in the Godhead itself, from the Father only; but from
that time they were obliged to confess only the external
mission of the Spirit into all creation, a mission which comes
to pass, not only from the Father, but also through the Son.
They preserved the external form of the faith, but they lost
the inner meaning and the grace of God; as in their confession, so also in their life.

§ 8. Having confessed her faith in the Tri-hypostatic Deity,
the Church confesses her faith in herself, because she acknowledges herself to be the instrument and vessel of divine grace,
and acknowledges her works as the works of God, not as the
works of the individuals of whom, in her visible manifestation
[upon earth], she is composed. In this confession she shows
that knowledge concerning her essence and being is likewise
a gift of grace, granted from above, and accessible to faith
alone and not to reason.

For what would be the need for me to say, 'I believe,' if I
already knew? Is not faith the evidence of things not seen?
But the visible Church is not the visible society of Christians,
but the Spirit of God and the grace of the Sacraments living
in this society. Wherefore even the visible Church is visible
only to the believer; for to the unbeliever a sacrament is
only a rite, and the Church merely a Society. The believer,
while with the eyes of the body and of reason he sees the
Church in her outward manifestations only, by the Spirit
takes knowledge of her in her sacraments and prayers and
works well pleasing to God. Wherefore he does not confuse her with the society which bears the name of Christians,
for not every one that saith, 'Lord, Lord,' really belongs to
the chosen race and to the seed of Abraham. But the true
Christian knows by faith that the One Holy Catholic and
Apostolic Church will never disappear from the face of the
earth until the last judgment of all creation, that she will

remain on earth invisible to fleshly eyes, or to the understanding which is wise according to the flesh, among the visible society of Christians, exactly in the same way as she remains visible to the eye of faith in the Church beyond the grave, but invisible to the bodily eyes. But the Christian also knows that the Church upon earth, although it is invisible, is always clothed in a visible form; that there neither was, nor could have been, nor ever will be a time in which the sacraments will be mutilated, holiness will be dried up, or doctrine will be corrupted; and that he is no Christian who cannot say where, from the time of the Apostles themselves, the holy Sacraments have been and are being administered, where doctrine was and is preserved, where prayers were and are being sent up to the throne of grace. The Holy Church confesses and believes that the sheep have never been deprived of their Divine Pastor, and that the Church never could either err for want of understanding,—for the understanding of God dwells within her; or submit to false doctrines for want of courage,—for within her dwells the might of the Spirit of God.

Believing in the word of God's promise, which has named all the followers of Christ's doctrine the friends of Christ and His brethren, and in Him the adopted sons of God, the Holy Church confesses the paths by which it pleases God to lead fallen and dead humanity to reunion in the spirit of grace and life. Wherefore, having made mention of the prophets, the representatives of the age of the Old Testament, she confesses Sacraments, through which, in the Church of the New Testament, God sends down His grace upon men, and more especially she confesses the Sacrament of Baptism for the remission of sins, as containing within itself the principle of all the others; for through Baptism alone does a man enter into the unity of the Church, which is the custodian of all the rest of the Sacraments.

Confessing one Baptism for the remission of sins, as a Sacrament ordained by Christ Himself for entrance into the Church of the New Testament, the Church does not judge those who have not entered into communion with her through Baptism, for she knows and judges herself only. God alone knows the hardness of the heart, and He judges the weaknesses of reason according to truth and mercy. Many have been saved and have received inheritance without having received the Sacrament of Baptism with water; for it was instituted only for the Church of the New Testament. He who rejects it rejects the whole Church, and the Spirit of God which lives within her; but it was not ordained for man from the beginning, neither was it prescribed to the Church of the Old Testament. For if any one should say that circumcision was the Baptism of the Old Testament, he rejects Baptism for women, for whom there was no circumcision; and what will he say about the Patriarchs from Adam to Abraham, who did not receive the seal of circumcision? And in any case does not he acknowledge that outside the Church of the New Testament the Sacrament of Baptism was not of obligation? If he will say that it was on behalf of the Church of the Old Testament that Christ received Baptism, who will place a limit to the loving-kindness of God, who took upon Himself the sins of the world? Baptism is indeed of obligation; for it alone is the door into the Church of the New Testament, and in Baptism alone does man testify his assent to the redeeming action of grace. Wherefore also in Baptism alone is he saved.

Moreover, we know that in confessing one Baptism, as the beginning of all the Sacraments, we do not reject the others; for, believing in the Church, we, together with her, confess Seven Sacraments, namely, Baptism, the Eucharist, Laying on of Hands, Confirmation with Chrism, Marriage, Penance, and Unction of the sick. There are also many other Sacraments; for every work which is done in faith, love, and hope, is suggested to man by the Spirit of God, and invokes the unseen Grace of God. But the Seven Sacraments are in reality not accomplished by any single individual who is worthy of the mercy of God, but by the whole Church in the person of an individual, even though he be unworthy.

Concerning the Sacrament of the Eucharist the Holy Church teaches that in it the change of bread and wine into the Body and Blood of Christ is verily accomplished. She does not reject the word 'Transubstantiation'; but she does not assign to it that material meaning which is assigned to it by the teachers of the Churches which have fallen away.[1] The change of the bread and wine into the Body and Blood of Christ is accomplished in the Church and for the Church. If a man receive the consecrated Gifts, or worship them, or think on them with faith, he verily receives, adores and thinks on the Body and Blood of Christ. If he receive unworthily he verily rejects the Body and Blood of Christ; in any case, in faith or in unbelief he is sanctified or condemned by the Body and Blood of Christ. But this Sacrament is in the Church, and for the Church; not for the outside world, not for fire, not for irrational creatures,[2] not for corruption, and

---

[1] Cf. the following passage from 'The longer Catechism of the Russian Church' (Blackmore's translation, p. 92.). '*Question*. How are we to understand the word *Transubstantiation*?' *Answer*. 'In the exposition of the faith by the Eastern Patriarchs [*i.e.* Peter Mogila's *Confessio Orthodoxa*, drawn up in Kieff in 1640, examined by the Synod of Jassy, and approved by the four Greek Patriarchs in 1643] it is said that the word transubstantiation is not to be taken to define the manner in which the bread and wine are changed into the Body and Blood of the Lord; for this none can understand but God; but only thus much is signified, that the bread truly, really, and substantially becomes the very true Body of the Lord, and the wine the very true Blood of the Lord. In like manner John Damascene, treating of the Holy and Immaculate Mysteries of the Lord, writes thus: *It is truly that Body united with the Godhead, which had its origin from the Holy Virgin: not as though that Body which ascended came down from heaven, but because the bread and wine themselves are changed into the Body and Blood of God. But if thou seekest after the manner how this is, let it suffice thee to be told, that it is by the Holy Ghost; in like manner as, by the same Holy Ghost, the Lord formed flesh to Himself, and in Himself, from the Mother of God; nor know I aught more than this, that the word of God is true, powerful, and almighty, but its manner of operation unsearchable* (S. Joh. Damasc. *De fide orthodoxa*, l. iv. cap. xiii. 7.)—[W. J. B.]

[2] Samarin (correspondence with Baroness de Rahden, p. 112; Moscow,

not for the man who has not heard the law of Christ. In the Church itself (we are speaking of the visible Church), to the elect and to the reprobate the Holy Eucharist is not a mere commemoration concerning the mystery of redemption, it is not a presence of spiritual gifts within the bread and wine, it is not merely a spiritual reception of the Body and Blood of Christ, but is His true Body and Blood. Not in spirit alone was Christ pleased to unite Himself with the faithful, but also in Body and in Blood; in order that that union might be complete, and not only spiritual but also corporal. Both nonsensical explanations concerning the relations of the holy Sacrament to elements and irrational creatures (when the Sacrament was instituted for the Church alone), and that spiritual pride which despises body and blood and rejects the corporal union with Christ, are equally opposed to the Church. We shall not rise again without the body, and no spirit, except the Spirit of God, can be said to be entirely incorporeal. He that despises the body sins through pride of spirit.

Of the Sacrament of Ordination [1] the Holy Church teaches, that through it the grace which brings the Sacraments into effect is handed on in succession from the Apostles and from Christ Himself: not as if no Sacrament could be brought to effect otherwise than through Ordination (for every Christian is able through Baptism to open the door of the Church to an infant or a Jew or a heathen), but that Ordination contains within itself all the fulness of grace given by Christ to His Church. And the Church herself, in communicating to her members the fulness of spiritual gifts, in the strength of the freedom given her by God, has appointed differences in the grades of Ordination. The Presbyter who performs all the Sacraments except Ordination has one gift, the Bishop who performs Ordination has another: higher than the gift of the

---

1893) explains this expression as follows: 'Ici l'auteur fait allusion à la question posée et discutée dans l'Eglise latine: à savoir si un rat qui aurait mangé le pain consacré aurait communié.'—[W. J. B.]

[1] The Russian word, Рукоположение, is equivalent to Χειροτονία. —[W. J. B.]

CONFIRMATION 209

Episcopate there is nothing. The Sacrament gives to him who receives it this great significance, that even if he be unworthy, yet in performing his Sacramental service, his action necessarily proceeds not from himself, but from the whole Church, that is, from Christ living-within her. If Ordination ceased, all the Sacraments except Baptism would also cease; and the human race would be torn away from grace: for the Church herself would then bear witness that Christ had departed from her.[1]

Concerning the Sacrament of Confirmation with Chrism[2] the Church teaches that in it the gifts of the Holy Ghost are conferred upon the Christian, confirming his faith and inward holiness: and this Sacrament is by the will of the Holy Church performed not by Bishops only, but also by Presbyters, although the Chrism itself can only be blessed[3] by a Bishop.

Of the Sacrament of Marriage the Holy Church teaches that the grace of God, which blesses the succession of generations in the temporal existence of the human race, and the holy union of man and woman for the organisation of the family, is a sacramental gift, imposing upon those who receive it a high obligation of mutual love and spiritual holiness, through which that which otherwise is sinful and

---

[1] This passage is meant to apply to the priestless sects amongst the Russian Old Believers, who, having lost the Apostolical Succession, and yet retained Catholic doctrine concerning the Sacraments, have not, like the Protestants, invented a new Ministry, but remain altogether without Sacraments.—[W. J. B]

[2] The word Мѵропамазаніе is a compound word, derived from мѵро, chrism, and помазати, to anoint. The word мѵро ($\mu\acute{\nu}\rho o\nu$) is used exclusively for the chrism consecrated by a Bishop (in Russia only by the Metropolitans of Moscow and Kieff) on Maundy Thursday, and never for the oil used for anointing the sick, or for that of the Catechumens, both of which are blessed by the priest or priests when they are required, and not, as in the West, once a year on Maundy Thursday by the Bishop. The Eastern Church, like the English Church, uses Chrism at the Coronation of the Sovereign, whereas the Roman Church uses the Oil of Catechumens.—[W. J. B.]

[3] благословенно, literally blessed, but according to Western usage 'consecrated' would be a better rendering.—[W. J. B.]

O

material is endued with righteousness and purity. Wherefore the great teachers of the Church, the Apostles, recognise the Sacrament of marriage even amongst the heathen : for while they forbid concubinage, they confirm marriage between Christians and heathens ; saying that the man is sanctified by the believing wife, and the wife by the believing husband (1 Cor. vii. 14). These words of the Apostle do not mean that an unbeliever could be saved by his or her union with a believer, but that the marriage is sanctified : for it is not the person, but the husband or wife, who is sanctified. One person is not saved through another, but the husband or/the wife is sanctified in relation to the marriage itself. And thus marriage is not unclean, even amongst idolaters ; but they themselves know not of the grace of God given unto them. But the Holy Church through her ordained ministers acknowledges and blesses the union, blessed by God, of husband and wife. Wherefore marriage is not a mere rite but a true Sacrament. And it receives its accomplishment in the Holy Church, for in her alone is every holy thing accomplished in its fulness.

Concerning the Sacrament of Penance the Holy Church teaches that without it the spirit of man cannot be cleansed from the bondage of sin and of sinful pride : that he himself cannot remit his own sins (for we have only the power to condemn, not to justify ourselves), and that the Church alone has the power of justifying, for within her lives the fulness of the Spirit of Christ. We know that the first-fruits of the Kingdom of heaven, after the Saviour, entered into the sanctuary of God by the judging of himself, that is to say, by the Sacrament of Penance ; for he said, 'for we receive the due reward of our deeds' ; and he received absolution from Him who alone can absolve, and who does absolve by the mouth of His Church.

Of the Sacrament of Anointing with consecrated oil[1] [*i.e.*

---

[1] The Slavonic word елеосвященie is derived from елей (ἔλαιον) *olive oil*, and священie, *to hallow*. Thus the very title of the Sacrament

Unction of the Sick] the Holy Church teaches, that in it is perfected the blessing of the whole fight (2 Tim. iv. 7), which has been endured by a man in his life upon earth, and of all the journey which has been gone through by him in faith and humility, and that in Unction of the Sick the divine verdict itself is pronounced upon man's earthly frame, healing it, when all medicinal means are of no avail, or else permitting death to destroy the corruptible body, which is no longer required for the Church on earth or the mysterious ways of God.

§ 9. The Church, even upon earth, lives, not an earthly human life, but a life which is divine, and of grace. Wherefore not only each of her members, but she herself as a whole, solemnly calls herself 'Holy.' Her visible manifestation

points to the fact that in the Eastern Church the oil is blessed each time by the priest or priests by whom it is administered, not once a year by the Bishop, as is the custom in the West. The Sacrament is also commonly called in Russian собороване, 'an assembling together,' from the fact that, in conformity with the direction of the Apostle (James v. 15) as many priests as it is possible to collect are summoned to bless the oil and administer the Sacrament. The ideal number is seven, in which case each priest reads one of the seven Gospels appointed, and administers one of the seven anointings. But this number is not necessary, and the oil may be hallowed and administered by fewer, or even by a single priest. In the East this Sacrament is not necessarily deferred until the man or woman is at the point of death, and may be administered in any serious illness, and, if desired, more than once during the same illness. As an illustration of the practice of the Eastern Church with regard to its administration I may mention the case of Archbishop Nicanor of Odessa, who, after hearing from a medical specialist at Moscow that his illness was incurable, returned to Odessa, and summoned the priests of his Cathedral and the Suffragan Bishop of his see to administer the Sacrament to him. The Suffragan Bishop and seven priests, assisted by seven deacons and the Cathedral choir, administered it, the Archbishop sitting throughout the ceremony in an arm-chair, and himself rising to give the blessing before the reading of each of the seven Gospels. His death did not take place until three months later, *i.e.* in January 1891.—[W. J. B.]

is contained in the Sacraments; but her inward life in the gifts of the Holy Spirit, in faith, hope, and love. Oppressed and persecuted by enemies without, at times agitated and lacerated within by the evil passions of her children, she has been and ever will be preserved without wavering or change wherever the Sacraments and spiritual holiness are preserved. Never is she either disfigured or in need of reformation. She lives not under a law of bondage, but under a law of liberty. She neither acknowledges any authority over her, except her own, nor any tribunal, but the tribunal of faith: for reason does not comprehend her: and she expresses her love, her faith, and her hope in her prayers and rites, suggested to her by the Spirit of truth, and by the grace of Christ. Wherefore her rites themselves, even if they are not unchangeable (for they are composed by the spirit of liberty and may be changed according to the judgment of the Church) can never, in any case, contain any, even the smallest, admixture of error or false doctrine. And the rites (of the Church) while they are unchanged are of obligation to the members of the Church; for in their observance is the joy of holy unity.

External unity is the unity manifested in the communion of Sacraments; while internal unity is unity of spirit. Many (as for instance some of the martyrs) have been saved without having been made partakers of so much as one of the Sacraments of the Church (not even of Baptism) but no one is saved without partaking of the inward holiness of the Church, of her faith, hope, and love: for it is not works which save, but faith. And faith, that is to say, true and living faith, is not twofold, but single. Wherefore both those who say that faith alone does not save, but that works also are necessary, and those who say that faith saves without works, are void of understanding; for if there are no works, then faith is shown to be dead; and if it be dead, it is also untrue; for in true faith there is Christ the truth and the life; but if it be not true, then it is false, that is to say, mere external knowledge. But can that which is false save a man? But if it be true, then it is also a living faith, that is to say, one which does works; but if it does works, what works are still required?

The divinely inspired Apostle saith: 'Show me the faith of which thou boastest thyself by thy works, even as I show my faith by my works.' Does he acknowledge two faiths? No, but he exposes a senseless boast. 'Thou believest in God, but the devils also believe.' Does he acknowledge that there is faith in devils? No, but he detects the falsehood which boasts itself of a quality which even devils possess. 'As the body,' saith he, 'without the soul is dead, so faith without works is dead also.' Does he compare faith to the body and works to the Spirit? No, for such a simile would be untrue; but the meaning of his words is clear. Just as a body without a soul is no longer a man, and cannot properly be called a man, but a corpse, so faith also that does no works cannot be called true faith, but false; that is to say, an external knowledge; fruitless, and attainable even by devils. That which is written simply ought also to be read simply. Wherefore those who rely upon the Apostle James for a proof that there is a dead faith and a living faith, and as it were two faiths, do not comprehend the words of the Apostle; for the Apostle bears witness not for, but against, them. Likewise when the Great Apostle of the Gentiles says, 'What is the use of faith without love, even of such a faith as would remove mountains?' (Cp. 1 Cor. xiii. 2) he does not maintain the possibility of such faith without love: but assuming its possibility he shows that it would be useless. Holy Scripture ought not to be read in the spirit of worldly wisdom, which wrangles over words, but in the spirit of the wisdom of God, and of spiritual simplicity. The Apostle in defining faith, says, 'it is the evidence of things unseen, and the confidence of things hoped for' (not merely of things awaited, or things to come), but if we hope, we also desire, and if we desire, we also love; for it is impossible to desire that which a man loves not. Or have the devils also hope? Wherefore there is but one faith, and when we ask, 'Can true faith save without works?' we ask a senseless question; or, better to say, no question at all: for true faith is a living faith which does works; it is faith in Christ, and Christ in faith.

Those who have mistaken a dead faith, that is to say, a false faith, or mere external knowledge, for true faith, have gone so far in their delusion, that, without knowing it themselves, they have made of it an eighth Sacrament. The Church has faith, but it is a living faith; for she has also sanctity. But if one man or one bishop is necessarily to have the faith, what are we to say? Has he also sanctity? No, for it may be he is notorious for crime and immorality. But the faith is to abide in him even though he be a sinner. So the faith within him is an eighth Sacrament; inasmuch as every Sacrament is the action of the Church in an individual, even though he be unworthy. But through this Sacrament what sort of faith abides in him? A living faith? No, for he is a sinner. But a dead faith, that is to say, external knowledge, is attainable, even by devils. And is this to be an eighth Sacrament? Thus does departure from the truth bring about its own punishment.[1]

We must understand that neither faith nor hope nor love saves of itself—for will faith in reason, or hope in the world, or love for the flesh save us? No, it is the object of faith which saves. If a man believes in Christ, he is saved in his faith by Christ: if he believes in the Church, he is saved by the Church; if he believes in Christ's Sacraments, he is saved by them; for Christ our God is in the Church and the Sacraments. The Church of the Old Testament was saved by faith in a Redeemer to come. Abraham was saved by the same Christ as we. He possessed Christ in hope, while we possess Him in joy. Wherefore he who

---

[1] As infallibility in a dead faith is an error in itself, so its deadness is expressed in the fact that this infallibility is bound up with objects of inanimate nature, with a place of residence, or with dead walls, or with diocesan succession, or with a chair. But we know who it was that in the time of Christ's sufferings sat in the chair of Moses.—[Author's note.]

desires Baptism is baptized in will; while he who has received Baptism possesses it in joy. An identical faith in Baptism saves both of them. But a man may say, 'if faith in Baptism saves, what is the use of being actually baptized?' If he does not receive Baptism, what did he wish for? It is evident that the faith which desires Baptism must be perfected by the reception of Baptism itself, which is its joy. Therefore also the house of Cornelius received the Holy Ghost before he received Baptism, while the eunuch was filled with the same Spirit immediately after Baptism (Acts x. 44-47, viii. 38, cf. ii. 38). For God can glorify the Sacrament of Baptism just as well before, as after, its administration. Thus the difference between the *opus operans* and *opus operatum* disappears. We know that there are many persons who have not christened their children, and many who have not admitted them to Communion in the Holy Mysteries, and many who have not confirmed them:[1] but the Holy Church understands things otherwise, christening infants and confirming them and admitting them to Communion. She has not ordained these things in order to condemn unbaptized children, whose angels do alway behold the face of God: but she has ordained this according to the spirit of love which lives within her, in order that the first thought of a child arriving at years of discretion should be not only a desire, but also a joy for sacraments which have been already received. And can one know the joy of a child, who, to all appearances, has not yet arrived at discretion? Did not the prophet, even before His birth, exult for joy concerning Christ? (St. Luke i. 41.) Those who have deprived children of Baptism and Confirmation and Communion are they, who, having inherited the blind wisdom of blind heathendom, have not comprehended the majesty of God's Sacraments, but have required reasons and uses for everything, and having subjected the doctrine of the Church to scholastic explications, will not even pray, unless they see in the prayer some direct

---

[1] Не мропомазывали ихъ : literally, 'have not anointed them with chrism.' See note on page 209.—[W. J. B.]

goal or advantage. But our law is not a law of bondage or of hireling service, labouring for wages, but a law of the adoption of sons, and of love which is free.

We know that when any one of us falls, he falls alone; but no one is saved alone. He who is saved is saved in the Church, as a member of her, and in unity with all her other members. If any one believes, he is in the communion of faith; if he loves, he is in the communion of love; if he prays, he is in the communion of prayer. Wherefore no one can rest his hope on his own prayers, and every one who prays asks the whole Church for intercession, not as if he had doubts of the intercession of Christ, the one Advocate, but in the assurance that the whole Church ever prays for all her members. All the angels pray for us, the apostles, martyrs, and patriarchs, and above them all, the Mother of our Lord, and this holy unity is the true life of the Church. But if the Church, visible and invisible, prays without ceasing, why do we ask her for her prayers? Do we not entreat mercy of God and Christ, although His mercy preventeth our prayer? The very reason that we ask the Church for her prayers is that we know that she gives the assistance of her intercession even to him that does not ask for it, and to him that asks she gives it in far greater measure than he asks: for in her is the fulness of the Spirit of God. Thus we glorify all whom God has glorified and is glorifying; for how should we say that Christ is living within us, if we do not make ourselves like unto Christ? Wherefore we glorify the Saints, the Angels, and the Prophets, and more than all the most pure Mother of the Lord Jesus, not acknowledging Her either to have been conceived without sin, or to have been perfect (for Christ alone is without sin and perfect), but remembering that the pre-eminence, passing all understanding, which She has above all God's creatures was borne witness to by the Angel and by Elizabeth, and above all, by the Saviour Himself, when He appointed John, His great Apostle and seer of mysteries to fulfil the duties of a son and to serve her.

Just as each of us requires prayers from all, so each person owes his prayers on behalf of all, the living and the dead, and even those who are as yet unborn : for in praying, as we do with all the Church, that the world may come to the knowledge of God, we pray not only for the present generation, but for those whom God will hereafter call into life. We pray for the living that the grace of God may be upon them, and for the dead that they may become worthy of the vision of God's face. We know nothing of an intermediate state of souls, which have neither been received into the kingdom of God, nor condemned to torture, for of such a state we have received no teaching either from the Apostles or from Christ; we do not acknowledge Purgatory, that is, the purification of souls by sufferings from which they may be redeemed by their own works or those of others: for the Church knows nothing of salvation by outward means, nor any sufferings whatever they may be, except those of Christ; nor of bargaining with God, as in the case of a man buying himself off by good works.

All such heathenism as this remains with the inheritors of the wisdom of the heathen, with those who pride themselves of place, or name, or in territorial dominion, and who have instituted an eighth Sacrament of dead faith. But we pray in the spirit of love, knowing that no one will be saved otherwise than by the prayer of all the Church, in which Christ lives, knowing and trusting that so long as the end of time has not come, all the members of the Church, both living and departed, are being perfected incessantly by mutual prayer. The Saints whom God has glorified are much higher than we, but higher than all is the Holy Church, which comprises within herself all the Saints, and prays for all, as may be seen in the divinely inspired Liturgy. In her prayer our prayer is also heard, however unworthy we may be to be called sons of the Church. If, while worshipping and glorifying the Saints, we pray that God may glorify them, we do not lay ourselves open to the charge of pride ; for to us who have received permission to call God 'Our Father' leave has also been granted to pray, 'Hallowed be His Name. His Kingdom come, His will be done.' And if we are permitted to pray of God that He will glorify His Name, and accomplish His Will, who will forbid us to pray Him to glorify His Saints, and to give repose to His elect ?[1] For those indeed who are not of the elect we do not pray, just as Christ prayed not for the whole world, but for those whom the Lord had given unto Him (St. John xvii.). Let no one say : 'What prayer shall I apportion for the living or the departed, when my prayers are insufficient even for myself ?' For if he is not able to pray, of what use would it be to pray even for himself ? But in truth the spirit of love prays in him. Likewise let him not say : 'What is the good of my prayer for another, when he prays for himself, and Christ Himself intercedes for him ?' When a man prays, it is the spirit of love which prays within him. Let him not say : 'It is even now impossible to change the judgment of God,' for his prayer itself is included in the ways of God, and God foresaw it. If he be a member of the Church his prayer is necessary for all her members. If the hand should say, that it did not require blood from the rest of the body, and that it would not give its own blood to it, the hand would wither. So a

---

[1] Khomiakoff is here referring to the passage near the commencement of the Great Prayer of Intercession after the Consecration of the Eucharist in the Liturgy of St. Chrysostom, in which the Eastern Church *prays for*, as well as asks to be assisted by the prayers of, all the Saints :—

'And further we offer to Thee this reasonable service on behalf of those who have departed in the faith, our ancestors, Fathers, Patriarchs, Prophets, Apostles, Preachers, Evangelists, Martyrs, Confessors, Virgins, and every just spirit made perfect in the faith ; especially the most holy undefiled, excellently laudable, glorious Lady, the Mother of God, and Ever-Virgin Mary, the Holy John the Prophet, Forerunner and Baptist, the holy, glorious and all celebrated Apostles, Saint N. (*the Saint of the day*), whose memory we also celebrate, and all Thy Saints, through whose prayers look down upon us, O God. And remember all those that are departed in the hope of the resurrection to eternal life, and give them rest where the light of Thy countenance shines upon them.'—[W. J. B.]

man is also necessary to the Church, as long as he is in her: and if he withdraws himself from communion with her, he perishes himself and will cease to be any longer a member of the Church. The Church prays for all, and we pray together, for all; but our prayer must be true, and a true expression of love, and not a mere form of words. Not being able to love all men, we pray for those whom we love, and our prayer is not hypocritical; but we pray God, that we may be able to love all, and pray for all without hypocrisy. Mutual prayer is the blood of the Church, and the glorification of God her breath. We pray in a spirit of love, not of interest, in the spirit of filial freedom, not of the law of the hireling demanding his pay. Every man who asks: 'What use is there in prayer?' acknowledges himself to be in bondage. True prayer is true love.

Love and unity are above everything, but love expresses itself in many ways: by works, by prayer, and by spiritual songs. The Church bestows her blessing upon all these expressions of love. If a man cannot express his love for God by word, but expresses it by a visible representation, that is to say by an image (*eikon*), will the Church condemn him? No, but she will condemn the man who condemns him, for he is condemning another's love. We know that without the use of an image men may be saved and have been saved, and if a man's love does not require an image he will be saved without one; but if the love of his brother require an image, he, in condemning this brother's love, condemneth himself; and if a man being a Christian dare not listen without a feeling of reverence to a prayer or spiritual song composed by his brother, how dare he look without reverence upon the image which his love, and not his art, has produced? The Lord Himself, who knows the secrets of the heart, has designed more than once to glorify a prayer or psalm: will a man forbid Him to glorify an image or the graves of the Saints? One may say: 'The Old Testament has forbidden the representation of God': but does he, who thus thinks that he understands better than

Holy Church the words which she herself wrote (that is, the Scriptures), not see that it was not a representation of God which the Old Testament forbade (for it allowed the Cherubim, and the brazen serpent, and the writing of the Name of God), but that it forbade a man to make unto himself a god in the similitude of any object in earth or in heaven, visible or even imaginary?

If a man paints an image to remind him of the invisible and inconceivable God, he is not making to himself an idol. If he imagines God to himself and thinks that He is like to his imagination, he maketh to himself an idol--that is the meaning of the prohibition in the Old Testament. But an image [*eikon*] (that is to say, the Name of God painted in colours), or a representation of His Saints, made by love, is not forbidden by the spirit of truth. Let none say, 'Christians are going over to idolatry'; for the spirit of Christ which preserves the Church is wiser than a man's calculating wisdom. Wherefore a man may indeed be saved without images, but he must not reject images.

The Church accepts every rite which expresses spiritual aspiration towards God, just as she accepts prayer and images [*eikons*], but she recognises as higher than all rites the holy Liturgy, in which is expressed all the fulness of the doctrine and spirit of the Church; and this not only by conventional signs or symbols of some kind, but by the word of life and truth inspired from above. He alone knows the Church who knows the Liturgy. But above all is the unity of holiness and love.

§ 10. The Holy Church, in confessing that she looks for the Resurrection of the dead and the final judgment of all mankind, acknowledges that the perfecting of all her members will be fulfilled together with her own, and that the future life pertains not only to the spirit, but also to the spiritual body; for God alone is a perfectly incorporeal Spirit. Wherefore she rejects the pride of those who preach a doctrine of an incorporeal state beyond the grave, and consequently despise the body, in which Christ rose from the dead. This body will not be a fleshly body, but will be like unto the corporeal state of the Angels, inasmuch as Christ Himself said that we shall be like unto the Angels.

In the last Judgment our justification in Christ will be revealed in its fulness; not our sanctification only, but also our justification, for no man has been or is as yet completely sanctified, but there is still need of justification. Christ worketh all that is good in us, whether it be in faith or in hope or in love ; while we only submit ourselves to His working: but no man submits himself wholly. Therefore there is still need of justification by the sufferings and blood of Christ. Who, then, can continue to speak of the merits of his own works, or of a treasury of merits and prayers ? Only those who are still living under a law of bondage. Christ works all good in us, but we never wholly submit ourselves, none, not even the Saints, as the Saviour Himself has said. Grace works all, and grace is given freely and to all, that none should be able to murmur, but not equally to all, not according to predestination, but according to foreknowledge, as the Apostle says. A smaller talent indeed is given to the man in whom the Lord has foreseen negligence, in order that the rejection of a greater gift should not serve to greater condemnation. And we do not increase the talents which have been intrusted to us ourselves, but they are put out to the exchangers, in order that even here there should not be any merit of ours, but only non-resistance to the grace, which causes the increase. Thus the distinction between 'sufficient' and 'effectual' grace disappears. Grace worketh all. If a man submits to it the Lord is perfected in him, and perfects him ; but let not a man boast himself in his obedience, for his obedience itself is of grace. But we never submit ourselves wholly : wherefore besides sanctification we ask also for justification.

All is accomplished in the consummation of the general judgment, and the Spirit of God, that is, the Spirit of faith, hope, and love, will reveal Himself in all His fulness, and every gift will attain its utmost perfection :—but above them all will be love. Not that it is to be thought that faith and hope, which are the gifts of God, will perish (for they are not separable from love), but love alone will preserve its name, while faith, arriving at its consummation will then have become full inward knowledge and sight; and hope will have become joy: for even on earth we know that the stronger it is, the more joyful it is.

§ 11. By the will of God the Holy Church, after the falling away of many schisms, and of the Roman Patriarchate, was preserved in the Greek Eparchies and Patriarchates, and only those communities can acknowledge one another as fully Christian which preserve their unity with the Eastern Patriarchates, or enter into this unity. For there is one God, and one Church, and within her there is neither dissension nor disagreement.

And therefore the Church is called Orthodox, or Eastern, or Greco-Russian; but all these are only temporary designations. The Church ought not to be accused of pride for calling herself Orthodox, inasmuch as she also calls herself Holy. When false doctrines shall have disappeared, there will be no further need for the name Orthodox: for then there will be no erroneous Christianity. When the Church shall have extended herself, or the fulness of the nations shall have entered into her, then all local appellations will cease; for the Church is not bound up with any locality, and neither boasts herself of any particular see or territory, nor preserves the inheritance of Pagan pride: but she calls herself One Holy Catholic and Apostolic; knowing that the whole world belongs to her, and that no locality therein possesses any special significance, but only temporarily can and does serve for the glorification of the name of God, according to His unsearchable will.

APPENDIX

TRANSLATIONS BY WILLIAM PALMER
OF POEMS BY KHOMIAKOFF ON GREAT BRITAIN AND RUSSIA.

'THE ISLAND.'

Isle of riches, isle of wonder,
Fairest thou beneath the moon;
Brightest gem of emerald verdure,
Studding Ocean's azure zone!

Guardian of thy vaunted Freedom
Round thy battlemented shores,
Whelming fleets of proud invaders,
Ocean dread his billows pours.

Fathomless, unmeasured ocean,
Foe to other lands is he:
But submissive and obedient
Fawns in blandishment on thee.

Yes! for thee he tames the madness
Of his storms that rage so high,
Till the waves in sunlit dimples
Kiss thy white cliffs lovingly.

Albion! Nature's [1] darling daughter!
Gracious land, what gifts are thine!
How with life thy streets are teeming!
How thy fields with harvests shine!

---

[1] Дочь любимая *природы*, literally, 'Daughter darling of nature.' So it appeared in the first edition of Khomiakoff's *Poems*, from which Mr. Palmer translated it. But the later Russian editions have, not природы but свободы = 'of Freedom,' and there is no doubt that this is the true text.—[W. J. B.]

How imperially thy Standard
O'er the billows rides afar !
How victoriously thy Armies
Wield the flaming sword of war !

What bright crowns of Art and Science
Circle round thy laurelled brow !
What high songs of heavenly rapture
Hath thy harp poured forth below !

Outwardly thou art all golden ;
Inwards all with mind doth shine ;
Thou art prosperous, thou art wealthy,
Luxury and power are thine :

And far distant lands and empires
Raise a timid eye to thee,
From thy potent will exacting
Laws to guide their destiny.

But,—for this that thou art wicked ;
But,—for this that thou art proud ;
That thou settest worldly greatness
Higher than the throne of God ;—

That with sacrilegious daring
Thou Christ's church hast trampled down,
Chaining her unto the footstool
Of a fleeting earthly throne ;—

There shall come, O Queen of Ocean,
There shall come, and soon, a day
That thy glory, gold and purple,
As a dream shall pass away.

From thy hands shall fall the thunder ;
Heaven shall speed thy arms no more ;
Nor shall mind, or art, or science,
Mark thy children as before.

Thy Imperial flag forgotten,
Once more terrible and free
Shall the waves at will disporting
Lift the wide and stormy sea.

God then to a land more humble
Marked with faith and signs of fear,
Shall the Empire and earth's thunder,
And the Word of Heaven transfer.

'TO RUSSIA.'

'Be proud, O Land !'—thus tongues have spoken. —
'And lift thy crownéd front on high !
'O giant land ! whose sword hath taken
'Half the wide world beneath the sky

'Bounds there are none to thy dominion ;
'And Fortune's self obedient stands,
'Slave-like, attentive to thy pleasure
'Awaiting thy august commands !

'Fair are thy steppes of boundless pastures
'Thy chains of mountains capped with cloud
'Thy sea-like lakes, thy broad deep rivers ! —
Believe not, hear not, be not proud.

Grant, that the waves of thy deep rivers
Roll mighty on the azure main,
Thy mountains teem with diamond treasures
Thy steppes wave bright with golden grain ;

Grant, that before thy sovereign splendour
The nations quail with timid eye ;
Grant, that seven seas, in one rough chorus,
Hymn ceaseless thy supremacy ;

Grant that afar thy battle thunders
Have pealed from War's empurpled cloud,—
At all this power, at all this glory,
At all this dust,—O be not proud!

More dread than thou was Rome Imperial,
The Monarch of the seven-crowned hill,
Embodiment of iron forces,
Embodiment of haughty will.

Resistless flamed the Tartar falchion,
That swept from Altai's plains of old;—
The Queen that rules the Western Ocean
Buries herself in heaps of gold.

And where is Rome? Where are the Mongols?
And Albion, Empress of the main,
She too, mid gathering signs of vengeance,
Hides in her breast a deadly pain.

Fruitless is every haughty spirit,
Gold fails, steel breaks and rusts away;
But strong is the bright world of martyrs,
And mighty are the hands that pray.

And lo, for this, that thou art humble,
Childlike and simple to believe,—
That in thy heart's deep silent treasure
Thy Maker's word thou did'st receive,—

To thee He gave a heavenly calling,
To thee He gave a glorious meed,—
To keep this heritage for nations,
High sacrifice, and holy deed;

To keep the tie of holy kindred;
The cup of quickening charity;
Warm faith's unpurchaseable treasure
Law without blood, and equity.

O then, remember thy high calling !
The spark within thy heart revive
Ask the deep Spirit therein abiding,
That spirit, by which alone we live !

Attend to it ! and so embracing
All nations with affection true,
Tell them of God's mysterious freedom ;
Pour faith's bright beams upon their view !

So shalt thou stand in glory marvellous
Above all tribes of earth ; as high
As this blue arch, that God's protection
Veils and reveals to mortal eye.

www.ingramcontent.com/pod-product-compliance
Lightning Source LLC
Chambersburg PA
CBHW032104220426
43664CB00008B/1133